Interdisciplinary Applications
of the Person-Centered Approach

Jeffrey H. D. Cornelius-White
Renate Motschnig-Pitrik
Michael Lux
Editors

Interdisciplinary Applications of the Person-Centered Approach

Springer

Editors

Jeffrey H. D. Cornelius-White
University of Missouri
Springfield, MO
USA

Renate Motschnig-Pitrik
University of Vienna
Vienna
Austria

Michael Lux
Neurologisches Rehabilitationszentrum
  Quellenhof
Bad Wildbad
Germany

ISBN 978-1-4614-7143-1   ISBN 978-1-4614-7144-8   (eBook)
DOI 10.1007/978-1-4614-7144-8
Springer New York Heidelberg Dordrecht London

Library of Congress Control Number: 2013939567

Printed on acid-free paper

Springer is part of Springer Science+Business Media (www.springer.com)

This book is dedicated to Carl R. Rogers and to people everywhere who reach to understand that which is within and beyond their own world, build bridges with others, and unfold new facts, feelings, ideas, and actions

Preface

The idea for this book was born at the PCE 2010 Conference in Rome. Over dinner and breaks the three of us editors started imagining a volume on the interconnections of the Person-Centered Approach (PCA) with other disciplines. Something like 'Becoming Interconnected: Perspectives of the Person-Centered Approach'.

In fact it didn't take us long to follow the crystallizing idea of building bridges from, as well as toward, the PCA. While the three of us work in quite different areas of engagement in the PCA—Jef in an academic counseling and educational leadership department, Michael at a neurological rehabilitation center, and Renate at the Faculty of Computer Science, engaged in knowledge engineering and learning technology—what united us was our felt confirmation that the PCA resonates with the way we want to relate to others, us, and our environment.

Certainly, Rogers and his colleagues helped us to grow in our relationships. Based on our experiences in person-centered climates and our knowledge of the PCA, we intend to support people to grow in various relationships, with themselves, their partners, children, students, teams, communities, nations, and the environment. This support or in other words "input" or "resource" for growth, in our view, can take on various forms and originate from various sources: sharing experience, knowledge, research processes and results, practices and selves. Therefore, we sought to invite authors from those disciplines and areas of engagement that we felt work toward the same or strongly related "ends" to help us to interconnect the PCA with related "siblings" and thus to produce a conceptual image that is more complete than any image from a separate perspective would be.

The authors whom we decided to invite for a contribution were mainly those whom we knew through personal contact or through publications. Thankfully, the vast majority accepted the invitation. So we created a (protected) book homepage with relevant information for contributors as well as the contributors' abstracts for the sake of orientation. For each chapter, one of the co-editors of this book acted as the primary chapter-editor to work with the author(s). Almost uniformly, the chapter editor's comments called for a minor or major revision of a chapter. Subsequently, each chapter was read and reviewed by at least two other persons of different nationalities—often but not exclusively the other two co-editors—so as to ensure an international review process of and for high quality.

As a complementary aspect, from the first beginning we were really keen to propose key issues of the research, theory, and practice of the PCA as a grounded meta-view for interpersonal growth in a person-centered climate. Forming, confirming, and sharing the forward directed, lived experience of the PCA provided us with the intrinsic motivation to engage in this book project by (re)searching, practicing, living, and writing within the PCA.

So while this book is limited by "speaking" through a printed medium only, it is centrally aimed at contributing to deep, significant learning in the readers' as well as authors' and editors' experiential fields. It seeks to transcend established disciplinary boundaries to reach out for better informed, more flexible, more self-organizing, and sustainable solutions that our rapidly changing societies and environment require. It was awkward in multiple ways and ended with etc. even though it began with few examples which is illogical. I suggest: Just to name a few examples, consider problems like climate change, lack of understanding between peoples, or uncompromising adherence to dogmas void of empathy. Elaborating solutions depends, we believe, on creative, open minds, and constructive, collaborative efforts between peoples and multiple knowledge sources.

We are deeply convinced that, to strengthen the constructive potential inherent in humans, we need to contribute to promoting those socio-environmental conditions that research and practice in the person-centered, humanistic orientation has been confirming worldwide, across all continents since more than half a century. Briefly, the conditions of experiencing and mutually communicating empathic understanding, acceptance, and genuineness have countlessly been confirmed across many disciplines to bring to the forefront the inherent, constructive talents in humans. This holds true for individual persons as well as for groups of small and large sizes, covering homogeneity as well as diversity. Hence we feel these socio-environmental conditions are key to the *solution of real problems*, even of problems and crises of enormous size that seem to require, first of all, (inter)personal immersion, encounter, mutual understanding, and a loosening of rigidly held mental models. This is because problems such as conflicts between nations, climate change, or financial crises cannot be solved by a single genius but call for sustained collaborative effort.

Historically, the socio-environmental conditions, which promote the constructive sides of humans and bring along the flourishing of persons and groups were described and investigated by Carl Rogers and his co-workers about 60 years ago. Rogers formulated a consistent theoretical framework, which embraces his humanistic view of mankind and growth-promoting interpersonal relationships. Over the last years, progress in the human sciences has yielded many significant research findings which are, from our point of view, closely related to key features (such as subception, organismic valuing, self-organization, etc.) of the theoretical framework of Rogers and thus the PCA. Several of these insights are communicated through the sibling book *Interdisciplinary Handbook of the Person-Centered Approach: Research and Theory*. It is intended to help readers understand the research and theories from multiple perspectives and to inform the *applications* of the PCA, the focus of this book, and support their social assimilation.

These and similar thoughts come up in our minds when trying to justify our initiative for editing this book on PCA applications along with its conceptual sibling, the *Interdisciplinary Handbook of the Person-Centered Approach: Research and Theory*. Frankly, however, the most inner sense, if we allow ourselves to share it, is our feeling, based on our own experience with and in the PCA and our being in this world that makes us sense that this project is the right thing to do at this time. It requires us to divide our limited time resources between this project and other responsibilities, but, in any case, it feels right to enjoy working on this book. Our huge supply of intrinsic motivation seems to come from each of our own experiencing, our knowledge, as well as from our appreciation of working together on a project we called into life. This is perhaps the more honest explanation of why we are editing these books and feel so fortunate that we found Springer as a renowned publisher as well as top contributors from several disciplines to help us in our bridge-building endeavor.

Not to be misunderstood, when we are saying that reciprocally perceiving person-centered attitudes of empathic understanding, acceptance, and congruence "are key to the solution of real problems" what we absolutely do not intend is to argue that they are all we need. That would be ridiculous. Equally, we do not intend to downplay the invaluable contributions of other disciplines, schools, and theories. What we do, however, endeavor is to build bridges from a person centered, experiential approach to many other disciplines. This is to join forces with them, thereby *never* losing or departing from our deepest human basis— a whole person approach, as originally expressed in the life work of Carl Rogers (1902–1987), or expressed even more broadly, an empathically attuned, self-organizing whole environment approach.

More theoretically, the PCA can be seen as providing one meta-model that can help connect many fields of study. It provides a parsimonious explanation and an astonishingly straightforward and elegant theory on how to move forward to address those dimensions of the unique challenges of the present and the future that concern interaction within and between people. It offers constructs that have been supported from many fields of study, but are largely unknown to other fields. To be fully assimilated and understood, however, the constructs of the PCA need to be experienced. This is a limitation of the/any book that readers can overcome only when experiencing a person-centered climate. Nevertheless, this book endeavors to highlight the parsimony, unknown research support, and links within the PCA and from it to various fields of study and practice.

The major contribution of this book is to identify and characterize key *applications*—so far often dispersed—of the PCA across disciplines. Consequently, the book's main themes and objectives are to:

- Explore the power, depth, and practical impact of the PCA through its relationship to a broad variety of disciplines.
- Articulate how the theory of PCA can be applied not only in the clinical fields but also in highly influential disciplines such as education, management, communication, thus significantly transcending its root applications.

- Propose an integrative framework and conceptual map to depict more of the "geography" surrounding the PCA.
- Respond to international calls for interdisciplinary studies that facilitate dialogue and cooperation with other disciplines to stimulate new ideas and solve twenty-first century problems, such as conflict resolution and intercultural understanding.
- Introduce people who are less or not familiar with the PCA to reveal it as a meta-approach with widespread scientific support, integrative potential, and influential applications
- Help those who identify research and practice within the PCA—largely psychotherapists, but also educators, consultants, negotiators, coaches, nonviolent facilitators, etc.—to engage with a broader literature, find scientific dialogue with compatible findings from other disciplines, and have increased appreciation for other disciplines.
- Stimulate further research and theory development by identifying open questions stemming from applications in practice.
- Inspire new applications and the sharing of experience and insight between practitioners.
- Contribute to help us move forward as a human species, regardless of which (knowledge) culture or spiritual tradition we may come from.

Overview and Structure of the Book

This book is set out to be a unique contribution to the literature in so far as it throws fresh light on the broad, practical *application,* and impact of the PCA. A "sibling book" focusing on the scientific contribution and foresight of the PCA accompanies it. That "sibling book" provides transdisciplinary chapters, linking diverse disciplines with the PCA, including cognitive and neuroscience, developmental relating, positive psychology, systems theory, and mindfulness, philosophy, and spirituality. The innovative approach taken in both books is to provide readers with a multidisciplinary and multi-perspective view.

This application book is structured as follows: The first section is an invitation to bridge-building, introducing the domains of application, including a few conceptual maps to help the reader organize and extend their understanding of the application chapters. It also provides an experiential example central to the roots of the PCA: A comprehensive transcript from a demonstration interview of Carl Rogers and Dadisi, an African-American volunteer. This interview had, to the best of the authors' knowledge, not been previously published in written form. Subsequently, the application chapters follow.

The application chapters are organized into five sections starting with clinical applications discussing person-centered and experiential psychotherapies, person-centered medicine, and care for special needs persons, continuing with education with and without technology integration, followed by developmental relating with children and in families, proceeding to the realm of organizations, business, and leadership and following on with conflict management and international, constructive communication. In brief, the main objective is to let the reader see how not only psychotherapy, but social systems, medicine, art, communication, economics, and other fields can benefit from an understanding of the PCA, particularly in today's knowledge-based society.

In the final chapter the editors propose an initial formulation of a meta-view of the PCA as an "overarching paradigm," drawing on not only the application chapters of this book, but also the research and theory chapters of the "sibling book". The meta-view is intended as a generic framework to be specialized for each area at hand so as to reach a broad understanding and be applied or explored through further research or application to stimulate further engagement with the PCA.

In a nutshell, this book aims to explore and testify how the PCA contributes to moving forward as a human species in a *multitude of application areas*. If this book facilitates letting you grasp and perceive a more complete, deeper picture of the interconnection of the PCA along with their implication for theory and/or practice, it will have fulfilled its purpose. The editors trust you will explore the book in the way that best fits for you. Moving through as designed or jumping from topic to topic as your interest or need motivates you! Readers who are new to person-centered thought may want to read the introduction and the initial section of the "sibling book" on research and theory first, and thereafter proceed whichever way they prefer. We trust each reader and contributor to find their own insights and significant revelations from each chapter as well as the book as a whole.

Acknowledgments

At this point let us express our deep gratitude to our contributors from all continents and to Springer for supporting this large-scale project to crystalize and bring together so many important and divergent views and practices. For decades, many scholars have argued for the importance of interdisciplinary collaboration as the primary means to solve difficult social problems and encourage the formation of new paradigms enriched by older traditions. Undoubtedly, without the openness of our contributors to the interdisciplinary adventure, their acceptance of our offerings and constraints, and their empathy toward our shared goals and needs as editors, this collaborative work and its thrust would not have been accomplished.

Thanks also go to Mike Bobbitt and Randi Davis, Graduate Assistants in the Department of Counseling, Leadership, and Special Education at Missouri State University, who helped with several miscellaneous tasks, and Dennis Kear, Tami Arthaud, and David Hough, administrators at Missouri State University for support of Jef Cornelius-White's sabbatical, which helped this project come to fruition. Thanks to the Faculty of Computer Science at the University of Vienna, Austria, for their openness to this interdisciplinary project and for providing part of the infrastructure to work on it. Special thanks go to Giorgia Silani, Colin Lago, Will Stillwell, Natalie Rogers, Jenny Bell, Tess Sturrock, and others who provided reviews of various chapters. Thanks to our families for supporting us through so many hours of work!

Renate expresses sincere thanks to Ladislav Nykl for his continuing collaboration and fresh sharing, both critical and appreciative, regarding all the difficult questions that come to the surface when you delve deep into person-centered theories and encounters. Thanks are also due to Sigrid Schmitz, who introduced Renate to concept mapping and hinted her to the tool CMapTools from the Institute of Human and Machine Cognition (http://www.cmap.ihmc.us).

Last but not least, we are deeply thankful to Sharon Panulla, Executive Editor at Springer, for her just perfect and friendly support and encouragement. She contributed significantly to making the genesis of the book an enriching and joyful experience throughout the whole process. Sharon, we appreciate your open-mindedness, prompt, friendly, and helpful responses and your patience with all our questions. For us, you were the best Editor we envisage in this project.

Contents

Part III Education

Part IV Children and Family

Part V Business and Leadership

Part I
Introductory Chapters

Introduction to Interdisciplinary Applications

Jeffrey Cornelius-White, Renate Motschnig-Pitrik and Michael Lux

The person-centered approach (PCA) is most known for its beginnings in psychotherapy and its contributions to psychotherapy, particularly in providing some of the first transcriptions of sessions, the first rigorous quantitative and qualitative research, and expanding insights from psychotherapy from the exclusive domain of psychiatry into psychology, counseling, social work, nursing, and other areas (Kirschenbaum 2007). However, early writings of Rogers and others related to the approach actually show that applications beyond therapy were present from its outset. Indeed, Rogers' first full-length work was a diary of his trip as a missionary, educator, and peace activist to China and other Far East countries in 1922 (Cornelius-White 2012). Likewise, research on nondirective (known more commonly as learner-centered today) education dates back to the 1930s, predating the seminal works by Rogers (1942, 1951) on psychotherapy and counseling (Cornelius-White and Harbaugh 2010).

Furthermore, throughout Rogers' mature professional life, he seemed to move his priorities beyond psychotherapy, particularly after the Wisconsin project in the early 1960s. He focused on encounter groups, personal power, cross-cultural work, peace workshops, education, business applications, nursing and medicine, legal work, and other areas. Likewise, he inspired other researcher to conduct extensive research strands beginning in the 1960s (e.g., Aspy and Roebuck or Anne-Marie

J. Cornelius-White (✉)
Counseling, Leadership and Special Education, Missouri State University, S. National Avenue 901, Springfield, MO 65897, USA
e-mail: JCornelius-White@MissouriState.edu

R. Motschnig-Pitrik
Computer Science Didactics and Learning Research Center, University of Vienna, Waehringer Strasse 29/6.41, 1090 Vienna, Austria
e-mail: renate.motschnig@univie.ac.at

M. Lux
Neurologisches Rehabilitationszentrum Quellenhof, Kuranlagenallee 2, 75323 Bad Wildbad, Germany
e-mail: luxbw@yahoo.de

J. H. D. Cornelius-White et al. (eds.), *Interdisciplinary Applications of the Person-Centered Approach*, DOI: 10.1007/978-1-4614-7144-8_1,
© Springer Science+Business Media New York 2013

and Reinhard Tausch) conducting dozens of studies in these areas. Other former colleagues of Rogers created applications that have been widely practiced and in some cases studied and offer as much empirical validation as the approach has related to psychotherapy [e.g., parent effectiveness training, filial/child–parent relationship therapy, Nonviolent Communication, Rogerian rhetoric (the latter two not covered in this volume)].

This section offers a collection of chapters describing the history, current practice, and future directions of a rich variety of applications of the PCA.

1 Clinical Applications

Of the five sections, the first one offers descriptions of applications closest to psychotherapy and intervention with persons identified as having clinical diffi-culties from traditional psychotherapy approaches to artistic empowerment and treatments within medical contexts. The section begins with an overview chapter by Stumm, depicted by Fig. 1. The map shows how person-centered and experi-ential psychotherapies include a wide variety of talk therapy orientations that integrate diversity and are challenged through continuous research and discussion.

Wagner provides a bridge chapter between person-centered therapies and moti-vational interviewing, which is described as "80 % Rogers" and a directive com-ponent focusing on change conflict that can encourage momentum toward specific

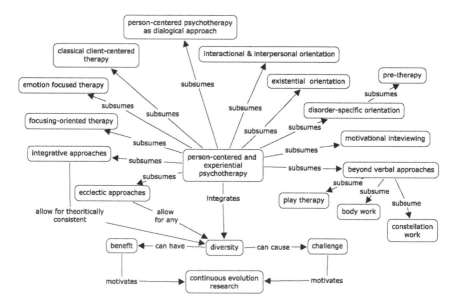

Fig. 1 Concept map visualizing the orientations within the person-centered and experiential psychotherapies (see Stumm, Chap. 3)

goals rather the broader personal growth goals of traditional person-centered approaches. Klein shows how person-centered expressive arts therapy grew throughout the life and career of Natalie Rogers (Carl's daughter). It highlights the empowerment process for individuals and groups, supplying several examples of practice from different regions and time periods.

Pörtner focuses on concrete guidelines for work with adults with special needs, including case examples and the consistency of this work with principles of traditional person-centered psychotherapy. Rao and Umesh describe counseling the spiritual awareness and integration (SAI) way, a popular approach to medical and counseling in India that bears striking resemblances to the PCA. As seen in Fig. 2, SAI counseling integrates spiritual practices like relaxation and mindfulness and cardinal human values like nonviolence, peace, love, and honesty, with person-centered core conditions of empathy, unconditional positive regard and congruence.

Botbol and Lecic-Tosevski show the close relationship of person-centered medicine, a movement in medicine which focuses on the whole person and promotes holistic well-being in addition to the treatment of disease, with the PCA. The authors assume that an enhanced collaboration between person-centered medicine and the PCA might foster the advancement of health care systems.

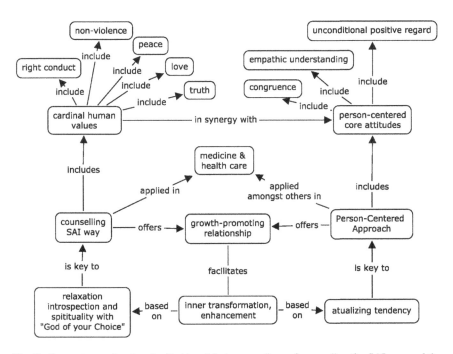

Fig. 2 Concept map showing the "bridges" between notions of counseling the SAI way and the PCA (see Rao and Umesh, Chap. 7)

2 Education

The five chapters of Section 2 provide foundations and extensions of person-centered work in educational contexts, including public schools, adult education, university education, and educational technology enhanced environments. As the "mother" of contemporary person-centered educational work, McCombs provides two chapters that provide an in-depth look at the learner-centered model both in context to classic person-centered concepts and popular mainstream education. She also discusses research methods and a vision for the future about how to improve education utilizing the lessons learned from this extensive work. Figure 3 shows person-centered/learner-centered education their links to research-validated principles related to learning processes and learners as well as classic concepts of organismic valuing and facilitation. It also shows the links between constructivism and collaborative education and that co-learning fosters the solving of authentic problems and develops social and team competence.

The remaining three chapters in this section develop concepts or explain practices within specific areas of education. Kunze shows how concepts apply within adult education. Motschnig-Pitrik describes generalizations from dozens of studies she and her colleagues have conducted within person-centered e-learning

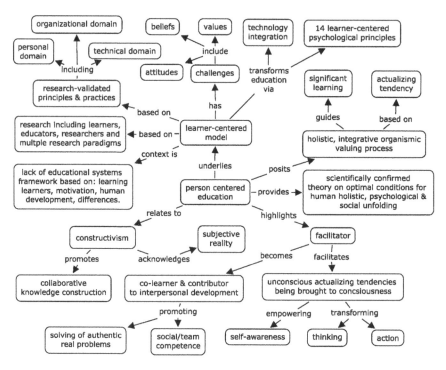

Fig. 3 Concept map highlighting essential issues of the PCA in education (see McCombs, Chap. 9)

in higher education environments. In particular, she points to the consistent value students themselves place on these learning environments when compared to other learning environments they are experiencing that do not include as many of the relational and autonomy supportive elements in both face-to-face and online components. Harbaugh and Cornelius-White provide further discussion on the role that technology can have within person-centered educational contexts. Their focus is on how a meta-review of research on ubiquitous educational computing (where every child and learner has an educational technology device) shows that these programs are most effective when fostered within a learner-centered climate and likewise how introduction of computers for each person can lead to learner-centered classrooms where face-to-face interaction is more facilitative.

3 Children and Family

The third section includes two short chapters. Rice focuses on how all oppression stems from the ways in which adults (especially parents) treat children. It also shows how nondirective person-centered practices represent a contrast and potential solution to a variety of power imbalances and unethical practices throughout the lifespan when this fundamental oppression is understood and improved. Nuding and Hüsson describe how person-centered practices have influenced family education, including the creation, proliferation, and empirically tested applications in parent effectiveness training and filial (child–parent relationship) therapy, and the integration of core concepts into mainstream early childhood principles.

4 Business and Leadership

The fourth section provides three chapters related to leadership and development in business and management contexts. Ryback and Motschnig-Pitrik discuss in an engaging, accessible dialog style chapter, Rogers' contributions in these areas including Ryback's own development and research. Sollárová and Sollár give an overview of applications in managerial and coaching contexts, particularly focusing on the concept of the fully functioning person and on applications in training contexts. Haasis provides a focus on innovation, creativity, and team collaboration using organizational climate concepts from the personal stance of a chief executive officer who has also become a person-centered counselor.

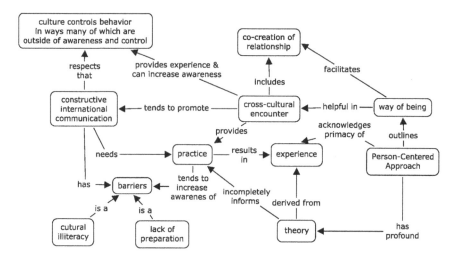

Fig. 4 Concept map visualizing the interconnections between constructive international communication and the theory and practice of the PCA (see Lago, Chap. 18)

5 Conflict and Constructive Communication

The final section of applications of the PCA focuses on conflict and peace. As seen in Fig. 4, Lago provides a description of how constructive cross-cultural and international communication includes a co-creation of relationship and removes barriers related to cultural illiteracy and lack of preparation. It focuses on the way of being that experiences of the PCA fosters.

Stillwell uses the concept conflict transformation to facilitate change in relationships between "parts" of a jeopardized entity through reconciliation, repair, renewal, or dispersal of a "whole" with just and satisfying replacements. He provides illustrative examples and links back to Rogers' original theories. O'Hara highlights the unique opportunities that encounter groups provide to developing collective styles and solutions within the wisdom of this practice. To conclude this section, Hopkins gives examples of how she has merged being a political activist with a clear agenda with being a person-centered counselor with a clear nonagenda in a compelling personal tale.

6 Concluding Thoughts

The editors invite you to engage with this collection of chapters on applications of the PCA across disciplines!

References

Cornelius-White, J. H. D. (Ed.) (2012). *Carl Rogers: The China Diary*. Ross-on-Wye, UK: PCCS Books.

Cornelius-White, J. H. D., & Harbaugh, A. P. (2010). *Learner-centered instruction: Building relationships for student success*. Thousand Oaks, CA: Sage.

Kirschenbaum, H. (2007). The life and work of Carl Rogers. Ross-on-Wye, UK: PCCS.

Rogers, C. R. (1942). *Counseling and psychotherapy: Newer concepts in practice*. Boston: Houghton Mifflin.

Rogers, C. R. (1951). *Client-centered therapy: Its current practice, implications and theory*. London: Constable.

An Experiential Example of the Person-Centered Approach: Carl Rogers at Work

William Stillwell, Antonio Monteiro dos Santos,
Renate Motschnig-Pitrik, Michael Lux
and Jeffrey Cornelius-White

1 Introduction

Below you can read and perhaps visualize Carl Rogers at work, embodying all the conditions of the person-centered approach (PCA), which makes for good psychotherapy and conspicuous communication, especially in an intercultural environment. We can see this deep communication in spite of cultural differences between the two people, leading the client to explore his deep fears and bring them out in the open, so that new beginnings and new ways of coping can open a new world of possibilities for that person. Therefore, we do not want to miss an opportunity in this book to provide a little space for the PCA "at work" by giving an extensive excerpt from Carl Rogers interviewing Dadisi, a black client. The interview was recorded at the Carl Rogers Institute for Psychotherapy and Training in 1985, and it was transcribed by

W. Stillwell (✉) · A. M. d. Santos
Center for Studies of the Person, 1150 Silverado St., La Jolla, CA, US
e-mail: awstillwell@sbcglobal.net

R. Motschnig-Pitrik
Computer Science Didactics and Learning Research Center, University of Vienna, Währinger Strasse 29/6.41, 1090 Vienna, Austria
e-mail: renate.motschnig@univie.ac.at

M. Lux
Neurologisches Rehabilitationszentrum Quellenhof, Kuranlagenallee 2, 75323 Bad Wildbad, Germany
e-mail: luxbw@yahoo.de

J. Cornelius-White
Counseling, Leadership and Special Education, Missouri State University, S. National Avenue 901, Springfield, MO 65897, USA
e-mail: JCornelius-White@MissouriState.edu

J. H. D. Cornelius-White et al. (eds.), *Interdisciplinary Applications of the Person-Centered Approach*, DOI: 10.1007/978-1-4614-7144-8_2,
© Springer Science+Business Media New York 2013

W. Stillwell and A. M. dos Santos. The whole transcribed interview[1] and the questions and responses from the audience can be obtained from the Center for Studies of the Person (http://www.centerfortheperson.org/), or by mailing to William Stillwell (awstillwell@sbcglobal.net). The editors who in this chapter are the primary authors of the introduction, comments, and conclusion thank Will and Antonio for contributing this authentic scenario from Carl Rogers' practice.

The interview is an example of counseling or psychotherapy, from where the field the PCA originates. It is meaningful to this book not only because it is a live presentation in intercultural communication but also because it shows how to build bridges among people instead of creating chasms that separates peoples and dehumanizes them so that they cannot be the best that they can be. Beyond psychotherapy, the basic principles have proven to be applicable to any growth-promoting relationship. In different contexts, some of the basic conditions of the PCA could be more valuable than the others although they function interdependently. Rogers (1980) talks about how each is valuable in their own right when he says that congruence is most important in partnership, working life, or educational settings. "It is a basis for living together in a climate of realness" (p. 160). By facilitating openness to experiences, unconditional positive regard promotes creativity and productive thinking. In addition, it is important if nonverbal aspects of communication are required, for example, during interactions with small children, psychotic persons, or the seriously ill. However, "when the other person is hurting, confused, troubled, anxious, alienated, terrified; or when he or she is doubtful of self-worth, uncertain as to identity" (Rogers 1980, p. 160), problems which are typically addressed in counseling or psychotherapy, empathic understanding has highest priority—a view which is consistent with both Bohart et al.'s (2002) and Elliott et al. (2011) meta-analyses.

Let us now give the word to Rogers and Dadisi so that we can learn in a practical example something about the experience of the PCA. Every time that we have gone through this interview, when we allowed ourselves to relax and attune our minds to it, we have learned something new in the nuances hidden within it which are behind the words spoken, in between the lines, or even by what was left unspoken. We hope sincerely that the reader will have a similar experience. This interview is a precious gift given to us by Rogers and Dadisi so let us listen to what they have to offer us.

2 The Demonstration Interview

Rogers 1: ...I'd be glad to hear about it.

---

[1] In fact, translations into French, Spanish, German, Russian, Portuguese, and Chinese are also available from the Center.

Dadisi 1: Well, what sort of concerns me right *now* is the direction I want to go in ahm, regarding school, (R. Um hum.) and my profession. (R. Um hum.) And my profession is I'm a youth and family counselor, as well as a community organizer at an agency called Harmonium."

Rogers 2: (looks to one of the organisers) Is there any chance of turning off that [background] noise? I'm having a little difficulty getting to hear. But I do understand it's, it's question of where to go in school, (D. Um.) where to go in your career, (D. Um hum.) as, as a counselor. (D. Right.) Marriage and what?...What kind of counselor did you say?

Dadisi 2: Youth, youth and family...

Rogers 3: Youth and family counselor, Okay. (D. Um hum.)

Dadisi 3: And I've been doing that at this agency for approximately four years and prior to that I've been the, um, Kid Counselor and Kid Counselor Supervisor at another agency in San Diego called the After Hours Program and I've worked there for 3 years.

Rogers 4: So you really feel "I've had a lot of experience, but still I'm not, not quite sure now where I want to go," is that...?

Dadisi 4: Right. I have a lot of *experience*, but I don't have the academic credentials (R. Uh huh, I see.) that match with the experience. (R. Uh huh, uh huh.) And that's been a issue as well as a concern for me, for, and it's something that I've been working on, for quite a while.

Rogers 5: Am I getting it right that you really feel quite competent in your work, but you don't have the paper credentials the academic credentials that would...– stand back of that?

Dadisi 5: Exactly.

Rogers 6: Um hum. Um...That sounds like a dilemma! (D. Um. Yeah.) {audience laughs}

Dadisi 6: Sometimes it is, um, and those times when it is, is when I want to do things that I know that I'm qualified for and have skills for, that, and I feel some limitations. Um, some of the things I do right now is um, with my agency, is what I do right now is what we call the New Agency *Counseling* which is above and beyond the scopes an' services of my agency, above my 40-h a week—and um, it's like doing private practice (R. Um hum.) under the auspices of the agency- since I don't have a licence or um, the uh degree. And the *limitations* that I feel sometimes with that, is that I can't, um, don't feel comfortable taking on certain kinds of clients, (R. Um hum.) don't feel comfort...and definitely can't uh, accept insurance. And one of the reasons I'm doing this other agency is to make more money, (R. Um hum.) based on the skills I know I have.

Rogers 7: So, it's, it's frustrating to have so many limitations when you really feel a good deal of personal confidence but uh, then find yourself limited in the things you can do.

Dadisi 7: Right. (R. Um Hum.) So I realize, that one of the things that I would, that I need to do is go back to school to *get* the credentials to do *that*, but, I've had a lot of resistance to doing that. (R. Um hum.)

Rogers 8: So, intellectually you know that the thing to do is to go to school and get the degree, but inwardly you feel "to hell with that."

Dadisi 8: Right. And sometimes it makes me *angry* that I have to do that.

Rogers 9: Um hum, um huh. Why should they be demanding that of you?

Dadisi 9: Right.

Rogers 10: It does make you mad. (D. Um huh.)

Dadisi 10: (18 s silence) I'm getting mad thinking about it.

Rogers 11: Um huh. Just thinking about it (D. Eh.) makes you really feel (slaps his hands together) "Damn it, it's really frustrating, it's unfair," or something like that.

Dadisi 11: Yeah, well, part of me feels like I need to do that, and it's quote unquote "paying the dues." (R. Um hum.) Um, I hear this quite often, to, to me with some staff people that I work with, (R. Um hum.) "Well, yeah you're good at what you do, but you gotta go back to school and 'pay the dues'." And, y'know I can laugh at that, and I at times agree with that and still it' frustrating to feel like I'd be backtracking, (R. Um hum, um hum, um hum.) *regressing*, to go back to do this, it feels like I can, a tremendous *sacrifice*.

Rogers 12: Um hum. Um hum. Yeah, it's gonna cost a lot, and you really feel as though you are really going backwards, like going back into elementary school or something, (D. Right.) to, to catch up on, on paper. Uh huh. (D. Yeah.) Uh huh, um.

Dadisi 12: I don't feel like it's gonna be catching up, I feel like it's just gonna be *documenting*, verifying (R. Uh.) what I feel like (R. Uh.) I already do well.

Rogers 13: Uh huh. Uh huh. Yeah, I see, uh huh, so the most it could do for you feels simply, to *show* that you *can* do, is what you already know you can do.

Dadisi 13: Right. And I am tempted to do that in a lot of ways, and, in a um, in a *sense* have type-of over-compensated for not having the educational background, ah, to back-up, um, the *skills*, and that's been, that's what got me more into the things I do out in the *world* which I all, always feel are much more important than the academic requirements. (R. Um hum, um hum.) Uh...

Rogers 14: Not quite clear on that, but partly *because* of your anger and frustration you do more things out in the world, uh, demonstrating your competence, is that (D. Right.) what you're saying?

Dadisi 14: Right. Part of it I think is demonstrating my *competence* and part of it is doing what I would do with deg the degree (R. Uh huh.) anyway, (R. Uh huh.) and part of I've mentioned, is over-compensation, what I really meant was, um, that what I do with the anger is, (R. Uh.) go out and "do," (R. I see.) uh, instead of feeling limited. (R. Uh huh.) Um, since I've been 21, I've been on several boards of directors of local organizations in the South-East as well as, um, um, working the Master's level position at this point, and got that job through a grueling, ah, interview session (R. Um huh.), three sessions, uh, six people, and I *felt* good that I was able to accomplish that (R. Um.), but also, kinda angry, um, that I had to go through six sessions—I mean, um, *three* separate interviews to verify (R. Um.) the skills I had 'cause I didn't have the degree.

Rogers 15: So does that uh—I get the feeling that you are saying too—that uh, you don't really expect anything out of the academic aspect, *except*, just to prove that you are who you are, that you *are* somebody, that you've held good positions, that you are competent. (D. Um um.) You don't expect to learn anything new.

Dadisi 15: Well... I do, I do. I feel there, there are a lot of things I could learn. I know how I am when I am a student, um, very um, inquisitive, in fact my name is "Dadisi" and what it means is "inquisitive and questioning."

Rogers 16: "Searching and Questioning?" (D. Right.) Um Hum. Um huh. So your very name is a, a "learning" name? (D. Yeah.) Um huh.

Dadisi 16: But I've chosen, often chosen to do that learning, and do that inquisitiveness in other arenas, (R. Um hum.) you know, real life, practical kinds of situations, working with um, *people*, and you mentioned all your living with, you know, your knowledge is (R. Um.), and for me it's living with my knowledge, and what my experience is, and sharing that with other people. (R. Um hum.) Um, I don't know that the academic is going to give me very much more, so my life is at tug and pull for, for my own self—yeah, I can get a lot more out of that, yeah, it's a lot of bullshit.

Rogers 17: Part of what I hear in all that is, your saying, "I'm not a conforming person, I do think in my own way, and I get there in my own way, if I have to conform and fit into an academic framework, that really pisses me off." (D. Yeah.) "I, I'll, I'll learn, I want to learn, but I want to learn in my own way, not in some conforming way."

Dadisi 17: Right. (20 s silence) That learning in my way, y'know when you say that touches for me that has a lot of significance (R. Um hum.) *for* me. Um, when I think, my way, I'm thinking of what I want to do, what I want to accomplish as a self-determining *person*, and that very, um, event of choosing this name that I now have for the last 8 years was a self-determining uh, *event*...(R. Um hum.) uh, has a lot of significance for *me* (R. Um hum.) in terms of who *I* am.

[..] Dadisi continues sharing how he feels about school and what kind of meaningful work he has done.

Rogers 20: Yeah. 'Cause you're getting, you're getting enough satisfactions outside, that, you can't help but feel "Oh, school. To hell with that."

Dadisi 20: Right. I criticize, re-prioritize, (R. Uh huh. Uh huh.) but I sometimes have this simultaneous feeling that some of the things I'm **doing** feel real **incongruent** with the educational level or the expectations (R. Uh hum.) of my educational level and what I should be able to do.

Rogers 21: Um hum. You realize there is a real, real is a mis-match between the amount of education you've had, and what you are doing. (D. Right.) And, the education thing is way low, and what you're doing is way high.

Dadisi 21: Um hum. (nods his head in acknowledgment) (79 s silence) There is another piece that I don't know if I feel comfortable sharing with you.

Rogers 22: I'd appreciate it if you would...if there *is* another piece that you haven't brought up. (23 s silence) I guess it's a real puzzle to know, whether you dare to bring it up.

Dadisi 22: You're puzzled? (smiles at Rogers). (R. Um?) You say you're puzzled?

Rogers 23: No. It sounds, it sounds though *you're* puzzled as to whether or not to bring it up. This other piece.

Dadisi 23: Yes I am. (R. Um hum.) (10 s silence) Part of it in some way has to do with not only who I am, but who you are. (R. Um hum, um hum, um hum.)

Rogers 24: What part of me? The fact that I'm *white*, or that I'm well known or what?

Dadisi 24: The fact that you're white.

Rogers 25: The fact that I'm white. You feel a little fearful in bringing up something that really has a lot of meaning to you because I'm a different color.

Dadisi 25: Right.

Rogers 26: Want to take a chance?

Dadisi 26: (feigns startle) I don't know yet! (laughs) {audience laughs}.

Rogers 27: I guess I'd appreciate it if you'd try me out.

Dadisi 27: It's a little hard, difficult for me because this is still a *live* issue (R. Um hum.) something I'm dealing with now. (R. Um hum.) Um, it has to do with you, the fact that you're *white*, it has to do with…also how I feel about *school*, (R. Um hum.) and the fact, um, how I've always felt about school, being a student predominantly in America (R. Um hum, um hum.) um, and, dealing with white educational systems (R. Um hum, um hum.) that never taught me anything about *me*, (R. Um hum, um hum.) and (R. Um *hum*.) for instance learning history, and not learning anything about black contributions to (R. Um.) American history, *world* history, in fact.

Rogers 28: So, part of the resentment against school is that it's a white system that hasn't taught you anything about yourself or about your background, or your race, your history, and that makes you mad!

Dadisi 28: Yeah it makes me mad, but it also motivates me to go and get it (R. Uh huh, uh huh.) for myself (R. Uh huh.) and not expect (R. Uh huh.) white people to …

Rogers 29: Not get it through the white system, but get it yourself.

Dadisi 29: Right. (R. Uh huh, uh huh, um, uh huh, um.) So some of my resistance with school has also been avoidance of *acceptance*, (R. Um hum.) avoiding *accepting*, um, *all* information that is transmitted in white institutions.

Rogers 30: (R. Um hum, um hum.) Yeah, that makes, that helps to clarify it; so underneath some dislike for school, is the fact that you're saying, "I don't like to take information or education from a white system. (D. Um. Yeah.) I resent that."

Dadisi 30: Um hum. (R. Um hum.) A totally white system with what felt like totally white interests at heart. (R. Um hum, um hum.) I never thought you'd have my interests at heart, (R. Um hum.) anyhow.

Rogers 31: We're interested just in the whites. (7 s silence) Mmm hum. So that's, that' much deeper than just a dislike of school, isn't it, I mean it's a real, real strong feeling about, strong feeling *against* a system that doesn't have your interests at heart.

Dadisi 31: Exactly. (21 s silence) And I feel that with the experience I've had in *public* school, I've been of the belief that the higher in the, this white educational system you be—you went, um, the more assimilated (R. The word.) *as-sim-i-la-ted* (R. Um hum.) that one became. (R. Um. Um hum, um hum.) So part of my avoidance is to being assimilated. (R. Um hum, um hum.)

Rogers 32: *Uh huh.* The higher you go, the more likelihood of being assimilated, and you don't want to be assimilated! (D. Nope.) You want to be a black *person.* (D. Yes.)

Dadisi 32: And learn and teach about what are *my* interests, (R. Uh huh, uh huh.) y' know, and assist and help and heal *my* people (R. Uh huh.). And, see, there are very few places where that's being taught, (R. Uh huh.) or where that interest (R. Uh huh, uh huh) is a priority.

Rogers 33: It narrows down a *lot* the places where you might get the kind of education you would want. (D. Um hum.) A very few. But you want to be of service to your people and help them, heal them. And you'd like to get the education *for* that. Not, not a white education.

Dadisi 33: (both drink, 36 s of silence) Some of the pieces have always been there, some of those pieces of information have always been there, but I think it's probably *taken* me I've turned thirty, yesterday (R. Um huh.)—*probably* just about to this time, to feel set in myself and set enough in my identity that I could take that on with a probably greater strength, (R. Um huh.) and, know that I won't necessarily *lose me*. (R. Uh huh. Uh huh. I *think* I'm getting that).

Rogers 34: Yet, (clears throat) you feel now, sufficient strength in your own identity (D. Um um.) that perhaps you could even take what you want, from a system you don't like, um, and not lose your identity, not be assimilated, is that..? (D. Um hum.) Yeah.

Dadisi 34: I realize I've been doing that all my *life* (humorously) 'cause I'm with white people all the time, y' know, and white institutions, and white information, everything.

Rogers 35: And now a white counselor, huh? {audience laughs}

Dadisi 35: Now a white counselor. (reaches out and touches Rogers' knee smiling) Yeah, I've always chosen black counselors. (R. Uh huh.) For sure. (R. Uh huh. Uh huh.) Yeah. (R. Uh huh.) And part of me is seeing that black counselors would understand me *better*, (R. Uh huh.) but, I've often times found myself in strange situations as being very understanding of *white* people…(continues but is interrupted)

Rogers 36: Do you mean understanding *of* white people or *by* white people?

Dadisi 36: By and for.

Rogers 37: By and for. Um hum. Um hum. So that, understanding between black and white isn't impossible? You, you've experienced that.

Dadisi 37: Right. No not that never really was the primary issue, (R. Um hum.) the understanding between races, but, um, just a, a racist, what I thought to be a racist *system* (R. Yeah, uh huh, uh huh.) which included education. (R. Um huh.)

Rogers 38: So with white individuals you've been able to understand and be understood but, but a racist white *system*, that's a different matter. (D. Um mm, yeah.)

Dadisi 38: And even with the, the prejudicial white people, that's been an evolution…ary unfolding kind of thing for me also. (R. Um hum, um hum.) Which has just been tied to my own personal development, y' know. Someone, uh, Maria, mentioned being an angry Mexican, a lot of times I'm an angry black, (R. Um hum.) I can't stand white people, (R. Um hum.) don't want to be around them. (R. Uh huh, uh huh.) Yeah.

But it, it also, when I'm feeling that about white people in general, there may be people who I have close relationships with, who I'm excluding from that general (laugh) "hatred," y' know. (R. Um hum). I hate all white people except...{all laugh as he points toward members of the audience}. {audience laughs} (R. Um hum, um hum.) I actually recall having done that since (R. Um hum) 'bout (R. Um hum) age (R. Um hum.) twelve.

Rogers 39: Um hum. So the feeling is "I hate all the whites, an', *well* except so and so, and so and so, and so and so."

Dadisi 39: Um hum...That *has* been the feeling, that's not (R. Uh.) so much where I am now. (R. Um.) But the issue with school in, is still something that, um, I, I deal with. (R. Um hum.) Yeah. (R. Um hum.) I probably know that *there will* be changes, there *are* changes, um, *happening* or me now, ahm, how *much*, I want to, ah, accept, or how much I want to, um, open up to those changes is still something I'm not certain I can still work on.

Rogers 40: But you know there are *changes* in you, going on, that, will make a difference, huh? (D. Um hum)

Dadisi 40: Um hum. Yeah. Now I have a real keen interest in *becoming* a therapist, I view myself as a therapist *now*, but I need to have the *credentials*. (R. Um hum.) Um, I have some similar beliefs as you in peace-making,

[..] Dadisi describes his experience form going through his struggles and his relationship with white people.

Rogers 43: So, there is, you have faced the possibility of, of, excluding white people, hating white people, and so forth, but you really have come to the conclusion, well, they need healing too, and, and, it's, you don't want to have a complete exclusion of, of white interests.

Dadisi 43: Right. Not just that white people need healing, but they need some of my and others like my (R. Uh huh.) particular kind of healing (R. Okay.) okay, maybe even more so.

Rogers 44: Okay. You realize within yourself "I could make a *contribution* to the white person, from myself." (D. nods) Okay. Shall we call it quits? (D. Yeah.) Okay. Um, what I'd like to do when you feel, ready, is if, if you would tell the group how our interview seemed to you, I'll tell them how it seemed to me, and then uh, we can take questions to you or to me. Uh, does that seem okay? When you thought about it a little, you might tell them how did this, how did this, how did this half hour seem to you.

Dadisi: Long! (problem with the microphone happens and nothing audible for approx 1 min) We really had a limited amount of time. And a lot of pieces of my personal history, but it seemed like, in line with what we were talking about, I was thinking a lot of things that did need to be said, but that was going on, um, back when we were discussing them. What was keeping me from talking about that were pretty broad, but dealt with a lot of things that I'm gonna have to see. (R. Um hum, um hum.) I, like I said that I had some discomfort about how much I wanted to *share*, um, other parts of me with you and the public, um, (waves hand toward audience) I work with some of these people {audience laugh with him}.

Rogers: Took a lot, it took a lot of courage. (D. Huh huh.) Um hum. Have you finished? (D. Yeah.) Uh, I think to me it seemed uh, one, one thing I felt keenly, I felt with you and for you, more than you might even know, because I'm a rebel too! (D. Mm mm.) I'm not black, but I'm a rebel and um… So I could *very well* understand your resentment on catching up on the paper credentials when you feel you are already have the competence. Uh, then I was very much interested in your silences because, after each silence, you went onto something more significant, and after the *longest* silence was when you were debating and debating whether to, really talk about the issue of, color; and uh I, I uh, I felt they were real "working" silences. I knew things were going on in you all the time that weren't being said, and I didn't need to know them. Um, uh, and I appreciated the uh, fact that, you didn't try to come to any *false* conclusions, you're, you're still uncertain of just where you'll go, but you're, you're thinking it through more clearly, I, I like that. Uh, and I was, I, I uh, I appreciated the fact that you were willing to talk to me, even though I was white. Um, I really appreciated that. And uh, I don't know whether you felt understood, I felt that I understood you pretty well. Um, but uh anyway, I felt, I felt in a half an hour, we did half an hour's worth, (D. Um.) I felt good about that. (D. Um hum.) Shall we let them ask us questions? [end of excerpt].

3 Reflection and Outlook

The above interchanges illustrate a real meeting between two persons and cultures. The person-centered attitudes which form the basis of a growth-promoting inter-personal relationship pervade the whole interview. Let us first take a look at empathy. It can be observed that Rogers' accompanying responses focus on checking understanding by summarizing the essence of Dadisi's statements. In this way, Dadisi can perceive that he is understood and can freely continue exploring his experience. Rogers accompanies Dadisi by "feeding back" important meanings from what he receives from Dadisi and thereby communicates his interest in Dadisi. Responses 14–17 provide an example.

In addition, Rogers expresses unconditional positive regard by communicating his curiosity and preference in a very respectful way, giving the impression of being on the same human level in the contemplation and decision process. Congruence is also salient. While Rogers communicates his inner world, he stays with Dadisi in his process that just has touched Rogers' experience. The exchanges show that Rogers gives a clear and transparent response to Dadisi. In this way, the puzzlement is clarified and the two do not get caught in potential transference. Responses 21–27 provide an example.

Finally, nondirectivity becomes evident in Rogers' abstention from exerting control—an expression from his deep trust in the actualizing tendency "doing its job." This is revealed, for example, by the way Rogers deals with silences. The silences are characterized by patience and humility from Rogers but are in fact working silences by Dadisi. After each silence, Dadisi goes one level deeper and explores something still more significant. Responses 20–23 provide an example.

Perhaps the most important moment of this interview came on the interaction beginning on response 21 by Dadisi where the relationship between the black-and-white cultures is at stake. It seems that at this point, Dadisi needed to make sure that he could go deeper within by testing if Rogers really means in a personal way what his theory says about equality, shared power as well as race and culture discrimination. Rogers answers swiftly motivating Dadisi to test it with no fear whatsoever opening new knowledge in a subtle way for Dadisi to understand that not all people practice discrimination and therefore discriminative practices must be checked in a person to person basis instead of generalizing it to a whole race. Not all whites discriminate against blacks and vice versa. We believe that this was a moment of movement in this interview, as Rogers (Bowen, Rogers and Santos, Rogers and Carl 2004) calls them, which, perhaps, took Dadisi to explore deeper levels of his experiencing and allowed for Dadisi's expression below many years later:

This interview changed my life.

It seems that the same constructive tendency and facilitative, person-centered climate pervades the relationships in various applications or settings of the PCA such as encounter groups, workshops, educational settings. However, while focus in on the client's experience in psychotherapy which guides the evolution of the relationship and meaning space between therapist and client, encounter groups, educational settings, and other applications typically have different or additional goals. What these are and in how far PCA can make a difference in a multitude of other fields will be discussed in several application-oriented chapters in third section of this book.

References

Bohart, A., Elliott, R., Greenberg, L. S., & Watson, J. C. (2002). Empathy. In J. C. Norcross (Ed.), *Psychotherapy relationships that work: Therapist contributions and responsiveness to patients* (pp. 89–108). New York: Oxford University Press.

Rogers, Carl R. (2004). A essência da psicoterapia—momentos de movimento. [The essence of psychotherapy: Moments of movement]. In M. C. Villas-Boas Bowen, C. R. Rogers., & A. M. dos Santos (Eds.), Quando fala o coração—a essência da psicoterapia centrada na pessoa [Spellbound: The essence of person-centered psychotherapy]. São Paulo: Vetor Editora.

Elliott, R., Bohart, A., Watson, J., & Greenberg, L. S. (2011). Empathy. *Psychotherapy, 48*(1), 43–49.

Rogers, C. R. (1980). *A way of being*. Boston: Houghton Mifflin.

Part II
Clinical Applications

Person-Centered and Experiential Psychotherapies: An Overview

Gerhard Stumm

The lecture "Some newer concepts of psychotherapy"[1] given by Carl Rogers in 1940 at the University of Minnesota can be seen as the date of birth of "client-centered psychotherapy." Since then, many more concepts have been developed by Rogers himself, his associates, and successors, this article is dedicated to demonstrate again that drawing from the notion of "newer concepts" today—more than 70 years after Rogers "groundbreaking innovation"—a vast variety of "tribes" of the person-centered "nation" (Warner 2000a) or "united colors" (Lietaer 2002) or "members" of the person-centered "family" now exist.

After classical client-centered therapy (CCT) was introduced by Carl Rogers and enhanced by him and his colleagues in the course of the years (Rogers 1951, 1959, 1961), a diversity of sub-orientations within the person-centered field has entered the stage. It is the goal of this chapter to illustrate, from a pluralistic perspective, the characteristics of the different brands and branches of the person-centered approach (PCA) in its application in psychotherapy (Bohart 1995, 2012; Keil and Stumm 2002; Sanders 2004, 2007; Kriz and Slunecko 2007; Lietaer 2008; Stumm 2008; Cain 2010).

At the outset of my venture, I present a schema that tries to catch and position the most prominent sub-orientations (see Fig. 1). Though this is quite a risky venture insofar as it attributes approximate categories to complex conceptions, nevertheless, for didactic reasons I believe this is tolerable. One underlying rationale of the following overview is that the diverse sub-orientations have different degrees of "(process) directivity." This follows the debate on "non-directivity," a crucial topic in the person-centered tradition. The theoretical orientations that advocate a non-directive style are to be found in the left hemisphere of Fig. 1,

---

[1] Chapter 2 of Carl Rogers' book 'Counseling and psychotherapy: Newer concepts in practice' (1942) is a revised version.

G. Stumm (✉)
Kalvarienberggasse 24/12, 1170 Vienna, Austria
e-mail: gerhard.stumm@tplus.at

J. H. D. Cornelius-White et al. (eds.), *Interdisciplinary Applications of the Person-Centered Approach*, DOI: 10.1007/978-1-4614-7144-8_3,

Suborientations	orthodox/traditional client-centered/person-centered orientation		various other sub-orientations	experiential orientation	
	(1) Classical Client-Centered Therapy ('non-directive')	(2) relational/ dialogic orientation	(3) interactional (interpersonal) orientation (4) existential orientation (5) disorder specific orientation (incl. pre-therapy) (6) creativity oriented (7) Motivational Interviewing (10) integrative orientation	(8) Focusing-oriented	(9) Emotion-Focused Therapy
Representatives (examples)	Brodley Bozarth Moon Levitt Warner Merry Sanders Sommerbeck	Mearns Thorne Cooper Pfeiffer Schmid Behr	(3) van Kessel, Lietaer, van Kalmthout (4) Swildens, Cooper (5) Swildens, Finke, Teusch, Speierer, Binder, Greenberg, Sachse, Prouty, van Werde (6) N. Rogers, Silverstone, Groddeck (7) Miller & Rollnick (10) Lietaer ["Leuven-school"], Bohart, Cain, Worsley, Keil, Gutberlet	Gendlin Purton Leijssen Wiltschko Iberg Weiser Cornell	Greenberg Rice Elliott Watson Goldman

Fig. 1 Overview of person-centered and experiential therapies

while others, including the experiential tribes that emphasize process-directive styles are located at the right-hand side.

The overview makes it clear that I have not only included approaches that stick to the classical tradition but also orientations that offer conceptualizations which go beyond the fundamental concepts elaborated by Rogers. The explicit inclusion of the experiential wing (focusing, emotion-focused therapy) particularly suggests that my starting point and outlook for the whole topic is PCE (as a person-centered/experiential approach). I will return to this issue in the conclusion.

Before I proceed to describe the essential characteristics of the sub-orientations of PCE, it seems appropriate to define my own orientation as a practitioner and as a trainer in person-centered psychotherapy. I regard myself as sympathizing with an integrative stance (Keil and Stumm 2002; Tuczai et al. 2008). I advocate for a broad palette of influences like classical, dialogic, interactional, experiential, existential as parts of an elastic (in contrast to rigid) person-centered identity. I am open to integrating pre-therapy, expressive media, body therapeutic elements, or a disorder-specific perspective. My guiding line is to steer a course that avoids both rigid orthodoxy on the one hand and complete "laissez-faire" on the other. What is required is integration with integrity! (see Sect. 10).

1 Classical Client-Centered Therapy

This tribe claims to be the genuine "incarnation" of what Carl Rogers himself has elaborated. Other labels for what one might call it are *non-directive, traditional, client-centered (as opposed to person-centered), orthodox, purist, literalist* or—with a distinct critical connotation—*conservative, dogmatic,* and *fundamentalist.* Barbara Brodley (2011b), Jerold Bozarth (1998), Tony Merry (2004) are prominent representatives of this strand. I will outline the main characteristics of this original perspective to establish a reference point for the different orientations (see Sects. 2, 3, 4, 5, 6, 7, 8, 9, 10) that deviate in one way or the other from this stance.

The main focus and thus characteristic of CCT is on the psychotherapist's basic attitudes, which serve to support the innate trustworthy growth potential of the client: known as the actualizing tendency, which is "the foundation block of person-centered therapy" (Bozarth 1998, p. 6). The therapist should be dedicated to go "with the client's direction, at the client's pace and in the client's unique way of being" (Bower and Bozarth; cit. by Bozarth 1998, p. 9). Many of the underlying principles follow Rogers' publications of 1951, 1957, and 1959. Especially in the two latter publications, he not only state the necessary conditions of personality growth but also declared these to be sufficient, while specifically citing the two arenas of diagnosis and specific treatments for defined disorders of the client as matters that did not concern the client-centered therapist. This is echoed by Brodley and Brody (1996) who claimed that the therapist should be guided by "a profoundly non-diagnostic mindset" (p. 371).

From this classical orientation, psychotherapy is seen by a number of representatives as an *ethical project*, that is, that the therapist does not interfere with the client's self-determination but provides a climate that facilitates autonomy, self-regulation, and self-agency. Crucial are values like "trust" in the capacities of human beings, deeply connected with the importance of freedom, an egalitarian aspiration, and caution to not disempower clients by exercising power over them. Such an understanding of Rogerian psychotherapy is very common among people who participate in the activities of the Association for the Development of the Person-Centered Approach (ADPCA), which has its center in the United States.

Figurehead of this stream was Barbara Brodley (1932–2007), who was also designated a "hardliner" (Wolfgang Keil; personal communication) due to her strict separation of "client-centered" and "experiential" as "different therapies" (Brodley 1990). In a chapter written briefly before her death, she has labeled her approach as *non-directive and non-experiential* (Brodley 2006b/2011b). Based on an empirical comparison, she concludes that her practice reveals a great deal of similarities with Carl Rogers' performance in therapeutic sessions.

Consistent with the later Rogers, the therapist might bring in responses from his/her own frame of reference (T-frame responses), but only on defined occasions like arrangements of therapy, addressing and encouraging "questions" and "requests" of clients (but "within the therapist's limits and ethics"), the therapist's own persistent resonance in terms of "loss of acceptance of empathy or incongruence" (like feeling bored or annoyed or disapproving the client), or spontaneous responses that are neither planned nor systematically intended (Brodley 1999/2011a, 2006b/2011b).

As I have mentioned above, the "power issue" is a delicate challenge for the therapist. Clients, "vulnerable" and easy to influence, may, just to oblige the therapist, follow process suggestions. Thereby therapists may risk damaging the potential of self-determination of the client, this being a central concern of client-centered philosophy.

As far as non-directivity is concerned, Grant (1990) distinguishes "instrumental" and "principled" non-directivity, stressing that the latter is a basic, permanent, and non-negotiable attitude which refrains from any therapeutic calculation (Brodley 2006a). This emphasizes an ethical principle to eschew any behavior that reduces the client's experience of equality within the relationship with the therapist. This ethical guideline supersedes even the idea of the actualizing tendency. For Levitt (2008), the actualizing tendency is just a "myth," a leitmotif that is only useful if it supports the "non-directive path" and the right of clients for self-determination. Also for Moon (2008), the actualizing tendency is not the first premise for her therapeutic endeavor: "I justify client-centered therapy by its ethical rightness in accepting and sheltering each individual intrinsically worthy and entitled to self-determination ... In fact my trust in the client is founded upon my respect for a person's *right* to be free and to self-determine" (p. 204).

Brodley, Grant, Levitt, and Moon belong to the same person-centered tribe. Of course, there are many others who feel attached to the classical branch but vary more or less in their interpretation of what "the late Rogers" has left as his legacy. Some of them highlight the feelings of clients or claim more space for the frame of reference of the therapist. A protagonist of an extreme position is Lisbeth Sommerbeck, a Danish psychologist, who has worked for over 30 years in psychiatric institutions. She argues that CCT should go "back to the roots" which are to be found in Rogers (1951). According to her conceptualization, "Rogers 1" (the *client-centered* Rogers) and "Rogers 2" (the later Rogers who is categorized as having been *therapist-centered* and *we-centered*) are differentiated (Frankel and Sommerbeck 2005, 2007). The main concerns of the authors are the inner frame of reference of the client, empathic understanding of the therapist, and the goal "to maximally minimize the risk of conveying conditional regard to the client" (Sommerbeck 2003 p. 16). Empathic understanding is aligned to "what the client wants the therapist to understand" (Sommerbeck 2003, p. 14). Interventions from the frame of reference of the therapist like feedback, confrontation, immediacy, or self-disclosure of the therapist (Finke 2004) distract the client from his/her own track. Congruence as it has been introduced by Rogers (1957) as one of the six necessary and sufficient conditions for therapeutic constructive personality change is denoted as "category error" (Frankel and Sommerbeck 2007), since it is already implied in the attitudes of empathic understanding and unconditional positive regard. The question which remains then is to what degree he/she reveals his/her experiences to the client, a question that has consequently spawned several different perspectives on therapeutic practice in the PCA.

Sommerbeck's point of view is thus a prototype of the therapist as mere "alter ego" of the client. Critics may say this is a regression or a fallback into a view of the therapist as "depersonalized," a criticism with which client-centered therapy had to struggle for years. But if we take into account that Sommerbeck's domain is work with highly disordered people, her warning might have good reasons to be considered at least in working with easily irritable clients. Nevertheless, the contrast of this perspective is made clear by the following sub-orientation, which advocates an explicit dialogic stance.

2 Person-Centered Psychotherapy as Dialogical Approach

As an existential-humanistic approach which has its roots in existential philosophy and in Buber's encounter philosophy, dialog, collaboration, and the *real* relationship have a long tradition in the PCA.

Starting with Wolfgang Pfeiffer in 1970's in Germany, an explicit relational perspective in person-centered theory has culminated in the work of the Austrian Peter Schmid who in the last two decades has published widely on the person in her/his relational quality and on psychotherapy as "personal encounter" (e.g., Schmid 2001). This position is also held in the "British school" of PCT, represented by the work of Dave Mearns, Brian Thorne, and Mick Cooper, who distinguished the role of the psychotherapist as an "other" and "counterpart" for the client, establishing PCT as a "two-person-centered therapy." Furthermore, for example, Michael Behr (2009), a person-centered child therapist from Germany, has presented the concept of "interactional resonance" that refers to and makes explicit use of the immediate experiencing of the therapist during the interaction with the child. Confronting the client with the therapist as a person demands the psychotherapist's presence, resonance, and disclosure of the therapist's frame of reference.

"Relational depth" was not only coined as a term by the Scottish colleague Dave Mearns (1996) but also introduced as a dialogic concept by him and is a good example to demonstrate what a dialogic PCA has to offer. Relational depth is defined as "a state of profound contact and engagement between two people, in which each person is fully real with the Other, and able to understand and value the Others's experiences at a high level" (Mearns and Cooper 2005, p. xii). In this orientation of PCT, such a profound contact and engagement between therapist and client is not only desirable, but it is a therapeutic goal to actively strive for. It is the therapist's intention to engage with the client on a deep level, transcending the technical aspects of the core conditions and establishing contact with the client beyond the surface level. The moment of encounter is paramount to facilitate change processes in the client. Far beyond focusing only on the frame of reference of the client, the spontaneous and active participation of the therapist is a means to offer relational experiences that can modify the client's relational patterns. The therapist is therefore required to offer a deep involvement and willingness to meet the client and share experiences with him/her. An affinity to existential thought is obvious here (see also Sect. 4).

This concept is based on a theoretical assumption of the fundamental need for relational experiences, attachment, and social interaction (Mearns and Cooper 2005). Ultimately, these needs seem to be superior to the need for the therapist's positive regard. In light of attachment theory, the need for positive regard can be reconsidered as an important element of the attachment system (Bowlby 1969).

From a clinical perspective, I express my reservation about such a deep engagement in the therapeutic relationship being required from the client. What is debatable at the philosophical level could prove to be an overwhelming experience for a patient with a fragile self-concept.

Some critique of this perspective has been expressed by people from the traditional client-centered camp, specifically suggesting a missing unintentionality and a directive practice (Wilders 2007). Tudor (2010) extended the critique. He argued that the concept of relational depth offends the principle of horizontalization, part of the phenomenological method. It implies a judgement, a depreciation for "superficial" experiencing of the client and a diagnostic expertise of the therapist in terms of the degree of relational depth.

I turn now to the next orientation whose focus lies also within the relational domain but situates the client's interactions to the fore.

3 Interactional/Interpersonal Orientation

This version of person-centered therapy predominantly deals with how the client relates to the therapist and co-creates the therapeutic relationship; thus, relational experiences and resulting relational schemata, which become transparent in relational expectations and performances, are seen as primary in contrast to the self-exploration of the client. The underlying idea of the utmost importance is the relational history of the client which then determines the practical implications for the therapist. Since interpersonal patterns are viewed as primary in the etiology of mental disorders, it is hypothesized that a change in interpersonal patterns of the client will also modify his/her intrapsychic structures.

Therefore, the emphasis of the therapeutic venture lies on the client's "way of offering a relationship," on how the client actualizes and handles relationships as it becomes visible during the therapeutic relationship.

The way the client gets in contact in the here and now of the actual therapeutic space points to the specific relational patterns he/she has acquired in the course of his/her life time, primarily in his/her childhood. Following this, the therapist might use the technique of "immediacy," an active intervention to refer to the actual client's relational behavior. Metacommunication on the relational experience in the here and now is used to explore the interpersonal patterns of the client and to modify his/her modes of relating (van Kessel and Lietaer 1998; van Kessel and Keil 2002). Finke (2004) indicates that the therapist ought to pay attention to relational issues only when the client brings in the topic explicitly or implicitly.

Though the dialogic exchange plays a certain role, the focus remains on the relational part of the client. It is up to the therapist to react in an "asocial," "non-positional," and "non-complementary" way, that is, to refuse to fulfill the (rigid) expectations of the client (van Kessel and Keil 2002). By not being a part of the intended "collusion," the therapist will not take over "roles" that the client (who is used to these "role-plays") wants him/her to play. In other words, by doing this, the therapist "throws back" the client upon him/herself to stimulate him/her to reflect upon his/her own relational style.

The "interpersonal approach" or "interactional orientation," based on Sullivan, Kiesler, and Yalom, makes the relationship "an arena for explicit interactional work" (van Kessel and Lietaer 1998, p. 157). By doing this, it goes far beyond providing a safe climate. It is directive insofar as it is the aim of the therapeutic work to focus on the relating of the client to the therapist and by implication, enhancing the client's awareness of their regular relational patterns.

Though it comes close to the analytic conception of a "transference-relationship," there are differences to a psychodynamic understanding: "The therapeutic relationship is not structured in such a way as to maximize regression and transference" and "the emphasis is not on working to achieve insight… but on the corrective emotional experience" (van Kessel and Lietaer 1998, p. 167f). Nevertheless the psychodynamic touch is evident which makes for the interactional orientation having an integrative tone—like other orientations that will be depicted (see Sect. 10).

4 Existential Orientation

Based on existential philosophy (Kierkegaard, Heidegger, Buber, Sartre and others), existential therapy comprises several approaches (Cooper 2003a; 2004). The PCA, however, is influenced by existential thinking, but it is not an explicit existential approach by itself, as I have also illustrated elsewhere (Stumm 2005). Rogers and some of his colleagues were interested in existential philosophy, but finally were rather attached to the American offspring, the humanistic movement in psychology. Concepts like an actualizing tendency or the particular emphasis on growth and autonomy do not get along easily with existential cornerstones like human existence as an innate "being with" or the significance of choice, meaning and responsibility, or elements like tragic dimensions and limitations such as death, transitoriness, existential anxiety, existential guilt, and even absurdity of the human existence (Cooper 2003b). Underlining these elements that have been rather neglected in the PCA, existential therapy transcends what Rogers and Gendlin (the latter equated existential with experiential) have already integrated from an existential background.

Nevertheless a few theorists like Swildens and Cooper have advocated the benefits of integrating an existential perspective into person-centered theory and practice. Swildens (1991) has presented a model of PCT that is grounded in existential thinking: "process-oriented client-centered psychotherapy" (see also Sect. 5). He has based his method on existential concepts like "facticity" (past, fixed givens, facts of life), "existentiality" (potentiality, future), intersubjectivity/ interconnectedness, and corporeality. He considers humans to be a process, and process-oriented psychotherapy is indicated if that process comes to a standstill or is being blocked. Moreover, he introduced concepts like *alibi* (reasons for not daring the process of being and becoming and not taking existential risks), *myth* (the subjective history), and *hindrance of choice* (different mechanisms of refusing authentic being) or *existential phase* (a possible stage in the therapeutic process), all of them rooted in an existential tradition.

Cooper (2003b) also underlines aspects that are not explicitly included in the classical tradition of client-centered/person-centered/experiential theory: these include (tragic) limits, contingency (chance), immanent tensions and antinomies of our existence, the permanent challenge of making choices, and a future orientation.

Given all these aspects, it is evident that a practice informed by an existential perspective implies a more challenging and confronting style, which includes the therapist clearly stating his/her position and revealing his/her perceptions, feelings and considerations (see also the existential touch in "relational depth" Sect. 2).

5 Disorder-Specific Orientation

Such an orientation is to be found mainly in continental Europe, particularly in the Netherlands, Germany, Belgium, Switzerland, and Austria. A number of theorists and practitioners, including psychiatrists like Swildens (1991), Finke (2004); Finke and Teusch (2007), and Speierer (1994), but also Greenberg and Sachse, for example, have argued for disorder-specific clinical knowledge (including classification of diagnoses) and the use of detailed and systematically structured treatment procedures within the person-centered framework. Depending on the disorder, for instance, different dominating themes (Finke and Teusch), stagnations (Swildens), or constellations of incongruence (according to the Differential Incongruence Model by Gert Speierer 1994) are postulated and, depending on the disorder, specific techniques as means of implementing the person-centered principles are recommended (e.g., Finke 2004).

Swildens' "process-oriented" approach uses diagnoses as categories which have a common aspect. They serve to offer specific therapeutic help for specific groups of individuals. Therefore, the model makes statements about how the person-centered attitudes have to be implemented by specific techniques in concrete (clinical) situations. "If the existential process, that is the human being as such, gets stuck because of a defect, then it takes more than a client-centered relationship to get things going again" (Swildens 1991, p. 62). Interventions (like empathic, actualizing, evocative, and confronting) vary due to the specific disorder of the particular client and the specific phase of the therapeutic process (premotivational, symptom, conflict, existential, and separation).

Binder and Binder (1991), Binder (2011) advocate the concept of "disorder-specific understanding." Ute Binder (1994, p. 17f) concludes that the more severely a client is disturbed, the more difficult it is to live the therapeutic core conditions. As a result—if the core conditions are not sufficiently set into practice—the treatment can be severely damaging for the client. Without clinical knowledge, the core attitudes might remain far below the necessary level. Apart from that she states: The more severely the client is disturbed, the more specific (and characteristic for each disorder) are the ways clients experience life. Knowledge of psychopathology would therefore be indispensable.

Though the emphasis of this orientation is on clinical aspects (e.g., knowledge about psychopathology, specifically with reference to the client's particular disorder, allied to a clinical practice that is suited to the category of that clients' disorder), its distinct outlook partly overlaps with other orientations. These include, for instance, an existential (Swildens) (see Sect. 4), a process-experiential/emotion-focused (Greenberg, Elliott) (see Sect. 9), or a hermeneutic view (Finke 1998), in which the therapist is regarded as an expert to understand (not to explain though) the client even better than the client him/herself is able to do.

In my opinion, Garry Prouty's *pre-therapy* is disorder specific as—referring to *psychological contact*, condition one in Rogers' six therapeutic conditions—it is meant to be applied with "out of contact" clients (psychotic, autistic, demented, cognitive-disabled, and brain-damaged people). As such pre-therapy is an approach that is offered before, if at all, psychotherapy can take place. There are a number of person-centered theorists who integrate pre-therapy into person-centered practice (Dion Van Werde, Marlis Pörtner, Hans Peters, Lisbeth Sommerbeck, just to mention a few).

The essential technique of pre-therapy are called contact reflections, which serve to establish contact with the world (reality contact), with oneself (affective contact), and with others (communicative contact) (Prouty, Van Werde and Pörtner 2002). These include as follows:

- *Word-for-word reflections*: Concrete echoing (even paralingual) of the (often fragmentary) utterances of the client.
- *Situational reflections*: Reflecting environmental aspects.
- *Facial reflections*: Reflecting verbally or physically facial expressions of the client.
- *Body reflections*: Reflecting verbally or physically expressions of the body of the client (gestures, movements, postures).
- *Reiterative reflections*: Repeat reflections that tended to be effective in terms of increasing contact.

I esteem pre-therapy as an eminent precious instrument to work with clients who otherwise would not receive an adequate psychological form of treatment. I regard it as one of the most remarkable innovations of the PCA in the post-Rogers era.

Finally, a few words on "difficult process" a diagnostic concept presented by Margaret Warner that outlines the problems of processing and provides useful inputs for a disorder-specific person-centered practice (Warner 2000b). Employing a phenomenological stance, she distinguishes "fragile process" and "dissociated process": While the first category (with an affinity to personality disorders) deals with problems of affect regulation (the intensity of experiencing is either too high or too low; affective reactions start all of a sudden or cannot be stopped; it is hardly possible to take the view of another person without losing one's own), the second is caused by traumatic experiences in childhood (e.g., sexual abuse). It is connected with states of trance, which allow relief, and splittings of different aspects of the self (similar to "dissociative identity disorder" in DSM IV).

6 Motivational Interviewing

With Keil (personal communication) and Bohart (at the PCE conference 2010 in Rome), I tend to include "motivational interviewing" (MI) into the person-centered family, though, for instance, their representatives do not perform as regular members at person-centered conferences. Introduced in the mid-1980s in the USA, by Bill Miller as a psychotherapeutic approach for people with addicted behavior, it was later extended as a tool to facilitate behavioral change in general (Miller and Rollnick 2002), and more recently with a disorder-specific perspective (Arkowitz et al. 2008).

The outstanding focus of the method is the motivation of the client. Miller and Rollnick (2002) define MI "as a client-centered, directive method for enhancing intrinsic motivation to change by exploring and resolving ambivalence" (p. 25). While for classical (non-directive) client-centered therapists, this is an obvious tension between client-centered and directive orientations, for Miller and Rollnick (Miller and Rollnick 2002) MI is "an evolution of the client-centered counseling approach that Rogers developed" (p. 25). They see "client-centered" and "directive" as compatible and offer guidance, for when the therapist is listening and following the client's path and when they should be open to directing the client in a subtle but not manipulative way.

Change is seen as a natural process which can be nurtured by the therapeutic attitudes described by Rogers (1957, 1959), with, above all, empathic attunement with the client's world.

Highlighting psychological concepts like reactance, resistance and ambivalence while simultaneously praising a humanistic value system (like accentuating the autonomy and self-determination of the client and the therapist's support for their intrinsic values) as underlying the "spirit" of the method, MI refrains from being confrontative. Instead it "is more like dancing: rather than struggling against each other, the partners move together smoothly" (p. 22). The label "interviewing" was chosen to underline the communicative and equal partnership of client and therapist. The model stresses "client advocacy" instead of "counselor advocacy."

According to Miller and Rollnick (2002), *ambivalence* is a natural step in the process of change. Clients never are unmotivated. They are always motivated to something even it is to stick to the situation as it is.

Resistance is understood as an interpersonal phenomenon, a view which goes back to Rogers (1951). As it occurs in the therapeutic relationship, it is characterized by a dissonance between client and therapist and as such it might be induced by (a counter-resistance of) the therapist.

The big difference compared to a classical client-centered stance is the particular regard for the motivational level of the clients, including a distinct attention to help the client to focus on their ways of dealing with the challenge of change. Staying with the frame of reference of the client is the baseline of the therapeutic work but when it comes to "change talk," utterances that reflect the ability, the readiness, the reasons, the wishes, and self-commitment to change, the therapist has no reluctance to steer and influence the client in order to facilitate their motivation to change, most often by dissolving their ambivalence. MI offers a guideline to indicate when MI can be applied with a directive touch, namely when change talk can be enhanced, reflected, summarized, and acknowledged.

The founders of MI distinguish three aspects of motivation:

- The intention expresses the *importance* of a change resulting from the discrepancy of how it is and how it should be.
- Hope and *confidence* refer to the assumed ability (self-efficacy) of the client to actually achieve a goal.
- Finally, it needs *readiness* and self-commitment of the client to start with the process of change. Once readiness is obvious, resembling behavior therapy, self-commitment is to be strengthened and change plans are to be negotiated.

My conclusion is that the method being quite simple and pragmatic offers a useful practical account, by being so selective as to put the motivation of clients and the impact of therapists as primary tasks of the therapeutic endeavor. However, I suggest that many other topics relating to the whole range of psychosocial processes are neglected. The strength of the method at the same time is its shortcoming. The specific focus on the motivational level is the merit and domain of MI, but other important aspects like relational or experiential remain un-elaborated. MI by itself seems a useful but incomplete method, but integrated into the person-centered frame work it adds a valuable dimension to the PCA.

7 Beyond the Verbal Level: Play Therapy, Expressive Arts, Body Work, and Constellation Work

The goal of person-centered/experiential therapy is to process experiences by symbolizing them, that is, making the implicit explicit. This frequently happens through verbalization, but there are many more modalities that facilitate the symbolization process. In the person-centered tradition, verbal communication has tended to be the primary medium but from as early as the 1940s (client-centered), play was being used as a means of child therapy.

Various modes of symbolizing are used in arts therapy, taking advantage of the creative human potential. It was Carl Rogers' daughter, Natalie, who developed "Expressive Arts Therapy" (N. Rogers 2000, 2011), but there are others who pioneered in this area (for instance, Liesl Silverstone in England and Norbert Groddeck in Germany).

N. Rogers' method leans on the theory of creativity by C. Rogers. That is the base for the "Creative Connection," the label for her unique model that values the interconnections between multiple means of expression: for example, Authentic Movement, dance, painting, drawing, writing, actively playing music, and using one's own voice.

The list of media and modalities is nearly endless: body work (Teichmann-Wirth 2002; Uphoff 2008), constellation work (Schmid 2010), or dream work (Koch 2012; Finke in press), imagination and fairy tales (Finke in press), role play or Psychodrama (Wilkins 1994), to mention a few more (see also Cooper and McLeod 2011).

8 Focusing-Oriented Therapy

This approach was developed in the 1960s by Gene Gendlin (born 1926 in Vienna, Austria), a colleague of Carl Rogers in the 1950s. In Gendlin's experiential philosophy, the emphasis is on the client's experiencing: "how our immediate lived experiencing relates to the concepts we use to express and carry forward that experiencing" (Purton 2004, p. 45). It is postulated that the client's progress depends on their level of experiencing: that is how she/he is dealing with his/her inner life (the intricate, the "soft underbelly" as metaphor for the rich but implicit wisdom of our body). In this respect, Gendlin made a shift both from the therapist's attitudes and the relational climate as *the* outstanding effective factor to the client's specific experiencing (in interaction), or, alternatively expressed, from the exploration of the self-concept to the self as process. Gendlin (1974) labeled his "experiential method" as a "method of methods" and eventually situated focusing as "meta-psychotherapy" (Gendlin 1996; Wiltschko 2010, 2011): "The basic principle of the experiential method is that whatever is said and done must be checked against the concretely felt experiencing of the person" (Gendlin 1974, p. 212). He thought this to be superior to approaches that neglect this moment, while Friedman (2003, pp. 40–42), a representative of focusing shows some reservation about such a "conquistador-stance." This requires a certain process-directivity, since the client's experiencing has to be initiated or even the method has to be taught to the client. Gendlin (1993, p. 55–58) himself sees only one single difference to the classical client-centered way of working: He explicitly intends with his answers to touch the client's direct referring to his/her experiencing, to what he terms the "felt sense."

Taking the "experiential theory" as a basis, recognizing that both experiential interaction and working with the implicit and pre-conceptual of the felt sense have an important impact and are decisive for therapeutic change, Gendlin (1978, 1996) elaborated a therapeutic practice which encompasses accurate listening, guiding (including focusing in a narrower sense), responses of the therapist, and giving focusing instructions or, more appropriately, "a gentle encouragement of attention to experiencing" (Purton 2004, p. 49). With its different "avenues" (e.g., experiments, dream work, imagination, and bodily access) focusing-oriented therapy reaches far beyond the six-steps model (clearing space, touching the felt sense, getting a handle, resonating, asking, receiving) (Gendlin 1978) with which it sometimes is associated in an abbreviated way.

9 Emotion-Focused Therapy

The origins of emotion-focused therapy (EFT) go back to the 1980s when Leslie Greenberg, mastermind of its further development, came to develop "process-experiential therapy," first of all with Laura Rice, and later on in cooperation with Robert Elliott, Jeanne Watson, and Rhonda Goldman (Elliott et al. 2004; Greenberg 2011). The term "emotion-focused" initially was used for "emotionally focused couples therapy"; Greenberg and Johnson (1988). For some time now, "EFT" has become the umbrella term for both the classical (two person) therapeutic setting (former "process-experiential therapy") and the application in couples therapy ("emotion-focused couples therapy"; Greenberg and Goldman 2008).

The principal cornerstone of this approach is the therapeutic relationship as outlined by Carl Rogers. Additionally, EFT provides interventions that stimulate, evoke, and activate emotions (which reveals its roots in and influence of Gestalt therapy),—as well as drawing from focusing—by working with the felt sense, and finally an existential color. From these, sources stem a differentiated therapeutic practice with a number of therapeutic tasks and distinct procedures. Different client behaviors, for example, problematic reactions, unclear felt sense, self-interruptions, conflict splits, "unfinished emotional business," and general vulnerability, require different therapeutic interventions and procedures which include evocative unfolding/exploration, focusing, two-chair dialog and enactments, empty chair work, and empathic affirmation. Recently, other tasks have been added, for example, new narratives with traumatized people and restoration of relational breaks.

EFT is an experiential approach that has its theoretical foundation in modern emotion theories and affective neuroscience combined with a systemic-constructivistic outlook. It emphasizes a process-oriented change theory (instead of incongruence which is seen as a static concept). The essential goal of the therapy process is to take possession (again) of experiences that have been dismissed so that these can be accepted as felt by oneself (Greenberg 2011).

Emotions like anger, grief, shame, disgust, anxiety, joy etc. are seen as elementary existential givens—hence, a contrast to Rogers and Gendlin who put experiencing into the center. In EFT, emotions are most important both at the level of experiencing and expression. While primary adaptive emotions have an orientating function like a biological compass (e.g., fear in case of danger, grief in case of loss, anger in case of hurt), EFT distinguishes three maladaptive categories of emotions: (1) *primary emotions* which become inadequate, (2) *secondary reactive emotions* replace either primary reactions (e.g., anger instead of grief) or they result from internalized conditions (e.g., self-contempt as a consequence of criticism or shame due to anxiety), and finally, (3) *instrumental emotions* are emotions with the intention to manipulate others. The main goal of EFT is to modify emotional schemas of the client—which have been either lacking in emotion or suffering with overstimulation. The therapeutic pathway is to transform maladaptive emotions by replacing them through primary adaptive emotions.

A pre-condition for that is to acknowledge the respective emotion. "The change of oneself requires the acceptance of oneself" (retranslated from Greenberg 2011, p. 84) or in other words: "You can't leave a place before you haven't arrived there" (retranslated from Greenberg 2011, p. 84). In this respect EFT, by echoing the Rogerian "paradox of change," clearly advocates a model which is in contrast to the cognitive behavioral perspective.

In summary, EFT is thus integrative, process-directive, guided by markers and a "multi-intentional" model of therapy (Greenberg 2011).

10 Integrative/Eclectic Approaches

Integrative approaches aim to integrate different therapeutic perspectives and procedures (Gutberlet 2008; Cain 2010; Cooper and McLeod 2011; Bohart 2012). Many person-centered therapists, in their practical work or in their theoretical framework, follow not only one of the above-listed orientations but integrate or combine, as I have already pointed out, two or even more sub-orientations or elements from different approaches. While an integrative approach requires theoretical consistency and an original elaboration of theoretical elements (e.g., EFT; process-oriented approach by Swildens), eclectic methods (constituting a hierarchy of unreflected/haphazard/intuitive, technical, pragmatic, and systematic interventions) delivered as a sort of a cocktail that is lacking a thorough and independent theory formation (Stumm 2011, pp. 265f and 289f). The demand of "integration with integrity" (Worsley 2004) corresponds with an ethical concern that cares about philosophical compatibility, theoretical consistency, and its practical implementation.

Depending on what is being integrated I distinguish two levels:

a *First-level integration*: Integration of various aspects from orientations within the person-centered "family," particularly from client-centered/person-centered, experiential, interpersonal, and existential aspects (Keil 2001; Bohart 2012) (see Sect. 11).

b *Second-level integration*: A combination of person-centered/experiential principles and concepts with theoretical elements or techniques from outside the "family" like Gestalt (as in the "process-experiential/emotion-focused approach"), relaxation methods (e.g., Reinhard Tausch), hypnotherapy (Gunnison 2003), or on a more theoretical-level Kriz's "Person-centered system theory" (Kriz 2010) or, for instance, operationalizing the link between person-centered and attachment theory (Höger 2007). At the practical level, such integration is often linked with a technical eclecticism.

The "Leuven-school" (Lietaer 2008), integrating client-centered, experiential (Rice, Greenberg, Gendlin), interpersonal (Kiesler, Yalom), and existential aspects (Yalom, Swildens), renders an example for (an eclectic) combination of both types of integration.

11 Conclusion

This article aims to illustrate diversity in person-centered/experiential psychotherapy at a theoretical and practical level. And, depending on basic assumptions (Lietaer 2002; Schmid 2003; Sanders 2004, p. 155; Worsley 2004, p. 129), the categories I have built and/or the approaches included in the list may not seem to be complete (e.g., Sachse's "clarification-oriented psychotherapy," a process-directive experiential method; see also Sect. 5) or are unacceptable to be included in the person-centered "nation." This leads us to a serious and far-reaching question: is there consensus about such a wide variety of therapeutic approaches? And the answer is, no, there is no consent about that in the person-centered community! The debate on the identity of "person-centered therapy" and about the relation of (classical) client-centered and orientations like experiential, existential, disorder specific, integrative-eclectic offered quite different answers. While Brodley (1990/2011), for instance—writing about the relation of "client-centered" and "experiential"—comes to the conclusion that they are different therapies (to me a "model of separation" or a "model of exclusion"), Keil (2001) takes the counter position claiming that "person-centered" and "experiential" belong together or are even one entity (I call this a "model of inclusion"). The question which still remains here is if "experiential" is included in "person-centered" or if it is the other way round. A position in the middle which, in my view, many share, including Bohart, Lietaer, and myself, acknowledges that there are differences between person-centered and experiential or other members of the family but insists that there is enough common ground to put them under one roof (for me a "model of [more or less] overlapping" or "intersection" of ideas). As far as person-centered and experiential are concerned Rogers and Gendlin, after all, seem to have shared an attitude which underlines the commonalities justifiying the notion of a "person-centered nation." Gendlin again and again has pronounced that focusing is deeply rooted in person-centered principles and prizes the quality of the therapeutic relationship as primary. To Art Bohart's question if Gendlin's focusing was a part of client-centered theory, Rogers in 1985 asserted: "That's were he belongs!" (Bohart 2012, p. 7). To do justice to all three models (separation, inclusion and overlap), which, of course, could be applied also for other tribes, in the controversial debate concerning person-centered and experiential approaches, a compromise is represented by the double-label "person-centered and experiential" (cf. "World Association for Person-Centered and Experiential Psychotherapy and Counseling" and its journal "Person-Centered & Experiential Psychotherapies"), in other words, PCE (person-centered and experiential approach) instead of PCA (person-centered approach)! This might be a formal step that echoes the sense of Warner's statement (2000a) that "we should solidify as a coalition of therapies under a common person-centered umbrella, celebrating and debating our diversity, while remembering that we are, at core, "one nation" whose commonalities far outweigh our differences" (p. 38).

Acknowledgments The author sincerely thanks Colin Lago for his support with the English version.

References

Arkowitz, H., Westra, H. A., Miller, W. R., & Rollnick, S. (2008). *Motivational interviewing in the treatment of psychological problems*. New York: Guilford Press.

Behr, M. (2009). Die interaktionelle Therapeut-Klient-Beziehung in der Spieltherapie—Das Prinzip Interaktionsresonanz. In M. Behr, D. Nuding, & D. Hüsson (Eds.), *Psychotherapie mit Kindern und Jugendlichen—Personzentrierte Methoden und interaktionelle Behandlungskonzepte* (pp. 37–58). Göttingen: Hogrefe.

Binder, U. (1994). *Empathieentwicklung und Pathogenese in der klientenzentrierten Psychotherapie*. Eschborn: Klotz.

Binder, U. (2011). *Störungsspezifische Verstehensprozesse versus diagnosegeleitete Einstellungen. Person, 15*(1), 37–43.

Binder, U., & Binder, J. (1991). *Studien zu einer störungsspezifischen klientenzentrierten Psychotherapie. Schizophrene Ordnung - Psychosomatisches Erleben - Depressives Leiden*. Eschborn: Klotz.

Bohart, A. (1995). The Person-centered psychotherapies. In A. Gurman & S. Messer (Eds.), *Essential psychotherapies: Theory and practice* (pp. 85–127). New York: Guilford Press.

Bohart, A. (2012). Can you be integrative and a person-centered therapist at the same time?. *Person-Centered & Experiential Psychotherapies, 11*(1), 1–13.

Bowlby, J. (1969). *Attachment*. New York: Basic Books.

Bozarth, J. (1998). *Person-centered therapy: a revolutionary paradigm*. Ross-on-Wye: PCCS Books.

Brodley, B.T. (1990). Client–centered and experiential: two different therapies. In G. Lietaer, J. Rombauts & R. Van Balen (Eds.), *Client-centered and experiential therapy in the nineties* (pp. 87–107). Leuven: Leuven University Press [Reprinted in Moon, K., Witty, M., Grant, B., & Rice, B. (Eds.) (2011). *Practicing client-centered therapy. Selected writings of Barbara Temaner-Brodley* (pp. 289–308). Ross-on-Wye: PCCS Books].

Brodley, B. (2006). Non-directivity in client-centered therapy. *Person-Centered & Experiential Psychotherapies, 5*(1), 36–52.

Brodley, B. (2011a). Reasons for responses expressing the therapist's frame of reference. In K. Moon, M. Witty, B. Grant & B. Rice (Eds.), *Practicing client-centered therapy. Selected writings of Barbara Temaner-Brodley* (pp. 207–238). Ross-on-Wye: PCCS Books. (Original work published 1999).

Brodley, B. (2011b). A Chicago client-centered therapy: non-directive and non-experiential. In K. Moon, M. Witty, B. Grant & B. Rice (Eds.), *Practicing Client-Centered Therapy. Selected writings of Barbara Temaner-Brodley* (pp. 4–27). Ross-on-Wye: PCCS Books (Original work published 2006b).

Brodley, B., & Brody, A. (1996). Can one use techniques and still be client-centered? In R. Hutterer, G. Pawlowsky, P.F. Schmid & R. Stipsits (Eds.), *Client-Centered and Experiential Psychotherapy. A Paradigm in Motion* (pp. 369–374). Frankfurt: Peter Lang

Cain, D. (2010). *Person-Centered Psychotherapies*. Washington, D.C.: American Psychological Association.

Cooper, M. (2003a). *Existential therapies*. London: Sage.

Cooper, M. (2003b). Between freedom and despair: Existential challenges and contributions to person-centered and experiential psychotherapy. *Person-Centered and Experiential Psychotherapies, 2*(1), 43–56.

Cooper, M. (2004). Existential approaches to therapy. In P. Sanders (Ed.), *The tribes of the person-centred nation. An introduction to the schools of therapy related to the Person-Centred Approach* (pp. 95–124). Ross-on-Wye: PCCS Books.

Cooper, M., & McLeod, J. (2011). Person-centered therapy: a pluralistic perspective. *Person-centered and experiential psychotherapies, 10*(3), 210–223.

Elliott, R., Watson, J. C., Goldman, R. N., & Greenberg, L. S. (2004). *Learning emotion-focused therapy: the process-experiential approach to change.* Washington, DC: American Psychological Association.

Finke, J. (1998). Hermeneutische Aspekte in der Psychotherapie am Beispiel der Gesprächspsychotherapie. *Zeitschrift für Klinische Psychologie, Psychiatrie und Psychotherapie, 46*(1), 1–13.

Finke, J. (2004). *Gesprächspsychotherapie. Grundlagen und spezifische Anwendungen.* 3., neubearb. und erweiterte Aufl.. Stuttgart: Thieme.

Finke, J. (in press). *Imaginationen, Träume und Märchen in Personzentrierter Psychotherapie und Beratung.* München: Reinhardt.

Finke, J., & Teusch, L. (2007). Using a person-centred approach within a medical framework. In M. Cooper, P. F. Schmid, M. O'Hara, & G. Wyatt (Eds.), *The Handbook of Person-centred psychotherapy and counselling* (pp. 279–292). Basingstoke: Palgrave.

Frankel, M., & Sommerbeck, L. (2005). Two Rogers and congruence: the emergence of therapist-centered therapy and the demise of client-centered therapy. In B. E. Levitt (Ed.), *Embracing non-directivity. Reassessing person-centered theory and practice in the 21st century* (pp. 40–61). Ross-on-Wye: PCCS Books.

Frankel, M., & Sommerbeck, L. (2007). Two Rogers: Congruence and the change from client-centered therapy to we-centered therapy. *Person-Centered and Experiential Psychotherapies, 6*(4), 286–295.

Friedman, N. (2003). Eugene Gendlin's theory and practice of psychotherapy: a personal account. *Person-Centered and Experiential Psychotherapies, 2*(1), 31–42.

Gendlin, E. T. (1974). Client-centered and experiential psychotherapy. In D. Wexler & L. N. Rice (Eds.), *Innovations in client-centered therapy* (pp. 211–246). New York: Wiley.

Gendlin, E.T. (1978). *Focusing.* New York: Everest House [updated version: London: Rider 2003].

Gendlin, E.T. (1993). *Focusing ist eine kleine Tür… Gespräche über Focusing, Träume und Psychotherapie.* Focusing-Bibliothek, Bd. 4. Würzburg: DAF.

Gendlin, E. T. (1996). *Focusing-oriented psychotherapy. A manual of the experiential method.* New York: Guilford Press.

Grant, B. (1990). Principled and instrumental nondirectiveness in Person-centered and Client-centered therapy. *Person-Centered Review, 5*(1), 77–88 [Reprinted in Cain, D. (Ed.) (2002). *Classics in the Person-centered Approach* (pp. 371–377). Ross-on-Wye: PCCS Books].

Greenberg, L.S. (2011). *Emotionsfokussierte Therapie.* München: Reinhardt. [English version: Greenberg, L.S. (2011). *Emotion-focused therapy.* Washington, D.C.: American Psychological Association.].

Greenberg, L. S., & Goldman, R. (2008). *Emotion-focused couples therapy: The dynamics of emotion, power and love.* Washington, D.C.: American Psychological Association.

Greenberg, L. S., & Johnson, S. (1988). *Emotionally focused therapy for couples.* New York: Guilford Press.

Gunnison, H. (2003). *Hypnocounseling. An eclectic bridge between Milton Erickson und Carl Rogers.* Ross-on-Wye: PCCS Books.

Gutberlet, M. (2008). Integration anderer Therapieformen in die personzentrierte Praxis—Wie viel Offenheit verträgt der Personzentrierte Ansatz? In M. Tuczai, G. Stumm, D. Kimbacher & N. Nemeskeri (Eds.), *Offenheit und Vielfalt. Personzentrierte Psychotherapie: Grundlagen, Ansätze, Anwendungen* (pp. 45–57). Wien: Krammer.

Höger, D. (2007). Der personzentrierte Ansatz und die Bindungstheorie. In J. Kriz & T. Slunecko (Eds.), *Gesprächspsychotherapie. Die therapeutische Vielfalt des personzentrierten Ansatzes* (pp. 64–78). Wien: Facultas WUV/UTB.

Keil, W. W. (2001). Das für Psychotherapie notwendige Erleben. Oder: Personzentrierter und Experienzieller Ansatz gehören zusammen. *Person, 5*(2), 90–97.

Keil, W. W., & Stumm, G. (Eds.). (2002). *Die vielen Gesichter der Personzentrierten Psychotherapie.* Wien: Springer.

Koch, A. (2012). *Dreams and the Person-Centered Approach. Cherishing client experiencing.* Ross-on-Wye: PCCS Books.

Kriz, J. (2010). Personzentrierte Systemtheorie. *Person, 14*(2), 99–112.

Kriz, J., & Slunecko, T. (Eds.). (2007). *Gesprächspsychotherapie. Die therapeutische Vielfalt des Personzentrierten Ansatzes.* Wien: Facultas UTB.

Levitt, B. E. (Ed.). (2008). *Reflections on Human Potential: Bridging the person-centred approach and positive psychology.* Ross-on-Wye: PCCS Books.

Lietaer, G. (2002). The united colors of Person-Centered and Experiential Psychotherapies. *Person-Centered and Experiential Psychotherapies, 1*(1), 4–13.

Lietaer, G. (2008). Das Klientenzentrierte/Experienzielle Paradigma der Psychotherapie im 21. Jahrhundert: Offenheit, Vielfalt und Identität. In M. Tuczai, G. Stumm, D. Kimbacher & N. Nemeskeri (Eds.), *Offenheit und Vielfalt. Personzentrierte Psychotherapie: Grundlagen, Ansätze, Anwendungen* (pp. 17–43). Wien: Krammer.

Mearns, D. (1996). Working at relational depth with clients in person-centred therapy. *Counselling, 7*(4), 306–311.

Mearns, C., & Cooper, M. (2005). *Working at relational depth in counselling and psychotherapy.* London: Sage.

Merry, T. (2004). Classical client-centred therapy. In P. Sanders (Ed.), *The tribes of the person-centred nation. An introduction to the schools of therapy related to the Person-centred approach* (pp. 21–44). Ross-on-Wye: PCCS Books.

Miller, W. R., & Rollnick, S. (2002). *Motivational Interviewing. Preparing people for change* (2nd ed.). New York: Guilford Press.

Moon, K. (2008). An essay on children, evil and the actualizing tendency. In B. E. Levitt (Ed.), *Reflections on Human Potential: Bridging the person-centred approach and positive psychology* (pp. 203–214). Ross-on-Wye: PCCS Books.

Prouty, G., Van Werde, D. & Pörtner, M. (2002). *pre-therapy. Reaching contact-impaired clients.* Ross-on-Wye: PCCS Books [orig. Version in German: 1998].

Purton, C. (2004). Focusing-oriented therapy. In P. Sanders (Ed.), *The tribes of the person-centred nation. An introduction to the schools of therapy related to the Person-Centred Approach* (pp. 45–65). Ross-on-Wye: PCCS Books.

Rogers, C. R. (1942). *Counseling and psychotherapy. Newer concepts in practice.* Boston: Houghton Mifflin.

Rogers, C. R. (1951). *Client-centered therapy.* Boston: Houghton Mifflin.

Rogers, C. R. (1957). The necessary and sufficient conditions of therapeutic personality change. *Journal of Consulting Psychology, 21*(2), 95–103.

Rogers, C. R. (1959). A theory of therapy, personality, and interpersonal relationships, as developed in the client-centered framework. In S. Koch (Ed.), *Psychology: A study of a science: Formulations of the person and the social context* (Vol. III, pp. 184–256). New York: McGraw-Hill.

Rogers, C. R. (1961). *On becoming a person: A therapist's view of psychotherapy.* Boston: Houghton Mifflin.

Rogers, N. (2000). *The creative connection: Expressive arts as healing.* Ross-on-Wye: PCCS Books [Orig.: 1993].

Rogers, N. (2011). *The creative connection for groups: Person-centered expressive arts for healing and social change.* Palo Alto, CA: Science and Behavior Books.

Sanders, P. (Ed.). (2004). *The tribes of the person-centered nation.* Ross-on-Wye: PCCS Books.

Sanders, P. (2007). The 'family of person-centred and experiential therapies. In M. Cooper, P. F. Schmid, M. O'Hara, & G. Wyatt (Eds.), *The Handbook of Person-centred psychotherapy and counselling* (pp. 107–122). Basingstoke: Palgrave.

Schmid, P. F. (2001). Authenticity: the person as his or her own author: Dialogical and ethical perspectives on therapy as an encounter relationship. In G. Wyatt (Ed.), *Rogers' therapeutic conditions* (Vol. 1, pp. 213–228)., Congruence Ross-on-Wye: PCCS Books.

Schmid, P. F. (2003). The characteristics of a Person-Centered Approach to therapy and counseling. *Person-Centered & Experiential Psychotherapies, 2*(2), 104–120.

Schmid, P. F. (2010). Für sich und andere etwas sichtbar machen … – Personzentrierte Aufstellungsarbeit. *Person, 14*(2), 125–134.

Sommerbeck, L. (2003). *The client-centred therapist in psychiatric contexts. A therapist's guide to the psychiatric landscape and its inhabitants.* Ross-on-Wye: PCCS Books.

Speierer, G.-W. (1994). *Das Differenzielle Inkongruenz Modell (DIM). Handbuch der Gesprächspsychotherapie als Inkongruenzbehandlung.* Asanger: Heidelberg.

Stumm, G. (2005). The Person-centered Approach from an existential perspective. *Person-Centered and Experiential Psychotherapies, 4*(2), 106–124.

Stumm, G. (2008). Einleitung. In M. Tuczai, G. Stumm, D. Kimbacher & N. Nemeskeri (Eds.), *Offenheit und Vielfalt. Personzentrierte Psychotherapie: Grundlagen, Ansätze, Anwendungen* (pp. 7–14). Wien: Krammer.

Stumm, G. (Ed.). (2011). *Psychotherapie: Schulen und Methoden. Eine Orientierungshilfe für Theorie und Praxis.* Wien: Falter.

Swildens, H. (1991). *Prozeßorientierte Gesprächspsychotherapie. Einführung in eine differenzielle Anwendung des klientenzentrierten Ansatzes bei der Behandlung psychischer Erkrankungen.* Köln: GwG [Original in Dutch: 1988; 2nd Dutch ed.: 1997].

Teichmann-Wirth, B. (2002). Zur Einbeziehung des Körpers in die Klientenzentrierte/Personzentrierte Psychotherapie: Der einzubeziehende Körper. In W. W. Keil & G. Stumm (Eds.), *Die vielen Gesichter der Personzentrierten Psychotherapie* (pp. 391–410). Wien: Springer.

Tuczai, M., Stumm, G., Kimbacher, D., & Nemeskeri, N. (Eds.). (2008). *Offenheit und Vielfalt. Personzentrierte Psychotherapie: Grundlagen, Ansätze, Anwendungen.* Wien: Krammer.

Tudor, K. (2010). Person-centered relational therapy – II: A critique of relational depth. Unpublished manuscript.

Uphoff, A. (2008). Touch and the therapeutic relationship: Shifting a paradigm. In S. Haugh & S. Paul (Eds.), *The therapeutic relationship: Perspectives and themes* (pp. 203–216). Ross-on-Wye: PCCS Books.

van Kessel, W., & Keil, W. W. (2002). Die Interaktionelle Orientierung in der Klientenzentrierten Psychotherapie. In W. W. Keil & G. Stumm (Eds.), *Die vielen Gesichter der Personzentrierten Psychotherapie* (pp. 107–119). Wien: Springer.

van Kessel, W., & Lietaer, G. (1998). Interpersonal processes. In L. Greenberg, J. Watson, & G. Lietaer (Eds.), *Handbook of experiential psychotherapy* (pp. 155–177). New York: Guilford Press.

Warner, M. (2000a). Person-centered psychotherapy: One nation, many tribes. *The Person-Centered Journal, 7*(1), 28–39.

Warner, M. (2000b). Client-Centered Therapy at the Difficult Edge: Work with Fragile and Dissociated Process. In D. Mearns & B. Thorne (Eds.), *Person-Centered Therapy Today: New Frontiers in Theory and Practice* (pp. 144–171). London: Sage.

Wilders, S. (2007). Relational depth and Person-centred Approach. *Person-Centred Quarterly, 1,* 1–4.

Wilkins, P. (1994). Can Psychodrama be Person-centred. *Person-Centred Practice, 2*(1), 14–18 [Reprinted in: Merry, T. (Ed.) (2000). *Person-centred practice: The BAPCA reader* (pp. 232–236). Ross-on-Wye: PCCS Books].

Wiltschko, J. (2010). *Hilflosigkeit in Stärke verwandeln.* Edition Octopus: Focusing als Basis einer Metapsychotherapie. Bd. I. Münster.

Wiltschko, J. (2011). *Ich spüre, also bin ich. Nicht-Wissen als Quelle von Veränderung. Focusing als Basis einer Metapsychotherapie. Bd. II.* Münster: Edition Octopus.

Worsley, R. (2004). Integrating with integrity. In P. Sanders (Ed.), *The tribes of the person-centered nation. An introduction to the schools of therapy related to the Person-centred approach* (pp. 125–147). Ross-on-Wye: PCCS Books.

Motivational Interviewing and Client-Centered Therapy

Christopher C. Wagner

Motivational Interviewing (MI) is an empathic approach that focuses on helping clients develop and enact plans for changing their lives in healthier, more fulfilling directions. A central focus in MI is helping clients resolve ambivalence about change. MI began when psychologist Bill Miller took a sabbatical from his position at the University of New Mexico to study and write in Norway. Invited by Norwegian clinicians to explain his thoughts and intentions while demonstrating his approach to working with alcohol problems, he began attempting to describe his practice, ultimately resulting in a 1983 descriptive paper in Behavioural Psychotherapy (Miller 1983). While the 30 years that have passed since that time have seen this therapeutic approach grow from one man's intuitive practice to a formal clinical method with hundreds of clinical trials of MI across problem areas, populations, settings, disciplines and cultures, the essence of the original insight remains intact.

Motivational Interviewing (MI) is "80 % Rogers" (Miller 2012). Like classic client-centered therapy (CCT), MI focuses on client perceptions and perspectives, using open questions, affirmations, reflections and summaries to help clients focus their attention and envision a more positive future. The underlying spirit of MI is one of a partnership between practitioners and clients, in service of clients' best interests and supporting clients' autonomy to define and pursue changes that will make their lives better. MI practitioners help by focusing more on evoking client perspectives than by providing information or guidance. While reflective listening is as crucial to MI as it is to CCT, in MI reflections are *used selectively* to highlight change talk and elicit additional momentum toward change. Change talk includes positive client expressions about change—the desire, need or reasons to change, ability to achieve change goals, and commitment to try.

C. C. Wagner (✉)
Virginia Commonwealth University, Richmond, VA, USA
e-mail: chriscwagner@gmail.com

J. H. D. Cornelius-White et al. (eds.), *Interdisciplinary Applications of the Person-Centered Approach*, DOI: 10.1007/978-1-4614-7144-8_4,
© Springer Science+Business Media New York 2013

1 Basic Processes and Topics in MI

MI uses four basic processes—engaging, focusing, evoking and planning (Miller and Rollnick 2013). Practitioners first *engage* clients into both a working relationship and a process of considering and discussing their concerns and interests. The next process is to develop a mutual *focus* on a specific area or areas of concern, ideally developing initial change goals and targeting specific behaviors that clients will change in pursuit of their goals. The heart of MI is in the third process, evoking, which involves eliciting clients' reasons, desires and sense of need for changes, along with an increased sense of confidence about implementing changes. With motivation to change thoroughly developed, the final process involves developing detailed *plans* for change, and getting started down the change pathway, while continuing to tend to any remaining or recurring ambivalence about change.

MI is not entirely process-oriented, however. Practitioners guide clients through a personalized series of topics that help clients focus and elicits their motivation to change. Most of these focus on the present and future, with little focus on the past. One past-oriented topic, however, involves "looking back" to earlier times, before therapeutic problems developed, as a way of recalling what life was like and eliciting a description of the pathway that led from then to now, then using that as a springboard to consider where current choices and behaviors are leading, to compare this to clients' future hopes and goals. Another past-oriented topic is "remembering successes"—ideally, times when clients identified desired changes and implemented them. Revisiting these successes allows practitioners to mine these experiences for client strengths and successful strategies and leverage them to enhance client confidence about the current challenges facing them.

MI practitioners guide clients to focus on present-day concerns and interests more than historical factors, however. Given the importance of the concept of ambivalence in MI, one conversational strategy is to explore clients' ambivalence in regard to their therapeutic focus—what's good and what's not-so-good about their current situation, choices, actions. Practitioners acknowledge and respect those elements of clients' lives that they may struggle to leave behind and that may draw them back into the less-than-optimal status quo if left unrecognized and untended. Mostly, however, the focus is on evoking momentum toward positive change, helping clients essentially talk themselves into implementing changes that will lead them toward their goals. One essential topic in MI is to consider client values, and the extent to which they currently live by them, alongside the possibilities for living more closely in line with them. Doing this in a client-centered, supportive manner helps elicit deeper motivation to change in positive directions.

An example of a future-oriented topic involves "looking forward." In this strategy, clients envision a more fulfilling future and this vision is used to help pull them forward toward it, rather than focusing on changing because they "should" or to escape current problems. One variation on this strategy is to contrast this envisioned future with the future clients imagine may develop should they continue down their current pathway without making any changes. This discrepancy between the sought-after future and the future that amplifies current problems can help enhance client motivations to change.

Optionally, MI includes formal change-planning, reviewing the specific change(s) to be made and client reasons for changing, clients' strengths and supports toward change, mechanisms for identifying if progress is being made toward goals and plans for righting the course if setbacks occur, and eliciting commitment to enacting specific short-term strategies leading toward client goals.

MI can be used as a therapeutic approach in its own right, or paired with other approaches or services to facilitate and initiate change. MI was not developed as a comprehensive therapy, intended to address all aspects of clients' lives or problems, but is empirically-supported for use with a wide range of client concerns across a wide range of settings and cultures (Hettema, Steele and Miller 2005; Lundahl et al. 2010).

2 Similarities and Differences Between MI and Classic Client-Centered Therapy

As mentioned above, MI is thoroughly grounded in Rogers' classic client-centered therapy (CCT). It shares with CCT the philosophy of client autonomy and self-determination; the commitment to a phenomenological, empathic approach; the acceptance and prizing of the client regardless of current or past choices or actions; the general perspective of client competence versus deficits; the use of reflective listening as the primary interactive method; and more. While these shared elements may go underappreciated, they pose a fairly stark contrast to both classic and third-wave contextual cognitive-behavioral approaches, psychodynamic approaches, and even to seemingly similar approaches such as solution-focused therapy, which rely more on therapist questioning (particularly closed questions), interpersonal control and expert guidance than CCT or MI (Ingersoll and Wagner 2010; Wagner and Ingersoll 2010).

At the same time, MI is more narrowly focused on eliciting change in relation to a particular problem or problem set than CCT, which focuses more generally on client well-being and personal growth. Wagner and Ingersoll (2013) discuss how MI practitioners can shape conversations in regard to depth, breadth and momentum toward change. MI practitioners can shape conversations to go deeper into values, emotions and identity or toward lighter, surface conversation; broaden conversations toward general themes or narrow to specifics as is more valuable in the moment; and accelerate momentum toward change goals and action versus decelerate into exploration of ambivalence regarding the situation at hand. Viewed through this lens, in a way, CCT prioritizes depth, while MI prioritizes momentum.

Rogers suggested that human suffering exists partly because people feel pressured to act, live and perceive themselves in ways that are incongruent with their personal values (real self) in order to gain positive regard from others. This incongruity between "I am" and "I should" fosters neurotic suffering, and one of the directions pursued in CCT is the resolution of this incongruence by helping clients lay down the burdens associated with introjected "I should" ideas that conflict with the sense of who they really are.

MI focuses on the notion of resolving intractable ambivalence between healthy or productive choices versus unhealthy or dysfunctional choices. While MI favors resolution in the direction of health and well-being, it currently lacks a well-defined theoretical basis to define what those are. While the direction may seem obvious at times (e.g., in an alcohol treatment center, the direction is clearly toward healthy use or abstinence versus unhealthy or dysfunctional use), MI still lacks a basis to determine which direction is preferred in complex situations (e.g., when drinking relaxes someone who otherwise might be violent toward family members; when taking a psychiatric medication may both help and hurt). Ethically, Miller and Rollnick (2002) suggest that to the extent that the practitioner has an investment in a direction that may not necessarily be in the client's best interests, MI should be used with caution. Further, they propose (Miller and Rollnick 2013) that there are situations in which practitioners should probably remain in equipoise (e.g., when a client is deciding whether to have a child), and thus offer non-directive CCT rather than the more directional MI. Yet to date, MI has offered little guidance for complex situations in which directionality may be useful, yet deciding which direction is preferable is clinically complex (Wagner and Ingersoll 2009). Using the approach of "client-centered direction" provides one possible resolution to this dilemma, in which MI practitioners elicit broadly from clients direction toward general well-being, satisfaction or life fulfillment, then collaborate toward narrowing focus toward specific changes clients may implement toward these general goals, thus keeping the process client-centered while pursuing the directional goals that lie at the heart of MI (Wagner 2012). Further exploration of Rogers' views on resolving conflicts between introjected patterns and the real self may yet provide additional guidance for the further development of MI, as may exploration of more contemporary person-centered theory. In return, MI provides a conceptually-consistent means for CCT practitioners to help clients resolve lingering ambivalence and move toward specific change goals, when desired.

References

Hettema, J., Steele, J., & Miller, W. R. (2005). Motivational interviewing. *Annual Review of Clinical Psychology, 1*, 91–111.

Ingersoll, K. S., & Wagner, C. C. (2010, June). *Relational and technical processes of client-centered, MI, and cognitive therapies in demonstration videos.* International Conference on Motivational Interviewing, Stockholm, Sweden.

Lundahl, B. W., Kunz, C., Brownell, C., Tollefson, D., & Burke, B. L. (2010). A meta-analysis of motivational interviewing: twenty-five years of empirical studies. *Research on Social Work Practice, 20,* 137–160.

Miller, W. R. (1983). Motivational interviewing with problem drinkers. *Behavioural Psychotherapy, 11,* 147–172.

Miller, W. R. (2012, June). *The client-centered heart of MI.* International Conference on Motivational Interviewing, Venice, Italy.

Miller, W. R., & Rollnick, S. (2002). *Motivational interviewing: Preparing people for change* (2nd ed.). New York: Guilford Press.

Miller, W. R., & Rollnick, S. (2013). *Motivational interviewing: Facilitating change* (3rd ed.). New York: Guilford.

Wagner, C. C. (2012). Client-centered direction: Or how to get there when you're not sure where you're going. *Motivational Interviewing: Training, Research, Implementation, Practice, 1,* 36–38.

Wagner, C. C., & Ingersoll, K. S. (2009). Beyond behavior: Eliciting broader change with motivational interviewing. *Journal of Clinical Psychology, 65,* 1180–1194.

Wagner, C. C., & Ingersoll, K. S. (2010, June). *Therapeutic processes in seven addiction treatment approaches.* International Conference on Motivational Interviewing, Stockholm, Sweden.

Wagner, C. C., & Ingersoll, K. S. (2013). *Motivational interviewing in groups.* New York: Guilford Press.

Linking the Person-Centered Approach to the Arts: Person-Centered Expressive Arts Therapy and Empowerment

Grace Harlow Klein

Linking the arts, creativity, healing, and the person-centered approach is the life work of Natalie Rogers who created person-centered expressive arts therapy (PCEAT). This chapter reviews the process of its emergence, the training that evolved from it and the applications of the approach beyond psychotherapy. Implications for future work are suggested in areas of science, which may have a dramatic impact in understanding how communication, connection, and community are facilitated by the arts in a person-centered context.

1 The Parallel Development of Natalie Rogers and Person-Centered Expressive Arts

Natalie earned a Master's degree in psychology with Abraham Maslow as her advisor. His deep interest in creativity and his support of women stimulated Natalie to do original research and write her Masters thesis, *A Play Therapist's Approach to the Creative Art Experience* (1960) in which her person-centered values joined expressive arts with children.

In writing of her personal transition, Rogers (1980b) shared her decade-long journey from married to single, from fulfilling cultural norms for women, especially in marriage in a male-dominated society, to breaking those norms—emerging as a person in her own right. In that process, she both examined her childhood family and drew on the two worlds she experienced growing up with her father, Carl, the psychologist and her mother, Helen, the artist who encouraged her children to draw, paint, and sculpt. She also remembered loving to "use movement for self-expression" when she was young (Rogers 1993, p. xv). She illustrated her talks about her transition with 100 personal slides of photos and her artwork in speaking of her journey in "The Right to be Me" (Rogers 1980b, pp. 13–29). The book was

G. H. Klein (✉)
Center for Human Encouragement, 15 Arnold Park, Rochester, NY 14607, USA
e-mail: ghc@rochester.rr.com

J. H. D. Cornelius-White et al. (eds.), *Interdisciplinary Applications of the Person-Centered Approach*, DOI: 10.1007/978-1-4614-7144-8_5,
© Springer Science+Business Media New York 2013

written "to give women courage and support to be full persons in our society, and to point out that what is personal is political. That is, what we choose to think and do as individuals has impact on our society as a whole (Rogers 1980b, p. 9)." Her father, Carl, was supportive though late in life he wished he had been more supportive (Kirschenbaum 2007). He wrote: "To learn from understanding *our own* experience is a difficult task, indeed, and to share it through writing and expressive art is courageous—this book confirms what I have long believed: what is most personal is most general" (Rogers 1980a, Book cover).

Natalie moved to California in 1974 in the midst of that transition to create a new life. She facilitated workshops worldwide with Carl and then created with her daughter, Frances, the person-centered expressive arts institute (PCETI). She invited Carl to participate in her program for the first three years. PCETI offered training programs drawing participants from around the world, from 1984 to 2005 when Saybrook University took over the sponsorship of her certificate program. In 2013, the certificate program will move from Saybrook to Sofia University (formerly Institute of Transpersonal Psychology). Former certificate graduates, with the assistance of PCETI faculty, have created similar training programs in Argentina, Hong Kong, Japan, South Korea, and the United Kingdom (current contact is tessdsturrock@gmail.com) (Rogers 2011, pp. 415–417).

Person-centered expressive arts use the arts as a process in both individual therapy and in workshops. The therapist offers the client experiences in movement, art, writing, or sculpture, among other modalities, for the purposes of "identifying and being in touch with feelings, exploring unconscious material, releasing energy, gaining insight, solving problems [and/or] discovering intuitive, mythological and spiritual dimensions of the self" (Rogers 1993, p 96). These modalities, included in the training of person-centered expressive arts therapists, draw on long traditions in other cultures which integrate arts with healing. The experiences are always offered, not required, and once engaged, the client shares the meaning of the experience, without interpretation by the therapist. In going beyond the current traditions of psychotherapy as a verbal process, Rogers notes the changing cultural environment in which persons are increasingly exposed to and comfortable with engaging in these other forms of expression (Rogers 1993).

In her writing (Rogers 1993), demonstrations and in an interview by Herron (2005), it is clear that Natalie has always based her work on the foundational principles of the person-centered approach: empathy, positive regard, and congruence. The expressive arts, by definition, include movement, art, sound, journal writing, and psychodrama. In using the words, "The Creative Connection," Natalie describes the process of the interplay between these media to bring individuals into their deep wellspring of creativity, spirituality, and self-empowerment. In making clear these connections among the arts and outcomes in the use of movement, dance, painting, etc., Rogers (1993) shares her personal experience of growth and healing through her father's death, emphasizing their facilitative role in both healing and the emergence of creativity.

In the interview, Rogers (Herron 2005) distinguishes PCEAT from other forms of art and expressive arts therapies as they reflect other forms of psychotherapy.

Rogers (2012, personal correspondence) described PCEAT as differentiated from some of the other forms of art therapy or expressive arts therapies in that "its values and methods are based in Carl Rogers' theories that each person has within him or herself the ability to find solutions for their difficulties if given a safe, empathic, non-judgmental environment" (p. 1).

As applied to the client's expressive art, it means the therapist does not analyze or interpret the client's art or movement or writing. The client is asked: "How did the process feel to you? What does it mean? As you look at your art what do you feel or experience? Does this color have any special meaning for you? You didn't mention this part, do you have anything to say about it?" When the client responds, the therapist finds ways to reflect back the essence of the client's meaning of their expression so that they are able to delve even deeper. If the client wants a response from the therapist or group facilitator, it is put this way: "If this were my painting, or my sculpture, or my dance, I would be feeling this way and wondering….." In this way, the therapist owns her own projections and is not telling the client who she is, by her expressive art. This is a subtle but very significant difference. Clients tend to accept a therapist's interpretation because he is the authority. The client, however, needs to find her own interpretation which is usually quite different.

Just as Carl rebelled against psychiatric methods of interpretation, or the medical model of believing the doctor had the answers, the person-centered expressive arts therapist separates herself from expressive arts therapists who interpret the client's art or believe they understand the inner workings of the client through their art without checking it with the client. Telling someone who they are by the art they have shared can have counter-productive effects (Rogers 2012, personal correspondence).

From that beginning, thousands of women and men have been exposed to Natalie's work as a process in their own inner development and as a process of psychotherapy with others. Natalie consistently refers to empowerment as an outcome of her work. In *The Creative Connection: Expressive Arts as Healing*, Rogers (1993) addresses both the healing aspects of PCEAT and its use with clients. The artwork of several persons is used to illustrate the process. One section addresses further applications of expressive arts for special client issues such as loss, grief, sexual issues, and addiction and describes its use with groups such as the twelve-step programs. She also addresses cross-cultural work and in the final chapter writes of creativity and consciousness in making a more peaceful world, thus completing the gamut of work by her father, Rogers (1977, 1980a).

2 Diverse Applications of Person-Centered Expressive Arts with Groups

In extending her work, Rogers (2011) addresses the process of using the arts in workshop format with groups, particularly focusing on healing and social change. She shares her experience in its use in erupting world tragedies, such as when the

United States was making a preemptive strike on Iraq and in Sweden when, in the midst of a workshop, their beloved Minister of Foreign Affairs was attacked by a deranged person and later died from her wounds. In each example, the shared experiences in the groups provided a safe outlet for deep emotions and brought healing in overwhelmingly painful situations that evoked enormous feelings of helplessness (Rogers 2011, pp. 223–225). How useful it might have been to have these experiences as a resource in some of our mass tragedies in the United States—September 11, Columbine, and other mass murder attacks which seem to be continuing as an ongoing occurrence in our way of life.

Graduates of the training program write of their applications of PCEAT in working with specialized populations, such as grieving children, adolescents with anger, elders, consultation groups for psychotherapists, eating disorders, loss and grief, developmental disabilities, cancer patients in China, victims of crime, grief among persons with mental disorders, children who stutter, and veterans. Others write of cultural and social groups focused on personal empowerment and inspiration, stress, transition, on education with teachers of social justice and English as a second language and with art with elementary school children. Finally, there are applications for the workplace and cross-cultural groups, including refugees (Rogers 2011). All of the applications describe the wide range of uses for PCEAT in groups and suggest the outcomes possible for such work.

Awareness is growing about the use of the arts in ways that transcend psychotherapy. A recent article, "Doctors of Arts" (Low 2012) describes the use of music, writing, poetry, pottery, and exercise activities as ways to manage stress and maintain cognitive alertness among physicians. The activities also add enjoyment to life.

3 Examples of Contributions to Expressive Arts

Bell, in her role as director of a university counseling service in England, used PCEAT in supervision with placement trainee staff. As presented in the Person-Centered Forum in Majorca in 2007, she presented, "This approach is particularly helpful in situations where the supervisee is feeling stuck and also struggling to identify and articulate the process of their work rather than just talk about the content." She describes inviting the counselor to visualize themselves and their client, to notice any images or colors or sounds or feelings that come up. They can then use paints or oil pastels to express whatever emerges in whatever way they wish. Sometimes a series of pictures or abstract colors emerge. They then are invited to write in a flow of consciousness and without censoring themselves for a few minutes. The aim of this process is to help the counselor access those feelings and thoughts that lay just below their awareness and to move through the sense of stuckness. Using these tools can be very empowering (Bell 2012, personal correspondence).

In another example, she writes about working with an experienced counselor who had become despairing about the usefulness of her long-term work with a very vulnerable abused client. The counselor did a series of drawings which eventually brought alive how much valuable work she had done with this client. The counselor had initially drawn the client as a closed-off black box. As the drawings progressed and enlarged, the counselor drew more colors for the client and for herself. The counselor described how much the client had achieved in the years they had worked together—and she then connected again with the positive feelings she had in working with this client. The counselor also found this exercise valuable in being able to go on then to explore how aspects of her process might parallel the client's experience. The person-centered expressive arts exercise had been a central factor in enabling the counselor to feel in touch with her own self-confidence again and to continue her sensitive and excellent work with this client (Bell 2007).

Tess Sturrock (2012, personal correspondence) shared her experiences with me in becoming a part of the very early PCEAT pathway:

> I began my training with Natalie Rogers in 1983, attending three week long intensives in Norway. At this time, I was training as a teacher of 11–16 year olds. Returning from one of the intensives, I was asked to offer a presentation on Carl Rogers to our group of trainee teachers. I did this, using expressive arts to explore thoughts and feelings of the group on Rogers' theory, especially the actualizing tendency and the core conditions. The resulting experiential learning, traveling from the personal to the universal via expression in the arts, was inspiring.

She continued, describing her ongoing activities, illustrating the richness and varied activities pursued within the PCEAT path:

> As a teacher of drama in a 70 % Muslim school, I included visual art, movement, sound and writing in addition to drama as avenues of expression for pupils with widely different language and social skills. This proved especially creative with the younger classes in the school, who gained confidence in their own expression and in their relating to others. We moved, made sounds, created imaginary worlds in drama and paint, and discussed the joys and sorrows of life as they flowed from these creations. It was a joy to be in the drama studio during these classes.
>
> During and after my training with Natalie, I facilitated an ongoing group which met once a month for several years, a mixed group of teachers, therapists and others in the helping professions. The group became extremely supportive of each other, and very responsive and at ease with Natalie Rogers' concept of the Creative Connection. We moved easily as a group between expression in movement and sound, visual art and writing and subsequent sharing. The arts simply became additional languages as we moved, painted and sang together—a powerful meld of deep trust and creative expression.
>
> I have offered many and various person-centered expressive arts workshops to counselor training courses in Britain and abroad spanning the last 22 years. For 11 years I co-facilitated person-centered expressive arts training in Britain. Within each group the familiar messages of 'I can't draw', or 'I hate my body', and 'I can't dance', etc. often emerge. At the same time, there are almost always students who are longing to explore other avenues of expression beyond the verbal. My work is to help to create a space that is safe enough for each person to explore and express—space for the creeping mouse and the raging bull, the high flying eagle and the pebble on the ocean floor—and space enough for us all to respect each difference. Challenging as this is, experiencing and helping to facilitate expression in this world is satisfying beyond all words. (Sturrock 2012, personal correspondence).

4 The Author's Personal Journey: Through Loss to Empowerment

At a critical juncture in my life, I began to write prose poetry and paint to express my experiences of death, loss, and transition. What emerged were books combining my prose poetry, art, and photography (Klein 2007; 2010a, b). Having developed and offered workshops on Empowering Nursing through the person-centered approach, I began to explore definitions and develop concept analyses and models for empowerment. These activities led me to link empowerment and person-centered expressive arts as a pathway through grief and loss (Klein 2010c). The books and paintings and photographs are a way to share my experience—with hope that others can connect through them with their own feelings and experiences.

Although I had been exposed to Natalie's work, the impetus for writing poetry, painting, and doing photography arose from my inner creative drive and was supported by Julia Cameron's *The Artist's Way* (1992) on recovering creativity which includes writing daily Morning Pages. A week-long intensive workshop alone with Tess Sturrock in Wales added deeply to my explorations and to my art.

The further I have come in my own process, the more clear it is to me that the writing, painting, and photography, as well as the making of books, are my own pathway to empowerment. Developing a language for feelings and experience is the most core and central issue in my life: to experience, to share in relationships, and to record my inner process. It is what helped me to recognize the writings of Rogers (1961) as the voice for my experiences and the one thing which ties together all of my longings and searching. It has also brought the most satisfaction to my life. To want to know myself and another brought great intimacy and love in my personal life, that "deep openness," which my husband, Klein (2001), wrote of in his poetry. And in the loss of him, it is music which helps me connect with the deepest part of my sadness and writing which helps me stay connected to the wonderful life we made together (Klein 2012). And in a recent retreat, it was painting which gave image and meaning to my changing experience of grief. Such deep openness in the therapist is also what creates the environment for healing in psychotherapy (Klein 2001).

This process is now one I share with my grandchildren in facilitating their making of books, remembering their grandfather, Armin. Their words and art are both beautiful and touching, and I hope, healing in their loss of him and empowering in their development of language to express their feelings.

5 Empowerment and Future Directions

There are many implied definitions and uses of the term empowerment which have evolved in our culture over the past 20 years. Emerging from my process, my definition is "Empowerment is the power to act—the foundation, meaning and direction coming from the connections within oneself, congruent with one's feelings, ideas, and experiences—and finding a voice and language to express all of that to others." (Klein 2010c).

The process of empowerment is like an energy field coming from the brain via feelings and emotions grounded in experience, but interpreted and given meaning in ideas which can be shared in language and in the languages of the arts as described by Rogers (1993, 2011).

Centered in the brain, both electrical and chemical signals transmit the messages of the brain (Lewis et al. 2000). The authors write in fascinating detail describing the functions of the three brains which govern this processing. The ideas, generated as cognitive processes in the left brain, can see phenomena in totally opposite interpretations. It is the intuitive, creative right brain where feelings are generated which gives grounding and validity to experience (Lewis et al. 2000). PCEAT draws on these processes through the verbal and feeling languages of expression— creating the basis for interaction with the therapist (Siegel 2012) and the languages of the expressive arts (Rogers 2011). The therapist responds through the use of those same languages, drawing also from those same processes (Cozolino 2002).

The use of movement, art, poetry, and journal writing, used in PCEAT, appears to increase experiences of flow (Csikszentmihalyi 1988)—thus expanding the data available in consciousness to the healing process. These mediums also provide for expression—such as movement, writing, singing, or drumming—that create ways of releasing energy in the healing process. Likewise, sharing in encounters with others can lead to a deeper sense of connection (Rogers 2011). Siegel (2010, 2012) explores the science of personal transformation and how relationships and the brain interact to shape who we are, providing new ways of understanding the processes of brain rewiring–healing.

In groups, the sharing of experience in all of these mediums appears to increase the sense of connection and community leading to healing and a deeper sense of belonging. Rogers (2011) writes of this shared energy as "collective resonance," (p. 225) which is not yet fully understood, but has, she believes, transformative power to change the world through group encounters. The fields of physics and neuroscience are beginning to evolve in such ways as to explain how these processes actually work in the brain (Cozolino 2002; Lewis et al. 2000; Siegel 2010, 2012). Rogers (1980a) sensed the direction of these connections in his work, especially citing physics—though the state of the science was much less developed or understood during his lifetime. Kriz (2013, this volume) has articulated some of the connections with new directions in physics through his description and bridges of interdisciplinary systems theory. How fascinating it would have been to have such resources (Siegel 2010, 2012) available to help answer a central question in my doctoral studies—"How do we become the person that we are?"

It is in these areas that science will increasingly provide answers to understand the connections possible in the human condition. We are in the forefront of dramatic change that will increasingly help us to understand the processes of growth, transformation, relationships, and healing and to foster community and peaceful interactions in our world. The arts cross the boundaries of culture, facilitating that process. Both the new science and the arts offer a rich and hopeful vision of the future.

References

Bell, J. (2007). Person centered expressive supervision. In K. Tudor & M. Worrall (Eds.), *Freedom to practice; Developing person centered approaches to supervision* (Vol. 2, pp. 59–71). England: PCCS Books.

Cameron, J. (1992). *The artist's way*. New York: Tarcher.

Cozolino, L. (2002). *The neuroscience of psychotherapy: Building and rebuilding the human brain*. New York: W. W. Norton.

Csikszentmihalyi, M. (1988). The flow experience and its significance for human psychology. In M. Csikszentmihalyi (Ed.), *Optimal experience: psychological studies of flow in consciousness* (pp. 15–35). Cambridge: Cambridge University Press.

Kirschenbaum, H. (2007). *The life and work of Carl Rogers*. Ross-on-Wye: PCCS Books.

Klein, A. (2001). Unconditional positive regard, deep openness. In G. Wyatt., J. Bozarth & P. Wilkins (Eds.), *Rogers' therapeutic conditions: evolution, theory and practice, unconditional positive regard* (Vols. 3 pp. 1–2). Ross-on-Wye, England: PCCS Books.

Klein, G. H. (2007). *Remembering junie*. Rochester: Grace Harlow Press.

Klein, G. H. (2010a). *A bridge of returning: An empowering journey*. Rochester: Grace Harlow Press.

Klein, G. H. (2010b). *Loss: A personal journey of empowerment*. La Jolla: Person-Centered Press.

Klein, G. H. (2010c). *Empowerment and a person-centered expressive arts pathway through grief and loss. Proceedings of the Presentation at the Annual Conference of the Association for the Development of the Person-Centered Approach*. Rochester, New York.

Klein, G. H. (2012). *A Person-Centered Life and Death. Proceedings of the Presentation at the Annual Conference of the Association for the Development of the Person-Centered Approach, Savannah, Ga*. Person-Centered Journal.

Kriz, J. (2013). Person-centered approach and systems theory. In J. Cornelius-White, M. Lux, & R. Motschnig (Eds.), *Interdisciplinary handbook of the person-centered approach: Connections beyond Psychotherapy*. New York: Springer.

Lewis, T., Lannon, R., & Amini, F. (2000). *A General theory of love*. New York: Random House.

Low, M. (2012). Doctors of Arts. *Democrat and Chronicle*, August 12, p. 1C.

Rogers, N. (1960) A play therapist's approach to the creative art experience. Massachusetts, USA: Brandeis University (Master's thesis).

Rogers, C. R. (1961). *On becoming a person: A therapist's view of psychotherapy*. Boston: Houghton Mifflin.

Rogers, C. R. (1977). *Carl Rogers on personal power: Inner strength and its revolutionary impact*. New York: Delacorte Press.

Rogers, C. R. (1980a). *A way of being*. Boston: Houghton Mifflin.

Rogers, N. (1980b). *Emerging woman: A decade of midlife transitions*. Santa Rosa: Personal Press, The Person-Centered Expressive Therapy Institute.

Rogers, N. (1993). *The creative connection: Expressive arts as healing*. Palo Alto: Science and Behavior Books.

Rogers, N. (2011). *The creative connection for groups: Person-centered expressive arts for healing and social change*. Palo Alto: Science and Behavior Books.

Siegel, D. (2010). *Mindsight: The new science of personal transformation*. New York: Bantam.

Siegel, D. (2012). *The developing mind: How relationships and the brain interact to shape who we are* (2nd ed.). New York: Guilford.

Person-Centered Work in Services for People in Need of Everyday Care

Marlis Pörtner

1 Is the PCA Suitable for Everyday Care?

Spreading into other areas than psychotherapy—such as social services providing care and assistance for people with disabilities, psychiatric patients, elderly persons as well as nursing and dementia care—opens challenging perspectives for the PCA.

Due to its humanistic orientation and theoretical foundations like the actualization tendency, self-concept, attitude of empathy, unconditional positive regard, and congruence, the approach proves particularly appropriate for clients hardly reachable on a cognitive–intellectual level, notably persons with mental disabilities—in psychotherapy as well as in everyday care. It is highly desirable that working with these clients becomes an integral part of person-centered psychotherapy training and more psychotherapists get interested in this field. It offers psychotherapists a singular chance to practice empathic understanding for the manifold—sometimes strange and incoherent—inner worlds of human beings and the variety of individual frames of reference. (Pörtner 1990; 2003)

However, in social services, person-centered work does not mean transforming care situations into psychotherapy sessions. Fundamental principles and the basic attitude are the same, yet conditions, circumstances, tasks, and roles of professionals in wider everyday care are different than in psychotherapy. They must be accounted for and made transparent. Person-centered work in social services basically implies

- *not going from ideas about how people should be, but from how they are and from their potential*
- looking for solutions, planning activities, and making decisions *with, not for them*

M. Pörtner (✉)
Seefeldstrasse 116, CH-8008 Zürich, Switzerland
e-mail: mpoertner@bluewin.ch

J. H. D. Cornelius-White et al. (eds.), *Interdisciplinary Applications of the Person-Centered Approach*, DOI: 10.1007/978-1-4614-7144-8_6,
© Springer Science+Business Media New York 2013

- taking persons seriously in their individual ways to express themselves and seeking to understand them
- helping people to find their *own ways*—within their limited possibilities—for adequately coping with reality
- according to them the most possible *personal responsibility*

To counter misunderstanding such principles as "laissez-faire" attitude, it needs more accurate definitions of what person-centered work means concretely in specific fields. The "practical foundations" and "guidelines for everyday care" I devised (Pörtner 2006; Pörtner 2012) describe adequate person-centered quality criteria for caregivers—not rigid rules, but a code of practice from which to orient, obliging yet at the same time leaving the necessary space to adequately respond to individual and situational particularities. With this concept, person-centered principles reached many professionals, not otherwise interested in PCA, with useful clues for their daily work.

2 Some Examples of Guidelines

2.1 Experience is the Key to Understanding

Most professionals are not used to attend and respond to a person's experiencing and rather pay attention to *what* happens than to *how* it happens and *is experienced.* They try to convince a confused resident that the situation is other than he believes instead of sensing how he feels about it and going from there. Thus, no appropriate care is possible. Change can only emerge from *within* a person's experiencing, not imposed from outside. That is why *empathic listening* is so important. Sensitivity for other persons' experiencing opens up new ways to relate and communicate.

Responding to a person's experiencing stimulates and reinforces what Prouty called "contact functions," the term he used to sum up his threefold definition of contact as "reality contact, affective contact, communicative contact" (Prouty 1994; Prouty et al. 2002). These contact functions are often impaired or not sufficiently developed. Affective contact, that is, being aware of and accept own experiences and feelings—including those considered "negative"—is essential for congruence. Congruence can be fostered by occasionally reflecting experiential aspects of a situation, such as "You are upset by having to do the dishes," "You smile," or at the shower "You enjoy the water trickling over your back." It helps the person being aware of her sensations and feelings, anticipates aggressive escalations, and—a widely neglected purpose—prevents involuntary reinforce-ment of incongruence by not being attentive and responding to how a person is experiencing.

2.2 Find the Person's Language

"Language" in this context embraces verbal *and* non-verbal expression. Particularly with persons who do not speak other ways to communicate must be found. Subtle body tensions, changes in facial expression, and a deep breath are signals to be observed and responded to. *Listening with all senses* is a precondition for sensible care. Prouty's contact reflections are extremely helpful here (Prouty 1994; Prouty et al. 2002).

2.3 The Road is as Important as the Destination

Aspiring fixed goals with a client is counterproductive. We never know *exactly* what a person can achieve. Goals must be defined as a road to take, for example, being *more* able instead of able to do something. *A stretch of way*—smaller or bigger—will be covered anyway. This is a far more encouraging experience than—once more—not attaining a destination. Each step proves capability of taking steps and bears hope for another step. Caregivers must *perceive and value each small step* (even when taking an unforeseen direction) in order to improve the person's self-concept.

2.4 Clarity

What seems clear to us is it not necessarily for others, especially if their capabilities of comprehension or thinking are impaired or slowed down. Clarity helps disabled, mentally ill, and disoriented or confused persons better orientating themselves in reality. Clear and understandable information respecting individual frames of reference is crucial. Even unpleasant situations must be transparent. People with mental problems or disabilities get confused by ambiguous situations or messages; they aggravate or even provoke behavior disorders and psychotic episodes.

2.5 Not the Deficiencies are Crucial but Personal Resources

The potential for growth and change lies in—may be buried, inaccessible, or undeveloped—*personal resources*. Those are to be discovered and developed. Often, people just cannot make a necessary link to manage something and must *be offered support to act independently*. Instead of taking over, caregivers must discover where exactly the gap is, help to bridge it, and thus enable the person to do the next step. An educator, instead of telling an adolescent not capable of tidying his room how he has to do, may show him different ways of doing it and let him choose the one that suits him best.

2.6 Offer Choices and Accord Personal Responsibility

Having choices, being allowed to take decisions and responsibility, fosters independency and self-esteem. Feeling as a person, not as an object determined by others, is essential for quality of life. Even for severely impaired or ill persons with considerably restricted possibilities, there is always *something* they are capable to decide about, be it only choosing the color of their T-shirt or how long they want the water running for their shower. Tiny details seeming irrelevant to us may be important for somebody enduring extremely restricted life conditions. It makes a difference whether a person can choose where she wants the wheelchair to be placed or caregivers decide it. Asking a person, unable to use the toilet by herself: "Is it ok to take you to the toilet now?" means respecting her human dignity. It matters for somebody who cannot eat without help, whether the spoon is put in his mouth without giving him a chance opening it or he is granted this tiny element of self-determination. It feels different for a person when in her presence people *talk with, not about her*. It is a deplorable custom of caregivers and relatives, in presence of non-verbal persons to talk among each other, as if they were not there. This reinforces a self-concept comprehending: "I am nobody" and "I don't exist "—no good precondition for mental health. We must perceive and respond to experiences and feelings of non-verbal persons too. Being asked means something for them, even if they cannot understand literally (though they frequently do), they sense the attitude behind the question and realize that they are taken seriously. With the very few who are not at all accessible by language, we must discover non-verbal ways to express a question.

2.7 Take the Other Person Seriously

This is the base for anything else to become possible. It implies a fundamental respect for other forms of human existence. May they appear strange, "crazy," or incomprehensible—they need acceptance and support and at the same time broaden our horizon of understanding human nature.

In daily life too, human beings must be taken seriously: their emotions, even if appearing inadequate or directed against us; their needs and wishes, even if we cannot always meet them. Even if we cannot understand what a person wants to express or her behavior appears bizarre, *trying* to feel into her—apparently unreal and incomprehensible—inner world is, in itself, beneficial. Feeling accepted as she is helps the person accepting herself and becoming more congruent.

2.8 Recognize One's Own Part

This demand is the most important and most difficult. The images in our heads influence feelings and behavior of our counterparts more than we believe. For better understanding their reactions and being able to respond adequately, caregivers must clearly recognize their own feelings and partialities.

Only congruent caregivers can foster congruence of others. Mentally ill or disabled persons are particularly sensitive to incongruence. They sense it immediately when what we say does not conform to what we feel and will rather respond to underlying feelings than to words. We should keep that in mind when dealing with "inadequate," "incoherent," or "excessive" reactions. Such clients strongly confront us with ourselves. In these fields, professionals cannot get around looking into themselves and reflecting their actions. This is not always easy, and sometimes tiresome, but on the other hand, is not it offering us an invaluable chance to grow?

There is also a simple and pragmatic aspect: Everybody involved, including the caregiver, has a part in the situation. One's own part is often the only clue for a change. By proceeding differently, we give the other person a chance to behave differently too. This is particularly true when situations tend to escalate or always reiterate the same way. To ask, "What could *I* change?" allows overcoming helplessness and acting sensibly. Reflecting a situation concretely—for example, "What exactly did I say?, At what point did he get so upset?, Was it too noisy when I spoke?, Was the door open?"—always reveals *something* to be changed in order to enable the other person to also change something.

3 Conclusion

Person-centered work requires not more time, but a shift of viewpoint and priorities. It is predominantly a matter of nuances greatly influencing quality of life and well-being of persons in need of care. Knowing about and considering these nuances diminish stress and render daily life more interesting and satisfying—for those getting care as well as for those who achieve this challenging task.

Organizations who adopted the concept confirm this experience. A most remarkable evolution takes place at the facilities for people with special needs of the Arbiter Samaritan Bund, Bremen (Germany). Since my first workshop there in 2001, they base their work consistently—including quality management—on the code of practice mentioned above. The excellent organizational structures and tools they created to grant long-lasting continuity are exemplary (for details see Pörtner 2006; Pörtner 2012) and led to amazing changes initially nobody had imagined possible. Implementation is a permanent improving process never coming to an end. It requires to continuously reflect and, where necessary, modify the line of action. Always anew the question is: What does person-centered mean *now, with this person, in this situation?*

References

Pörtner, M. (1990). Client-centered therapy with mentally retarded persons: Catherine and Ruth. In G. Lietaer, J. Rombauts, & R. Van Balen (Eds.), *Client-centered and experiential psychotherapy in the nineties* (pp. 659–669). Leuven: Leuven University Press.

Pörtner, M. (2012). Ernstnehmen, Zutrauen, Verstehen-Personzentrierte Haltung im Umgang mit geistig behinderten und pflegebedürftigen Menschen (8th Edition). Stuttgart: Klett-Cotta.

Pörtner, M. (2006). Trust and understanding-the person-centred approach to everyday care for people with special needs (2nd Revised and Expanded Edition). Ross-on-Wye, UK: PCCS Books.

Pörtner, M. (2003). *Brücken bauen. Menschen mit geistiger Behinderung verstehen und begleiten* [*Building bridges. Ways for a better understanding and supporting of persons with special needs*]. Stuttgart: Klett-Cotta.

Prouty, G. (1994). *Theoretical evolutions in person-centered/experiential therapy–applications to schizophrenic and retarded psychoses.* Westport: Praeger.

Prouty, G., Van Werde, D., & Pörtner, M. (2002). *Pre-therapy. Reaching contact-impaired clients.* Ross-on-Wye: PCCS Books.

Counselling the SAI Way

Umesh Rao and Gita Umesh

1 Introduction

A staggering 222 million out of 833 million people living in rural India are illiterate, attributable partly to their low socio-economic status. People in this marginalized group when stricken with serious illnesses—a brain tumour or heart disease—cannot afford modern medical care; the Sri Sathya Sai Institute of Higher Medical Sciences (SSSIHMS) is often their only hope. Founded by Sathya Sai Baba in 2001, this "Temple of Healing," as it is commonly called, provides tertiary-level care for patients suffering from serious cardiac and neurological illnesses necessitating major surgical interventions. This care is totally free enabled by unsolicited donations from diverse sources touched by the selfless work being done. Patients and accompanying attendants are typically characterized by having experienced high levels of stress and trauma.

Modern medicine needs a spiritual dimension to patient care for progressing from curing to healing, which necessitates addressing the body, mind and spirit (e.g. Benson 1996; Puchalski 2001; Rao 2010). In the SSSIHMS hospital, "Counselling the SAI Way"—Spirituality Awareness Integration in Counselling—addresses the spiritual dimension of patients using the PCA as a therapeutic framework. Being complementary to normal hospital care, SAI counselling is a short-term therapy focused on inner transformation or "the actualization process" in the patients to help achieve healing. SAI counselling provides emotional support and spiritual care to patients suffering from serious cardiac and neurological illnesses necessitating major surgical interventions. Patients are counselled before surgery, post-surgery and before discharge. A psycho-spiritual patient profile is maintained. Extensive

U. Rao (✉) · G. Umesh
Department of Counselling, Sri Sathya Sai Institute of Higher Medical Sciences, Whitefield
EPIP Area, Bangalore, India
e-mail: urao.lotus@gmail.com
URL: http://wfd.sssihms.org.in/

J. H. D. Cornelius-White et al. (eds.), *Interdisciplinary Applications*
of the Person-Centered Approach, DOI: 10.1007/978-1-4614-7144-8_7,
© Springer Science+Business Media New York 2013

clinical experience—over thirty thousand patients counselled since inception in 2001—indicates significant benefits for patients.

SAI counselling is based on the collective wisdom gleaned from ancient Indian scriptures and the teachings of enlightened spiritual leaders. Sai Baba's humane secular philosophy advocating prayer to the God of your Choice is the bedrock of SAI counselling which is founded on the supremacy of Love and the omnipresence of God:

> *There is only one caste, the caste of humanity. There is only one religion, the religion of love. There is only one language, the language of the heart. There is only one God, He is omnipresent.—Sathya Sai Baba.* (1985)

2 Spirituality-Based Counselling

Spirituality has been variously defined as being linked to societal harmony, giving life a purpose or meaning and a connection to God and nature. If so, there may be intrinsic qualities to human nature driven by man's inner spirit, the *Atma* in Hindu philosophy, the actualizing tendency in the person-centred approach, that propels man towards a harmonious coexistence with fellow human beings and the environment, ultimately for individual inner peace.

In Indian culture, a very strong belief prevails that Divine Grace is bestowed when one prays to a personal favourite deity, intertwining religion and spirituality. Prayer catalyses the inner spiritual strength and strengthens faith in Divine Grace and acceptance–the first step towards surrender to God's Will. A belief system conditions the mind to transcend body consciousness and to reach a higher spiritual level, in which one then perceives life's trials and tribulations as passing clouds.

In looking back at the history of mankind, we observe that people irrespective of culture, religion, race or creed have exhibited some common traits attributable to inherent values. Our ancient Vedic scriptures and our spiritual leaders have propounded that human beings are endowed with five innate, intrinsic values—Truth, Right Conduct, Peace, Love and Non-Violence (Fig. 1). When practiced, they promote harmony in the individual, society and environment, and hence, these five core human values can be defined as attributes of spirituality—a pragmatic definition for our patients and counsellors.

There is a remarkable seamless synergy between the person-centred approach and SAI philosophy. Empathy, unconditional positive regard and congruence are resonant with the five innate human values—Love, Truth, Right Conduct, Peace and Non-Violence. They create the vital *growth-producing climate* in a therapeutic relationship (Fig. 2).

At SSSIHMS, the basic theory of the PCA and the SAI philosophy is taught during counsellor training, but the emphasis is on experiential learning and practical knowledge. Aspiring counsellors must inculcate the core human values,

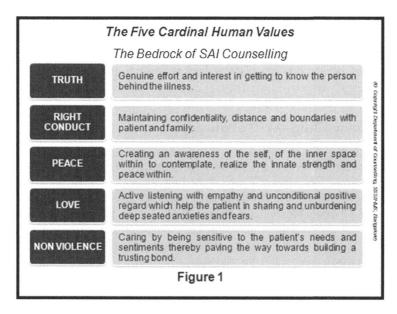

Fig. 1 The five cardinal human values: the bedrock of SAI counselling

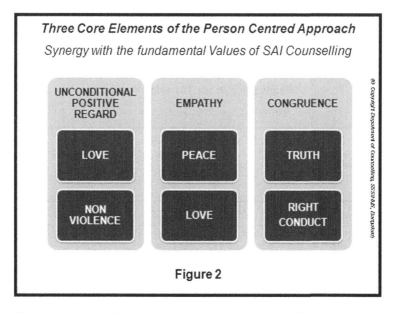

Fig. 2 Three core elements of the person-centred approach: synergy with the fundamental values of SAI counselling

developing the right body language and cultivating humility—all of which are vital for creating a growth-producing climate in a therapeutic relationship. The love element has touched the patients most; very often the counsellors are asked whether they behave this way always, even at home!

3 SAI Counselling—A Walkthrough

The saying *Mind alone is the cause for either bondage or liberation* is an ancient, simple yet powerful, adage. Change or healing happens by inner transformation through the dynamics of the actualizing tendency, social mediation and the actualizing process (Mearns and Thorne 2007), or as per the SAI philosophy through the hierarchy of the Atma (conscience, inner spirit), the intellect, the mind, the senses, the body and the outer world, catalysed by a therapeutic relationship creating a growth-promoting climate (Sathya Sai Baba 1976).

SAI counselling facilitates the transformation of the patient's feelings through a process of body relaxation, mind cleansing and mind conditioning leading the patient towards a state of mindfulness, thereby awakening innate inner strength. The psycho-spiritual healing process—helping the patient overcome outer influences while heightening the awareness of inner equanimity—thus begins. Figure 3 defines these process qualities and identifies relationships between them. Figure 4 provides photographs of the process at work and depicts how different people commune in their own ways yet together.

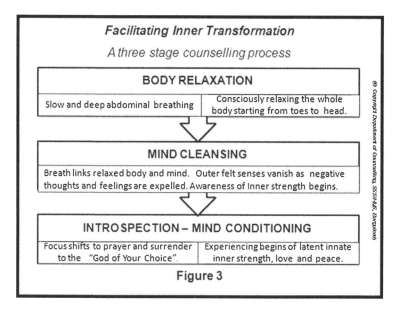

Fig. 3 Facilitating inner transformation: a three-stage counselling process

Inner transformation – without boundaries
This photo highlights the secular spirituality of SAI Counselling - Two patients of different faiths in group counselling together, both immersed in prayer.

Figure 4

Fig. 4 Inner transformation—without boundaries

Maintaining the hierarchy of the Atma (inner spirit), the intellect, the mind, the senses, the body and the outer world is paramount, making the mind subservient to the intellect, and the Atma (inner spirit) is the key to inner transformation.

The psycho-spiritual needs of the patient are addressed by the counsellor at various stages of the medical treatment process in the hospital. The first interaction between counsellor and patient/family establishes the vital rapport and trust wherein common language, love, empathy and body language are the key elements. The first-stage pre-surgery counselling focuses on allaying the fears and anxiety in the patient's mind. Will there be pain? Will I survive? Counsellor's reassurances, body relaxation, mind cleansing and mind conditioning help overcome these. Very often, active listening helps the patient ventilate suppressed feelings, which in itself is therapeutic. The counsellor gets to know the person behind the illness.

The second-stage post-surgery counselling happens after the patient is shifted to the ward from the ICU. The counsellor understands the patient and family at a deeper level as they generally unburden deep-seated feelings and emotions at this stage. The healing of the spirit begins through prayers, introspection and silent contemplation; this inner healing is reflected in their outer form and action. However occasionally, when the outcome is unfavourable, the counselling has to be intensified as illustrated in the second case history.

The final counselling session is prior to discharge when chronic stressful issues affecting health and well-being are addressed. The futility of trying to change attitudes and mindsets of others is emphasized; instead, one can change oneself through practicing the core human values, body relaxation, mind cleansing, mind conditioning and prayer to their favourite deity.

A psycho-spiritual profile is thus generated for every patient from these counselling sessions; eliciting patient information is through close and open-ended questions. Who do they rely upon during a crisis? What are the current or past happenings in their lives that may be related to their stress and anxiety? What are their sources of happiness and relaxation? What motivates them in their daily lives? What is their religion and who is their favourite deity? Do they pray daily, periodically or occasionally? Does prayer reinforce their faith, their inner strength and help surrender to the Divine Will? Does it provide inner peace? Did they pray more, or less, when confronted with this illness? The profile, which becomes part of the patient's hospital medical record, helps track the patient's progress based on the simple premise that when you capture and record information you can improve.

4 Case Histories

4.1 A Patient Traumatized by a Brain Tumour Recurrence that Mandated a Second Brain Surgery

4.1.1 Faith is the Bird that Sings When Dawn is Still Dark—Rabindranath Tagore

A bubbly, young 23-year-old Muslim woman, Mumtaz (name changed), from a traditional lower-middle-class family in a small town had lost her vision from a damaged optic nerve within a year of her marriage. One can imagine the mental agony experienced by Mumtaz and the family at this sudden and most unexpected calamity. She developed severe headaches and was diagnosed with a life-threatening tumour requiring neurosurgery which the family could not afford. Being a very devout family, their only recourse was their faith in Allah, which eventually brought them to our hospital, almost a thousand miles away from home. The tumour was successfully removed; her life was saved, but her vision could not be restored. However, the post-operative histopathology report warranted a follow-up course of radiation therapy to prevent recurrence—the family was advised to get this done at a medical facility closer to home. Complacency from a feeling of general well-being led to neglecting the radiation therapy.

Seven years later, the deadly tumour resurfaced to torment Mumtaz and her family once again. She was readmitted at our hospital for another surgery. She was now the mother of a four-year-old daughter, whom she loved intensely. Motherhood strengthened her will to survive and paradoxically became the main impediment. Toxic emotions kindled an intense fear of dying from the second surgery; yet she desperately wished to live for her child's sake. In this confused state of mind, she consented to the second surgery. However, when taken to the ICU to prep for surgery, she felt isolated, lonely and had a panic attack; she became very agitated, restless, illogical, aggressive, angry, frustrated, insecure and filled with remorse and resentment at her fate. She stubbornly refused surgery. Her mind held her in total bondage; she even forgot to pray, her main source of support at that point. At this juncture, the surgeons sought the counsellor's intervention.

The counsellor's empathic familial love soothed the patient as she gradually relaxed. She unburdened her main concern—fear of dying and depriving her child of a mother's love. The counsellor's persuasive gentle reasoning helped the patient to reflect and recollect all that which was meaningful in her life, and the possibility of losing it all if she refused surgery. Understanding dawned that she held the key to her life; there was a definitive shift in her perception. The mind that had held her in bondage now began to pave the way for her liberation. Through introspection, contemplation and prayer, she learnt to untie the knots; faith and belief replaced fear and worry, and prayer restored her inner strength. Her implicit faith in Allah made her surrender to the Divine Will. With her spiritual strength revived, she spontaneously consented to the surgery that saved her life.

Today, Mumtaz is a happy mother with a new-found zest for life and never forgets to convey her greetings to the counsellor through the doctors during the periodic telemedicine follow-up sessions.

4.2 A Patient Suffering from Trigeminal Neuralgia

4.2.1 When Did the Healing Begin and When Did the Cure Come?

The patient, Ram (name changed), a 44-year-old man, was admitted to neuro-surgery for trigeminal neuralgia, a neuropathic disorder characterized by periodic extremely painful facial spasms. Ram had been living with this illness for over two decades since the complex surgery required to cure him was beyond his means. His prayers brought him and his brother to our hospital—with high hopes.

The patient was relaxed and optimistic after the pre-surgery counselling—body relaxation, mind cleansing and mind conditioning. The second-stage post-surgery counselling after transfer-in from ICU was, however, very different. During surgery, certain complications had developed, which necessitated a second surgery to be scheduled. While the surgeons were confident of the second surgery effecting a cure, the patient's perception was different. With his hopes dashed, a sense of foreboding filled him; he flatly refused the second surgery. The counsellor found him very subdued, worried and disappointed; his expectation of an instant cure after surgery had not materialized. The patient was filled with frustration, anxiety, anger, sadness, depression and helplessness. How does one help a person who has lost all hope? A silent presence with a body language exuding love effectively reassured the patient that there is somebody who cares for his feelings with unconditional love. Proceeding thereafter in a soothing tone, the counsellor helped

Fig. 5 Counselling—the SAI way: a spiritual practice exuding love

the patient and his brother relax through deep breathing as they processed their fear, anxiety, worries, and apprehension and started expelling them from their mind. The counsellor perceived a remarkable peace and calm in their facial expressions as their minds stilled. Silence once again pervaded as the patient was left to introspect, realize his inner spiritual strength and pray to his God. At the end of the counselling session, the patient was mentally and emotionally ready for the planned second surgery. Cured and healed in body, mind and spirit after the second surgery, the patient's brother expressed their feelings as follows in his letter of gratitude to the hospital: "We had given up hope when Ram refused the second surgery. The counsellor revived our spiritual strength through which the patient rediscovered his lost courage. I am grateful to God for having provided this counselling which has taught us how to lead a spiritually empowered life."

5 Conclusion

In conclusion, the core elements of PCA and the core human values of SAI counselling are facets of Love that binds humanity, affirming the universal reality that in this world there is only one caste, the caste of humanity and there is only one religion, the religion of Love. Figure 5 depicts this with a montage of adages and photographs.

References

Mearns, D., & Thorne, B. (2007). *Person-centred counselling in action* (3rd ed.). London: Sage Publications.

Puchalski, C. M. (2001). The role of spirituality in health care. *Baylor University Medical Center Proceedings, 14*(4), 352–357.

Benson, H. (1996). *Timeless healing: The power and biology of belief.* NY: Simon and Schuster.

Rao U (Ed.). (2010). *Spirituality in Healthcare—Perspectives.* http://www.sathyasai.org/files2010/spiritualityInHealthcareEBookRED.pdf. Accessed on 14 March 2012.

Sathya Sai Baba (1985). *One God: Basic Truth of All Faiths, Sathya Sai Speaks,* Vol. 18, *Discourse* 30—25/12/1985. Puttaparthi, A.P., India, SSSBPT.

Sathya Sai Baba. (1976). *The mind and its mysteries, Puttaparthi.* SSSBPT: A.P., India.

Person-Centred Medicine and Subjectivity

Michel Botbol and Dusica Lecic-Tosevski

1 Introduction

In this chapter, we will give a brief characterization of person-centred medicine (PCM) and refer to connections with the person-centred approach (PCA), which are as of yet barely noticed (but see Mezzich et al. 2009). Born of the desire to bring back medicine to what it should always be, PCM primarily promotes a medicine that puts the whole person, and not just his or her illness, at the centre of its goals and treatment. Thus, formulated this principle seems to be so obvious that it is sometimes assumed to be almost trivial. The idea of creating a movement to defend a thesis no one denies has even become one of the criticisms put against the concept by considering it a truism or commonplace. The main real criticism comes, however, from practices that—in response to advances in science and the efficiency of biomedical therapeutic techniques—tend to focus on the disorders. These practices relegate to the status of adjuvant, folk medicine or persistence of picturesque obscurantism the interest shown in the *person* of the patient, in his subjective irreducible singularity. Certainly, the individualization of treatments is a categorical imperative of medicine in general, and in disease-centred medicine in particular, because recent scientific data show its relevance and scope, as it is the case more generally in biological sciences, from human biology to veterinary medicine (Banzato et al. 2005; Schwab et al. 2010).

Tremendous progress has also been made when it comes to the respect of patients' rights, that is to say, applying to suffering persons needing medical care,

M. Botbol (✉)
Université de Bretagne Occidentale, CHU de Brest, Hôpital psychiatrique
de Bohars, Bohars 29820, France
e-mail: botbolmichel@orange.fr

D. Lecic-Tosevski
Belgrade University School of Medicine Director, Institute of Mental Health,
Palmoticeva 37, 11000 Belgrade, Serbia
e-mail: dusica.lecictosevski@eunet.rs

J. H. D. Cornelius-White et al. (eds.), *Interdisciplinary Applications*
of the Person-Centered Approach, DOI: 10.1007/978-1-4614-7144-8_8,
© Springer Science+Business Media New York 2013

democratic and legal rules valid for everyone. Of course, such respect is of major importance for the patients, just like it is for any users regardless of the service they need and it does not imply in itself the recognition of the individuality of the person of the patient, as is the stated ambition of PCM. PCM should not therefore, be reduced to the individualization of care or the respect for patients' rights, as it aspires to something more: the recognition of the individual subjectivity of the whole person of the patient beyond what characterizes his or her illness or the status of a patient. What is of interest here is dealing with the inner world of a patient in his particular situation of suffering and dependence caused by illness, like in Aristotle's Nicomachean Ethics: "Cure of a unique person and not a generalized nosological case, in a specific situation, within a specific, unrepeatable period of one's life" (Warne 2007). What becomes crucial here is the commitment of the physician to approach the patient's subjectivity in his singular vital situation. In this regard, PCM shares with PCA the conviction that it is of central importance for clinical practice to empathically understand the inner world of the other and to accept that there are as many realities as there are persons (Rogers 1980).

2 What is Needed to Meet These Requirements?

In this perspective, the modernity and originality of PCM resides in the fact that it does not content itself with asserting its principles but strives to define conditions for the effective implementation of this ambition, in each medical situation. What counts the most here is to meet real patients' needs and not those of more or less paradigmatic entities defined by each medical speciality to allow the reductionist approach imposed by the research methodology in a "classical" evidence-based medicine (EBM) approach.

Three conditions must be met to reach this goal (Mezzich et al. 2010a, b; Botbol 2012):

- To take into account the whole being of the patient [I am myself and my context (Lain-Entralgo 1982)].
- To consider the diagnosis and therapeutic choices as a joint process involving the person of the patient, the persons of the carers (family and caregivers in general), and the person of the clinician (trialog).
- To consider as essential the subjective aspects of the person's health situation and not only the objective aspects of the illness.

Again, although not originally referred to Roger's work, this last PCM principle is shared with PCA. It matches very well proposition five of Rogers' (1995/1951) originally stated theory of personality and behaviour: "Behaviour is basically the goal oriented attempt of the organism to satisfy his needs as experienced, in the field as perceived" (p. 491).

2.1 Taking the Whole Person into Account

As said above, one should primarily move beyond the pathological aspects of the person's illness and focus also on the positive aspects of his health status by recalling that whatever the illness, a symptom always results from the interaction between the positive and the negative aspects of the person's health situation (Cloninger 2004). In other words, we are always dealing with an interaction between pathological processes and recovery mechanisms. This idea, which forms the basis of both psychodynamic and person-centred concepts in psychiatry, also applies to all pathological situations and symptoms, which the individualization of medicine takes only partially into account. It should also be recalled here that objective and subjective dimensions come into play in all these cases and inter-actions, as long as it is true that there is no such a thing as a disease alone, that is to say without the person of the patient. Data (biological and psychological, sub-jective and objective, standardized, or monographic) confirming this assumption is plentiful and varied in all fields of medicine (Heath 2005).

2.2 Considering Diagnosis and Therapeutic Choices as a Joint Process

Even beyond the legal reasons that now tend to impose it, but so often are reduced to formal attitudes with limited subjective consideration and impact, PCM con-stantly strives to leave to the patient and to his family, sufficient space in diag-nostic processes and in therapeutic choices. It implies giving enough attention to what they say and show. This attention requires much more than the physician's expertise, that is, his or her personal commitment in their relationship with the patients and their carers, a commitment which reveals the presence of the principle of unconditional positive regard within PCM (Hochmann 2012). Here again, PCM meets PCA principles as emphasized by Rogers in psychotherapy as well as in the field of education (1983). In PCM, likewise in PCA, the interpersonal relationship is recognized as a pivotal factor in healing and growth. In Rogers' (1983) words: "We know… that the initiation of [significant] learning rests not upon the teaching skills of the leader, not upon scholarly knowledge of the field, not upon curricular planning, not upon use of audiovisual aids, not upon the programmed learning used, not upon lectures and presentations, not upon an abundance of books, though each of these might at one time or another be utilized as an important resource. No, the facilitation of significant learning rests upon certain attitudinal qualities that exist in the personal relationship between the facilitator and the learner" (p. 121).

2.3 Taking into Account the Subjective Aspects of the Person's Health Situation

In addition to the attention paid to the medico-biological aspects of the person's health status, a person-centred assessment needs to give enough consideration to the patient's subjective feelings. Whether or not we suspect a psychic or psychosomatic causality to the disorder which a patient brings to us, it is essential to keep in perspective the factors involved in the patient's health situation. Beyond reasserting this principle, we need to utterly enhance the methodology for accessing these subjective dimensions among the different partners involved in the diagnostic process and the therapeutic relationship. For the professionals, the only way to access these subjective dimensions is through what the patient (and or his carers) says in words or shows in acting, as long as these words or acts can trigger in the professionals enough empathy to approach the patient's subjective feelings to which these expressions are related. In this way, PCM and PCA go hand in glove concerning the relevance of the clinician's empathy for the development of a health-promoting relationship.

3 What Methodology Then?

Answering this question is finally the main goal of the PCM ongoing work. This is particularly true for those who take part in the International College of Person-centred Medicine, which brought together a large number of world associations of health professionals (World Medicine Association, World Association of Family Doctors, representatives of important sections of the World Psychiatric Association, International Association of Nurses, Social Workers, Pharmacists, Medical Students, etc.), of patients (International Federations of Patients' Associations), and of caregivers (EUFAMI, World Federation of Mental Health). Since 2008, the College organizes an annual international conference on PCM in Geneva, under WHO auspices since 2009.

The overall mission of the International College includes the following:

- To make refocusing on the patient a major cross-cutting medical challenge.
- To reflect on the conditions required to meet this cross-cutting challenge.
- To develop directly or indirectly, tools to adapt to the PCM practical conditions and principles.
- To adapt these tools to all these contexts and pathologies.

Working on the diagnostic approach has become an important element to meet this methodological ambition. That is why on the basis of previous experience promoted by the World Psychiatric Association, the college developed a *Person-Centred Integrated Diagnostic (PID) model* (Mezzich et al. 2010a, b). Its main objective is to take into account the subjective aspects (positive and negative) of the health situation of persons seeking care and not just an objective description of their illness. This diagnostic model includes, besides the objective elements about the patient and his or her context, the subjective elements reported by the idiographic formulations of the person who is being cared for, their carers, and assisting professionals.

This approach naturally led us to a closer examination of *the role of the professional's empathy in the methodology to access the subjectivity of the patient*, trying to go beyond the general assertions on the importance of this concept in therapeutic relationships and care activities.

At first seen as the professional's ability to listen sympathetically to the comments of the patient and to consider his wishes and needs, the notion of empathy has gradually widened to include representations that the physician (or the health professional) makes of the clinical situation in which the person in need of care is involved. In short, these are representations that the professional makes of the health situation of the person suffering through his/her (the professional) own empathy, triggered by the words and the acts of the patients and of their carers. This mechanism is well described by the concept of "metaphorizing empathy" proposed by Lebovici (1999) from his work with babies and their mothers. It is also close to the notion of "narrative empathy" proposed by Hochmann (2012) based on his work with autistic children and on the philosophical ideas brought by Paul Ricoeur, a famous French phenomenologist, in his book "Time and Narrative" (Ricoeur 1983). This important development in PCM marked the full recognition of the role of the physician's subjectivity as a diagnostic and treatment tool in the physician–patient relationship.

4 Concluding Remarks and Future Perspectives

PCM thus evolved from mirroring the patients' opinion on their selves or their health status to struggling to approach the **subjectivity of the person** (in both its conscious and unconscious aspects) through the personal commitment and metaphorizing empathy of the professional. Moreover, by establishing the subjectivity of the physician as a tool for understanding the patient and his disorder, it gives back to the subjective involvement of the professional the positive status it has lost with the progress of objective technical medicine. In this perspective, this dimension can be properly reflected in practice and training if enough space is given to work it through. Rather than training the professionals to fight against their subjective movements or to deny it and to prevent them from getting closer to the patient's personal needs, PCM proposes to train them to use these subjective movements as their best tool to access the patient's subjectivity. Thus, PCM acknowledges the relevance for clinical practice, of the clinician's congruence in the relationship, that is, his or her access to experiences arising in resonance with the patient (see the chapter "Essence of the Person-Centered Approach"). A required condition is for these professionals to be trained to work it through properly and develop enough reflexive capacities. This would enable them to take their subjective movements as one of the bricks of the interactive construction they have to build with the patient and for him or her, involving all those who are contributing to their health care and health status. The team work and peer supervision are crucial to enhance and sustain this interactive process.

Finally, this brief presentation of PCM in the context of this book, allowed us to study more directly the relationships between Rogers' work and the perspective we have been developing in the last 10 years (Mezzich et al. 2009) following the path of many more or less congenial theories and practices (Rogers 1961; Cassel 1999; Kleinman 1988; Mezzich et al. 2009). Retrospectively, we can see striking similarities between PCM and PCA. Consequently, we expect that synergistic effects will arise from further elaborating the connections and complementary insights into PCM and PCA, contributing to an urgently needed positive development of health care systems.

References

Banzato, C. E. M., Mezzich, J. E., & Berganza, C. E. (2005). Philosophical and methodological foundations of psychiatric diagnosis: Introduction. *Psychopathology, 38*, 159–161.

Botbol, M. (2012). Du manifeste au subjectif: ce qu'est la médecine de la personne [From objectivity to subjectivity: What is Person Centered Medicine]. In S. D. Kipman (Ed.), *Manifeste pour la médecine de la personne [Manifesto for Person Centered Medicine]*. Paris: Dunod.

Cassel, E. J. (1999). Diagnosing suffering: a perspective. *Annals of Internal Medicine, 131*, 531–534.

Cloninger, C. R. (2004). *Feeling good: the science of well-being*. New York: Oxford University Press.

Heath, I. (2005). Promotion of disease and corrosion of medicine. *Canadian Family Physician, 51*, 1320–1322.

Hochmann, J. (2012). *Une histoire de l'empathie* [A history of empathy]. Paris: Odile Jacob.

Kleinman, A. (1988). *The illness narratives*. New York: Basic Books.

Laín-Entralgo, P. (1982). *El Diagnóstico Médico: Historia y Teoría* [The medical diagnostic: history and theory]. Barcelona: Salvat.

Lebovici, S. (1999). *L'arbre de vie—éléments de la psychopathologie du bébé*. [The tree of life— Principles of infant psychopathology]. Toulouse: Erès.

Mezzich, J. E., Snaedal, J., Van Weel, C., & Heath, I. (2009). *The international network for person-centered medicine: background and first Steps*. http://www.personcenteredmedicine. org/mission.php. Accessed 21 July 2012.

Mezzich, J. E., Snaedal, J., Van Weel, C., & Heath, I. (2010a). Introduction to conceptual explorations on person-centered medicine. *International Journal of Integrated Care, 10*, 330–332.

Mezzich, J. E., Salloum, I., Cloninger, R., Salvador-Carulla, L., Kirmayer, L. G., Banzato, C. E. M., et al. (2010b). Person-centred integrative diagnosis: conceptual bases and structural model. *Canadian Journal of Psychiatry, 55*(11), 701–708.

Ricoeur, P. (1983). *Temps et récit* [Time and narrative]. Paris: Le Seuil.

Rogers, C. R. (1961). *On becoming a person*. Boston: Houghton Mifflin.

Rogers, C. R. (1980). *A way of being*. Boston: Houghton Mifflin Co.

Rogers, C. R. (1983). *Freedom to learn for the 80's*. Columbus: Charles E. Merrill Publishing Company.
Rogers, C. R. (1995). *Client-centered therapy*. London: Constable (Original work published 1951).
Schwab, M., Kaschka, W. P., & Spina, E. (2010). *Pharmacogenetics in psychiatry*. Basel: Karger.
Warne, C. (2007). *Aristotle's Nicomachean ethics: Reader's guide*. London: Continuum.

Part III
Education

The Learner-Centered Model: From the Vision to the Future

Barbara L. McCombs

> *The emotions of this time are the deepest ones we humans experience—loss, grief, fear. Yet it helps us immensely if we can share these emotions and not push them away or pretend they're not present. I find that sharing our common experiences of grief, anger, anxiety allows us to move closer together in support of one another. It also helps quell the natural tendency to transfer impotence and grief into anger and rage. For the university, as in other organizations, I feel it is essential to name these emotions and to use them as an opportunity for solidarity. I've experienced how much capacity, creativity and even joy we humans can experience when we're sharing our despair and grief. It's essential that we don't let our strong reactions to this time drive us farther apart.*
>
> Margaret Wheatley (2011, June).

1 Introduction

The person-centered concept is finally reaching its intended destiny: the vision of Carl Rogers and his colleagues and supporters over the past decades has proven its validity and usefulness to practice. The supportive data now cannot be ignored. Further, there is sufficient acknowledgment by a growing number of researchers and educators that the research and theory meet quality research standards for this age of multi-method research in education (see chapters in this book for many examples). The person-centered model and its derivatives offer a philosophical foundation focused on the whole person and their perceptions and experiences of learning that are now seen as valid after decades of anti-self-report criticisms by the research community. My purpose in this chapter is to describe our work with the American Psychological Association since late 1989 and the early 1990s (cf. McCombs 2013, in press; McCombs and Miller 2007, 2008). This work has involved experts in educational psychology and its associated fields in defining research-validated principles and practices that can transform our current educational system in keeping with what is needed in our twenty-first century world.

B. L. McCombs (✉)
Applied Research and Technology Institute (ARTI), University of Denver (DU),
2135 E. Wesley Avenue, Denver, CO 80208, USA
e-mail: bmccombs@du.edu

J. H. D. Cornelius-White et al. (eds.), *Interdisciplinary Applications of the Person-Centered Approach*, DOI: 10.1007/978-1-4614-7144-8_9,
© Springer Science+Business Media New York 2013

To address how our work with research-validated learner-centered principles and practices for the past nearly 25 years can take the person-centered vision of Carl Rogers into the present and propel us to a new educational future requires a deeper look at our current educational context. We are in an era of rapid change (Brady 2011; Duffy 2011a, b; Fullan 2011; Hannum and McCombs 2008; Hargreaves 2011; McCombs 2011; McCombs and Miller 2007, 2008; Molloy 2010). This contextual variable suggests that old ways of thinking and doing are changing at a pace unprecedented and accelerated by rapidly changing technologies (Bransford 2001; Dede 2011) and student uses of technology for learning (Barton and Coley 2010; Fox 2012; Duffy 2011b; McCombs 2010; McCombs and Vakili 2009). What are considered to be the gold standards for research quality are also rapidly changing (cf. McCombs 2013, in press) along with what experts are suggesting are the most appropriate research models and research methodologies in educational research. Experts are acknowledging that the most important and valid research is increasingly conducted in real school and learning settings (cf. Horowitz and McEwan 2012; Phelps 2011) of all mixes (blended, qualitative, quantitative, etc.).

Another significant milestone that has been achieved is in the area of how experts are now defining the interconnectedness of learners and the value of relationships in helping learners of all ages achieve their potential and pursue learning for a lifetime (cf. Frakes and Linder 2012, February 8; Jourdain 2012; Radel et al., 2010; Wheatley 2011; Wheatley and Frieze 2011). The new systems view is ecological and holistic; it is a living systems perspective that outs the person at the center and the learner as the individual who is naturally curious, motivated to learn, and eager to discover self and personal life purpose. Research is growing that supports collaborative approaches among researchers from multiple disciplines and research locations nationally and internationally as evidenced by recent efforts by Hargreaves and Fullan as well as systems thinkers such as Scharmer (2011), Senge (2011), Wheatley (2009, 2010 2011, 2012) and Williams (2011). There is also increased recognition that learners are leaders and all leaders in a learning system need to be supported in flexible ways as they demonstrate their leadership skills and special talents (e.g., Harris 2012; Fullan 2010a, b; Fullan 2011). Finally, there are advances in emerging technology- and web-supported tools for learning that are aligned with current twenty-first century learner needs to connect with others in their personal environments and in virtual environments around the globe (cf. Duffy 2011b; Fox 2012; Hannum and McCombs 2008; Sisk 2011).

To better understand the importance of these developments, it is necessary to understand today's learners and learning contexts. How contextual variables connect with theoretical assumptions and research-validated principles confirming the validity of person-centered theories presents challenges to researchers, practitioners, and policymakers. We are now poised to meet these challenges with a new vision that can transform our thinking and educational systems. Subsequent sections further articulate how Rogers' person-centered model (PCM) has contributed in the past, where it has led us in the present, and into the future.

The transformation so urgently needed in our educational systems toward learner-centered models is described, and a call to action for empowering the natural learning of all learners is presented.

1.1 The Context

No one paying attention to education and the upheavals occurring in our systems nationally and globally can miss the calls for transformation in outdated systems built on old assumptions no longer valid for producing the highest educational outcomes for individual learners (see McCombs 2012). Our claim, shared by a numerous committed and experienced educators and researchers, is that the *basic features of learning, learners, human development, motivation, and individual differences are being ignored* (see McCombs 2009). Reasons for ignoring this well-established knowledge base share a common core: *We do not have an educational systems framework that is based on individual learners and how they naturally learn.* What we have and continue to promote is a system unwilling to change its basic assumptions and work from the inside out rather than the outside in. Evidence from both researchers and practitioners indicates that the problem can be solved rather simply by addressing new policies and practices in the education of our future educational researchers.

For the purposes of this chapter, the argument is broadened to include taking a deeper look at what person- and learner-centered models of the twenty-first century can contribute to educating not only the researchers in our field, but also the public. The public includes those who value the future of our children and our nation and world, including parents, concerned community members, business partners, and media representatives. What is clear is that until all of us understand what the research says and why we must transform our thinking and our systems, the political will to transform outdated learning systems will remain our biggest challenge.

It is clear that the current educational system is based on assumptions and values that no longer serve us as learners, or our students. These assumptions and values do not match the reality of the research and theory base on learning and individual natural learners nor do they match our practical wisdom and the experience of quality teachers and school leaders. Reformers who have attempted to improve a one-size-fits-all system have necessarily been compelled to work on the fringes, from the outside in, resulting in endless debates about standards, curriculum, testing, and accountability. From my own work on learner-centered educational systems, the *solution to the fundamental problem of choosing a research-validated set of assumptions and transformational paradigm for all research, practice, and policy* has to start with an understanding of individual learners and what we know about learning.

That is the reasonable approach and one originally advocated by person-centered theorists and researchers (Cornelius-White and Harbaugh 2010). In our rapidly changing landscape that is likely to accelerate in years to come, the educational system must be viewed as organic and living in service to the natural learning of students, teachers, administrators, and parents alike. It must be grounded on a core belief in the inherent tendency of all people to learn for a lifetime. It must start with a value all can embrace: *schooling and education are the fundamental means to develop each learner's unique potential to contribute in a way that is meaningful and relevant to him or her.* Any other approach will recreate the problems evident in the current system: Too many dropouts, too many disengaged students, too many students who simply comply with more shallow learning and testing to "get through," too many students who are depressed and lack the self-confidence to be successful, and too many students who believe they can learn more of what they need in life outside of school.

The transformation approached needed, as I have argued elsewhere (cf. McCombs 2011; McCombs 2012; McCombs and Miller 2007, 2008), is one that reflects all learners as naturally self-regulated and self-motivated agents of their own learning. We need to rethink whether we want to do things *to* and/or we want to do things *with* the natural learners that we are for a lifetime. We need to move away from our fears about giving students and teachers choices and agency as argued by Walls and Little (2005) and Zimmerman and Schunk (2001), for without choice, learners are unable to develop, learn, and demonstrate self-regulation and responsibility regardless of their age or stage of development.

The increasingly urgent achievement gap (Barton and Coley 2010; Ceci and Papierno 2005; Hannum and McCombs 2008; Horowitz and McEwan 2011; McCombs 2001, 2007, 2009; Phelps 2012; Sisk 2011) cannot be closed within current school policy testing and accountability environments. The changing demographics about school-age learners and what they need for fostering their natural curiosity, love of learning, and excitement about pursuing personal interests is another contextual variable that is well described in recent publications (e.g., McCombs 2011; Pink 2011; Tulgan 2009, 2010). These changing demographics are also impacting how young people are contributing to the workforce and how they expect to be engaged in purposeful and innovative projects and are more loyal than preceding generations while also wanting to identify problems no one else has identified, solve problems no one else has solved, and invent new things that can make existing things better.

1.2 The Theory

As described in this book, the PCA was founded by Carl Ransom Rogers (1902–1987), and has for Rogers (1980), the central hypothesis that individuals are capable of forming their own self-understanding and determining their own futures. Rogers has the vision and insight into formulate his theories as hypotheses that could be verified by scientific research. This was counter to the reigning logical positivists of the time and allowed him to explore the potentials of his approach in social and political domains (Rogers 1980). His theory took actualization to new levels and identified it as a central tenet of his theory that has endured from then through the present—the assumption that every being seeks to maintain and enhance self. The PCA theory identified the optimal conditions under which the actualizing tendency guides the human learners toward a constructive development of their inherent potentials as social beings who need social conditions for the unimpeded unfolding of the actualizing tendency (Rogers 1977).

As described in this book, the PCA is a parsimonious explanation of how people grow and change and an opportunity for interdisciplinary research and practice at biological, psychological, social, cultural, political, and artistic levels. The original PCA theories provide a well-grounded foundation of whole-person concepts such as actualization, empathy, congruence, and unconditional positive regard. This encourages us to pursue new findings and theories that can refine core person- and learner-centered concepts.

1.3 The Research

Research continues to emerge that enlightens the field for all constituents. For example, Caine and Caine (2011) have now taken their original principles of learner-centered natural learning into the fields of neuroscience and appropriate uses of new technologies for empowering learners and their teachers. This work has had a major impact on practice and is beginning to be heard by policymakers and politicians as our nation and world confronts failures in the current educational and learning paradigms.

Others in multiple fields continue to inform practitioners, researchers, and policymakers about the power of PCA for transforming current practice. These include authors in this volume as well as researcher in the United States and abroad, working collaboratively toward a new paradigm informed by quality research that is also being redefined to include perceptual data (cf. McCombs 2013, in press; McCombs 2012). Details are in subsequent sections of this chapter.

1.4 The Challenge

One of our biggest challenges is *our attitudes, our beliefs, and our values*—the way we choose to think about education and the preparation of educators for a rapidly evolving global society (McCombs 2012). There are many countries around the world moving in this direction, rebelling against the current standards-based, testing, and accountability-driven systems. They are having successes that validate the necessity of a new way forward—a way that transforms rather than reforms the educational system and the way we prepare educators to teach and lead others in those systems.

1.5 The Vision

It is safe to say that the time for a new vision is here and that this vision is shared in whole or in part by a growing number of others from all walks of life. Parents are an increasingly vocal group who are protesting current one-size-fits-all curricula, mandates for increased state and national testing, and lack of quality teachers for the most underprivileged learners of all races and cultural groups. For example, in the state of Colorado, many groups are collaborating to fight new state education policies and their efforts are beginning to pay off in groups such as Uniting 4 Kids (Engel 2011) and Feeding America (2011, September 15). There is growing recognition by policymakers, media groups such as PBS, and philanthropists that federal policies must be changed if we are to avoid the perils of too many children living in poverty and not being served by an outdated system. At this historic time for all of us, it is clear that voices are being heard and that these include our children and their families.

2 The Vision of the Past

The original and evolving PCM is consistently being embellished with research-validated practices that lead to lifelong learning motivations and dispositions for success in personalized and individually relevant ways. The PCM vision was obviously ahead of its times thereby justifying a brief review of what this model had to offer us up to this time. A systematic review of these contributions, the current research, and what a learner-centered approach can offer us for the future leads to implications that are elucidated in subsequent sections of this chapter.

2.1 The Person-Centered Model

For Rogers (1942, 1959), the self or the self-concept is central to intra-personal and inter-personal processes. He had the insight into see that the self is a gestalt available to awareness as a fluid and changing gestalt, as a process that at any given moment is a specific entity partially definable in operational terms by means of a Q sort or other measure. Rogers also recognized that the flexibility of the self is constrained by socialization experiences during the childhood emergence of the self when a need for positive regard appears. The person-centered theory was visionary in positing that the totality of individual experiences is a holistic-integrative evaluative process, the organismic valuing process (OVP) that has the potential to enhance the individual personal development of the individual and others in his or her community and to make for the survival and evolution of the human species (Rogers 1964, 1995).

The validity of the PCM theory, principles, and practices provides a basis for changing a status quo that consistently favors the advantaged students with more incentives to be lifelong learners. What is most telling in our national and international debates on education is that we can no longer ignore the children and families living on the streets or in cycles of poverty that are politically, socially, and morally hard to break. The political and social will is changing, however, and the focus now on the whole child is evidenced by efforts such as those of Richardson (2013).

2.2 What Current Research Says

The phenomenological philosophical underpinnings of the PCA theory relates to current theories of constructivism. Prior theories such as behaviorism looked at variables outside the person to explain learning and learning achievement. The PCA theory, on the other hand, acknowledged that personal experiences and the individual's subjective reality are crucial for how learners orient and relate in the world. Knowing what each learner experiences helps in understanding the role of the learning facilitator as someone who empathizes from his or her own experiences in understanding each learner as a whole person. Facilitation is seen as a dialectic process in which unconscious actualizing tendencies are brought to consciousness, and this self-awareness empowers and transforms thinking and actions.

We now understand that the basic attitudes of the PCA include (a) autonomy support to empower self-regulation and agency over one's decisions and life choices, (b) empathy, transparency or realness; (b) acceptance, or unconditional positive regard and are interwoven and mutually interdependent. Michael Fullan, Professor Emeritus at OISE/University of Toronto, has for decades argued for change through leadership development of educators at all system levels. In an article for the HOPE Foundation in Bloomington, Indiana, Fullan (2010a) stated that we now have the knowledge and practice base to bring about large-scale or whole system change and that it is becoming more valid and accessible. Fullan further asserts that we have learned there are simple principles that apply equally in diverse public and private sector organizations.

Those who agree with Fullan include Pink (2009) who presents a wide range of evidence drawn from research and human experiences that the key to success at personal and organizational levels are three drives or natural human higher instincts Pink affirms what motivation researchers such as Deci and Ryan (1991; Ryan and Deci 2000) have been saying for decades: autonomy or ability to direct our own lives, mastery or competence to get continually better at something that matters, and purpose or belonging so that we act in service to something larger than ourselves.

2.3 What the Implications are for Practice and Policy

From current research, it is clear that *individual diversity cannot be effectively addressed by education that is based on uniformity.* This implies that educational practice and policy need to include the following:

- Programs need to provide participants with opportunities to experience as well as learn the knowledge base on human learning, motivation, development, and individual differences.
- Programs need to embrace collaborative and real-world learning experiences that get educators involved in the real world of teaching and leading.
- Programs need to encourage visionary leadership and the ability to share leadership in the pursuit of quality teaching, learning, and leading in their particular contexts.
- Programs need to help participants form lifelong relationships and networks of support as they embark on transforming the current system to one that serves all learners in the pursuit of their personal purpose and life work.

These program and policy suggestions are a good start but must be acted upon to insure the vision of learner-centered education becomes a reality.

2.4 Where the Theory Led the Field

The PCA theory reminds the field that enhanced organizational functioning (functioning that supports meaningful learning and engages all learners in lifelong learning processes) *requires a personally supportive learning environment.* This requirement has been shown to be effective in educator preparation programs as well as for younger learners—the students in the schools in which they serve. As research demonstrates, a personally caring and supportive environment gives researchers, teachers, and all school leaders the time to reflect, discuss, share experiences, and receive social and emotional support (Deakin-Crick et al. 2007; McCombs 2004). In fact, our research has shown that a caring and supportive learner-centered environment in even a single classroom is what allows all learners to be able to deal with nonlearner-centered school policies and practices as well as how to deal with negative student reactions to these policies (McCombs and Miller 2007, 2008).

To move the theory into the present vision, the following section describes our learner-centered vision. It builds on Roger's PCA vision and is designed to lead us into the present time of deep reform and educational transformation in keeping with twenty-first century learning needs.

3 The Vision of the Present

In 1990, the American Psychological Association (APA) appointed a Task Force for Psychology in Education. One of the primary goals of this task force was to review over a century of research relevant to education. This review of research on learning, motivation, development, and individual differences led to the development and dissemination of the learner-centered psychological principles (LCPs). Originally, the task force identified 12 principles (APA 1993) and later added two principles in response to rising interests in understanding cultural diversity and the assessment of student learning outcomes (APA 1997). The new document can be downloaded at http://www.apa.org/ed/lcp.html.

According to the Preamble (p. 2), "These principles emphasize the active and reflective nature of learning and learners. From this perspective, educational practice will be most likely to improve when the educational system is redesigned with the primary focus on the learner." Not surprisingly, the principles are consistent with the principles advocated by Rogers and his PCM (McCombs 1999; Rogers et al. (2012, in press) and its learner dispositions and personal potential perspective.

The credibility of the LCPs comes from the consensus of a taskforce of researchers who identified principles that have stood the test of time in countless studies using a variety of research methodologies. The research on effective educational principles and practices based on the LCPs characterizes learning as a whole-person phenomenon (McCombs 2003). This involves cognitive and metacognitive as well as motivational and affective, social and developmental, and other individual difference factors important to optimal learning, motivation, and development. Practices based on these principles are consonant with recent discoveries from psychology relating to positive youth development and prevention interventions (Kristjansson 2010; Larson 2000; Seligman and Csikszentmihalyi 2000; Lazarus 2000; Lazarus 2003). To align this research with current federal guidelines about what constitutes "scientifically based evidence" is needed, however, in order to influence current educational policy and practice.

3.1 From Person-Centered to Learner-Centered

Recent research reveals the social nature of natural learning along with sociocultural and contextual factors. Lee and Shute (2010) explored personal and socio-contextual factors affecting the performance of K-12 students. The resulting integrative framework stresses the importance of personal factors (behavior, affect, attitude, and cognition) and their socio-contextual environment as predictors working together to create optimal school performance, particularly in reading and mathematics. Social and emotional skills were found to be essential for the successful development of cognitive thinking and learning skills. In addition, research is also confirming that learning is a natural process, inherent to living organisms (APA 1997; Caine and Caine 2011).

From our research and that of others who have explored differences in what learning looks like in and outside of school settings, several things become obvious (e.g., McCombs 2009; McCombs and Miller 2007, 2008; Zimmerman and Schunk 2001). Real-life learning is often playful, recursive and nonlinear, engaging, self-directed, and meaningful from the learner's perspective. Research increasingly shows that self-motivated learning is only possible in contexts that provide for choice and control (see Ackerman 2010; Deakin-Crick et al. 2009; Green and Azevedo 2010; Jukes et al. 2011; Patall et al. 2010). When students have choice and are allowed to control major aspects of their learning, they are more likely to achieve self-regulation of thinking and learning processes.

We believe that *a learner-centered foundation based on solid research validated by experience is the right approach to simplifying our research models and methods*. The learner-centered framework provides a foundation for transforming education and the role of distance learning. Many researchers associated with the application and assessment of technology in education recognize that the current system must be transformed to accommodate what students need to succeed and help shape the future (e.g., Levine 2007; Stewart 2007; Suarez-Orozco and Sattin 2007). Technology changes the role of teachers to that of co-learners and contributors to the social and interpersonal development of students, and can further promote student connections to the community around them and to working in groups on real-world projects across time and space.

Online delivery of education can also provide a means to centralize course development so that it achieves necessary economies of scale while linking intergenerational learners, teachers, and facilitators on a global scale. Rigorous research in all these areas is beginning to emerge (e.g., Duffy and Kirkley 2004; Penuel and Riel 2007) but more research needs to be done to systematically address the above issues and the critical features needed for wise decisions about data storage, data reduction, system use, and other associate leadership and change issues.

3.2 Learner-Centered Principles and Practices

The most recent version of the (APA 1997) LCPs are now being distributed widely to educational psychologists and included in the best-selling educational psychology textbooks (see McCombs 2009 and McCombs and Miller 2007, 2008 for more information about this trend). We invite readers take a look at the 14 principles in Table 9.1 and what we have done in our work shown in Table 9.2 where these principles of learning were posited at principles of change that apply to all living systems levels (personal, technical, and organizational (Hannum and McCombs 2008; Lambert and McCombs 1998; McCombs 2004; McCombs and Miller 2007, 2008).

Table 9.1 Learner-centered psychological principles (APA Work Group of the Board of Educational Affairs, 1997)

I. Cognitive and metacognitive factors

Principle 1: Nature of the learning process

The learning of complex subject matter is most effective when it is an intentional process of constructing meaning from information and experience

Principle 2: Goals of the learning process

The successful learner, over time and with support and instructional guidance, can create meaningful, coherent representations of knowledge

Principle 3: Construction of knowledge

The successful learner can link new information with existing knowledge in meaningful ways

Principle 4: Strategic thinking

The successful learner can create and use a repertoire of thinking and reasoning strategies to achieve complex learning goals

Principle 5: Thinking about thinking

Higher-order strategies for selecting and monitoring mental operations facilitate creative and critical thinking

Principle 6: Context of learning

Learning is influenced by environmental factors, including culture, technology, and instructional practices

II. Motivational and affective factors

Principle 7: Motivational and emotional influences on learning

What and how much is learned is influenced by the learner's motivation. Motivation to learn, in turn, is influenced by the individual's emotional states, beliefs, interests and goals, and habits of thinking

Principle 8: Intrinsic motivation to learn

The learner's creativity, higher-order thinking, and natural curiosity all contribute to motivation to learn. Intrinsic motivation is stimulated by tasks of optimal novelty and difficulty, relevant to personal interests, and providing for personal choice and control

Principle 9: Effects of motivation on effort

Acquisition of complex knowledge and skills requires extended learner effort and guided practice. Without learners' motivation to learn, the willingness to exert this effort is unlikely without coercion

III. Developmental and social factors

Principle 10: Developmental influence on learning

As individuals develop, they encounter different opportunities and experience different constraints for learning. Learning is most effective when differential development within and across physical, intellectual, emotional, and social domains is taken into account

Principle 11: Social influences on learning

Learning is influenced by social interactions, interpersonal relations, and communication with others

IV. Individual differences factors

Principle 12: Individual differences in learning

Learners have different strategies, approaches, and capabilities for learning that are a function of prior experience and heredity

Principle 13: Learning and diversity

Learning is most effective when differences in learners' linguistic, cultural, and social backgrounds are taken into account

Principle 14: Standards and assessment

Setting appropriately high and challenging standards and assessing the learner and learning progress—including diagnostic, process, and outcome assessment—are integral parts of the learning process

Table 9.2 Principles of learning and change©

In Living Systems, change and learning are flip sides of the same psychological processes. Each are characterized by a transformation in thinking, each are engaged in at a personal level, and each are based on research-validated principles of human learning, motivation, and development. The following principles represent what we know about personal and organizational change. They are grouped into the three domains in all living systems: personal, technical, and organizational.

PERSONAL DOMAIN:

- Change is a new way of thinking—it starts in the hearts and mind of individuals, and results in seeing learning and learners differently
- Change is seen differently by different people—to be successful, it must be built on areas of agreement
- Focusing on learners and learning creates a common vision and direction for change
- Change begins with hope—believing it is possible
- Change requires permission to make mistakes and engage in conflict resolution and negotiation skills

TECHNICAL DOMAIN:

- Substantive change seeks answers to perplexing issues and must be supported by opportunities for inquiry, dialogue, learning, reflection, and practice
- Honoring the learner's ability to make choices about and control his or her own learning facilitates change
- Change occurs when each person sees him or herself as a learner and sees change as basically a learning process
- Like learning, change is a lifelong and continuous process
- A critical outcome of the change process is the creation of learning communities that enhance, support, and sustain the motivation for ongoing learning and change

ORGANIZATIONAL DOMAIN:

- Change is facilitated when individuals feel personally empowered by feelings of ownership, respect, personal support and trust
- Key stakeholders musts be involved in the change and know precisely what is to be changed
- Like learning, change occurs best when it is invitational and not mandated
- Change requires commitment of resources, including time, knowledge, and leadership skills
- Change is facilitated by leaders who share power, facilitate communication, and are inclusive of all learners

© Copyright 1999 Barbara L. McCombs, Ph.D., Senior Research Scientist, University of Denver, Applied Research and Technology Institute, 2135 E. Wesley Avenue—Room 212, Denver, CO 80208

When learner-centered is defined from a research perspective that includes the knowledge base on both learning and learners, it establishes a foundation for clarifying what is needed to create positive learning contexts and communities at the classroom and school levels so that the likelihood of success is increased for more teachers and students. In addition, a research-validated foundation that focuses on both learners and learning can lead to increased clarity about the dispositions and characteristics of those people in our schools who are in service to learners and learning. Without this dual focus, we run the risk of contributing to and heightening the growing alienation, fear, and stress evidenced in our schools today.

Previous research with learner-centered practices and self-assessment tools based on the *Principles* for teachers and students from K-12 and college classrooms confirms that "learner-centeredness" is not solely a function of particular instructional practices or programs (McCombs and Lauer 1997; McCombs and Whisler 1997. "Learner-centeredness" is a function of learner perceptions which, in turn, are the result of each learner's prior experiences, self-beliefs, and attitudes about schools and learning as well as their current interests, values, and goals. Learner-centered as a concept also relates to the beliefs, dispositions, and practices of teachers. Thus, the quality of learner-centeredness does not reside in programs or practices but on sound research evidence demonstrating the effectiveness of learner-centered practices (see McCombs 2013, in press; McCombs 2012).

3.3 Self-Assessment and Reflection Tools for Teachers

Those using the term "learner-centered" in the context of teachers' professional development (Cornelius-White 2007; Darling-Hammond 1996, 1997, 2006; McCombs 2013, in press; Sparks and Hirsh 1997) refer to learning new beliefs and visions of practice that are responsive to and respectful of the diverse needs of students and teachers as learners. This means that professional development strategies must mirror those that support diverse learner needs and perspectives and must provide time for critical personal reflection. Reflection allows opportunities for teachers to re-create their practices and beliefs about students and instruction. Teachers, like their students, must be actively involved in their own learning and change processes in a collaborative process with other educators, teachers, and experts from higher education and the community. For Sparks and Hirsh and others, this view of "learner-centered" is a research-validated paradigm shift—a transformational view that is needed in professional development. The new paradigm and a deeper understanding of current research challenge misconceptions about learners and learning, identify common elements of successful programs, and create better ways to prepare quality teachers (e.g., Darling-Hammond 2006; Feistritzer 1999; Fullan 2011; Putnam and Borko 2000).

The learner-centered model (LCM) in its applied form consists of a variety of materials and guided reflection and assessment tools that support teacher effectiveness and change at the individual and school levels. LCM materials include staff development workshops and videos exemplifying learner-centered practices in diverse school settings. In addition, to assist teachers in changing their practices, McCombs and her colleagues developed a set of self-assessment and reflection tools for K-20 teachers (the assessment of learner-centered practices, ALCP). This set includes surveys for teachers, students, and administrators, which facilitate reflection and a willingness to change instructional practices. Early validation results (McCombs 2001, 2003; McCombs and Lauer 1997, 1998; McCombs and Whisler 1997) are confirmed and expanded in recent research both here in the United States and internationally (Deakin-Crick 2012) .

3.4 Research Results with the Learner-Centered Model and Self-Assessment Tools

The ALCP surveys have been validated beginning in 1995 and continuing through the present with more than 5,000 K-20 teachers and more than 25,000 students taught by those teachers. Different versions were validated for grades K-3, 4–8, 9–12, and college. For students in grades kindergarten through 3, three domains of classroom practice are most predictive of motivation and achievement: (1) establishing positive relationships and classroom climate; (2) provides motivational support for learning; and (3) facilitating students' learning and thinking skills. For middle (grades 4–8) and high school students (grades 9–12), there are four domains that include the three for K-3 students, but with the addition of (4) honoring student voice and providing individual choice and challenge. For college students, the domains of practice include a somewhat different structure that corresponds to prior structures but are entitled (1) establishes positive interpersonal relationships; (2) adapts to class learning needs (3) facilitates the learning process; (4) provides for individual and social learning needs; and (5) encourages personal challenge and responsibility.

Researchers today are challenged to provide visible and credible evidence to determine whether implementing these types of practices makes a difference in student achievement and motivation. A current challenge is to raise the visibility of research concerning the learner-centered principles by sharing results using the strongest possible statistical tests to examine evidence across a wide age span. At the same time, there is a need to define the types of additional scientifically based evidence which would be considered credible by practitioners and policymakers committed to goals of high levels of achievement for all learners. These are the issues that must be addressed by all researchers involved in studying the effects of learner-centered practices with different age groups of students.

3.5 Current Research on the Learner-Centered Model

Our research with the LCM and its self-development tools based on research-validated principles and practices takes a transformational approach (cf. McCombs 2013, in press; McCombs 2012). Our stance acknowledges that while single and simple solutions are not the answer, neither are overly complex outside-in solutions. Engaging communities in creating their own solutions and empowering them with person- and learner-centered options is the answer we know can work a certain kind of magic. The unacceptable option for us is one that takes 50–100 years and one that waits for intractable issues and changes in national policy to slowly unfold. We agree with Barton and Coley (2010) that the first need is for large-scale thinking and action that helps all of us better understand the problem and its magnitude and its consequences if not addressed now by solutions crafted with the community and the involvement of all constituents including young people whose voice has been ignored. We are committed to addressing these issues with validated practices, careful thought, action, and speed.

Leading the field as a researcher who has long integrated the best learning principles into the design of emerging technology-supported learning system, Dede (2009; Sabelli and Dede 2001) foresaw the Web 2.0 trends that would change the learning and research landscape for years to come. Web 2.0 tools can be customized for research and provide virtual setting for collaboration among stakeholders from many diverse communities and perspectives and levels of expertise. The tools can provide enhanced ways for sharing, thinking, and co-creating as learning partners using their collective wisdom and "an opportunity to experiment with a superset of scholarly norms that provide leverage on wicked problems" (p. 263). If schools do not keep up with this new digital generation of school-aged children, Rosen (2011) suggests that kids will pass teachers by in their learning and understanding of their world through advanced and emerging technologies that immerse them 24/7 in the tech world at all personalized levels that follow students' natural curiosity and love of learning.

3.6 Needed New Directions

From my perspective, we must begin with a new way of thinking about education and schooling. We need learning and change models at all system levels that educate (and remind) our future and current educators and student leaders about research-validated principles of learning, motivation, development, and individual differences that operate naturally in us all. What is unnatural is assuming anyone does not want to learn, is not motivated to learn, and does not want to develop their true potential.

Our research on learner-centered principles and practices has verified the truth of the following assumptions that apply to all learning experiences (McCombs 2013, in press; McCombs 2012):

1. *What happens to learners in school is that they begin to engage in unnatural learning in unnatural contexts and with unnaturally organized and fragmented curriculum and content divisions.* It is no surprise that learners quickly become disengaged and display noncompliance when learning events do not match their needs or views of the types of knowledge and skills they must master to succeed.

2. *What we learn about teaching, learning, and motivation from researchers is not necessarily what common sense would tell us. Truth(s) might match what we intuitively believe or they can run counter to these intuitive and experiential understandings (our tacit knowledge).* When research findings run counter-intuitive to our tacit knowledge, we must discover where the error lies.

The error may lie in our tacit knowledge or in the assumptions and methodology that underlies the research findings.

3. *Learners of all ages, from cradle to grave, naturally learn in self-organizing
   ways that are holistic and unending.* All learners come into life with an insa-
   tiable curiosity and motivation to learn. In fact learning is self-organizing by its
   nature.
4. *Choice and the permission to be a natural learner are essential to lifelong
   learning dispositions.* Without choice and some level of control, any learner is
   tempted to give up personal responsibility and conform to a routine.
5. *The way we think about motivation, learning, and teaching must change if we
   are to change the current state of affairs for students and those that teach them.*
   Assumptions about human capacity, learning, teaching, and motivation must be
   revised and reformed so that a transformational paradigm for education can
   emerge.

Our research and suggestions for practitioners need to be kept simple if we are
to have an impact on the field and on practice (McCombs 2000). By keeping it
simple but sophisticated, the chance of influencing policymakers who live in
different worlds than ours is enhanced. Policymakers need to hear research results
as stories of real educators who succeed with holistic, learner-centered, and
inclusive educational systems.

4 The Vision of the Future

The need for a new vision that can transform learners into leaders and highly
developed people who value lifelong learning is a challenge recognized by many
in our field. The educational testing service (ETS) has taken on this challenge in
addressing achievement gap issues between various cultural and racial groups here
in the United States and abroad.

At the ETS Addressing Achievement Gaps Symposium (2011, June 14), it was
reported that at least 15.5 million United States children live in poverty with more
than 40 % of these children under the age of 5 and poor. More than 40 % of these
children are black and at 9 months old, they are already behind higher income
peers in their cognitive development and this gap is even wider by the time they
are 24 months old. When poor black children attend kindergarten, they must break
the odds to catch up and sadly, many poor black youth never do catch up. All of us
are urged to address this issue now and are focusing attention of challenges and
opportunities facing 3.5 million black boys in their early years, under the age of
nine years old. In a partnership with the Children's Defense Fund, they are
exploring the larger picture of black male achievement and how high-quality
seamless PreK–third-grade education can better support the cognitive and social/

emotional development with realistic policies and strategies that can affect the path of these black male children.

Many of us have invested our research energies in developing comprehensive person- and learner-centered frameworks that are research validated and based on a solid theoretical set of principles and practices. While there are those who might disagree, there is great value to be achieved in focusing attention on those classes of variables that are common to all learners and those that are more intractable in terms of contextual variables and a host of other economic, social, and political issues and ways of thinking that must be challenged.

Most important from our own research and experience is helping deprived communities find ways to honor their cultural roots while also avoiding getting stuck in either their same neighborhood or others where the effects of deprivation and isolation continue to be passed down to subsequent generations. When four out of five black children who started in the top three income groups actually experience downward mobility while three out of five white children who started in the bottom two groups experience upward mobility compared to only one out of four black children—Barton and Coley (2010) rightly joint out that any generational improvement in a huge challenge and require solutions that allow the time necessary to change what are sometimes called neighborhoods of misery. Many system levels must be simultaneously addressed, going beyond the individual, family, neighborhood, and larger ancient heritage of slavery that has limited the intergenerational mobility and new worth of black families as compared to white populations.

Early childhood and family literacy approaches need to be combined with the political will to combine public, private, and nonprofit efforts according to Barton and Coley (2010). These efforts must include improving social and economic capital, school quality, and recreational and health infrastructures. Our current economic times and job losses for the lowest levels of our social structure are urgent challenges that will require all of our collaborative efforts.

4.1 Changes in Learners and Learning that have Emerged

Our own research in the decade from 2000 to 2010 has shown us that the achievement gap issue can be addressed with learner-centered principles and practices (e.g., McCombs 2013, in press; McCombs 2012). What is required, however, it courage and transformational leadership that acknowledges hope in times of economic hardship for too many of our children and families. Significant statistics of relevance to our field include:

- At the national level, 14 million children, about 1 in 5, are hungry and undernourished, with no significant rise in the numbers in recent years.
- At the individual state levels, the number and percentage of hungry and undernourished children varies significantly.

- For school-age children, there are 46 million who come to school hungry and undernourished.
- A growing problem in schools located in high-poverty districts is the number of children who do not qualify for free and reduced lunch or other effective programs.
- Most existing funded programs only effectively deal with school-age children and not their families.

Of those, most urgently needed corrections in policy and regulations are those pertaining to (a) qualification criteria for what defines poverty level in current economic times; (b) criteria for determining whether minimum wage or part-time employed parents can qualify for food stamps, health insurance, and other needed services during these economic times; (c) criteria currently set for who qualifies for free and reduced lunch given growing numbers of hungry children coming to school; (d) ways to fund the development of a client-centered system wherein vital information and records are the central point of services that are given to individual family members and children, thereby short-circuiting cost-inefficient and ineffective shared records at the program or agency level—not at the individual person in need level; and (e) ways to fund (on local, state, and federal levels) the twenty-first century systems that help community leaders create the infrastructure needed for connecting appropriate agencies to cross-agency services being provided to individual clients (children and their families that are impoverished and hungry), thus reducing time needed to get services to needy families and children in local neighborhoods, schools, and communities throughout our nation.

4.2 The Role of New Technologies for Learning

Strom (2010) recently commented that many experts are finding useful information in the technology failures that have occurred across our nation and world. These failures have been highly instructive in terms of understanding what variables need to be present for technology tools to be most effective and useful for education and learning. This is particularly true in third-world nations funded by nonprofits as Strom explains. What has been learned has helped to transform practices to be more culture and gender conscious and to pay more attention to contextual variables that might be overlooked without a systemic and holistic perspective. This perspective must also be one that values and respects the views and voices of the people in each unique community and sees them as capable learners who can control their own destinies with respectful and collaborative help. Expanding the internet for developing countries has now become an international effort that involves private and public investors.

One of the industry leaders in seeing youth as the fundamental resource in implementing technology tools in learner-centered ways, Harper (2012, February 5) recently commented that the issue of finding resources for technology support should come from the population of youth in schools which makes up 93 % of every school and of which probably 95 % have the tech skills to handle technology support issues plus they work for free. His research with the GenYes program includes more than 100 studies over the past 15 years (see http://genyes.org/programs/genyes/research) and has shown that from the teachers' perspectives, students provide better professional development in technology than adults. And because students are doing meaningful things in schools, they are prepared to be leaders in the integration of technology in learner-entered ways into learning and into transforming schools to better serve individual students.

Similarly, Hobar (2012, February 5) supported Harper's post and commented that in leadership roles, those in authority need to be involved in creating and supporting the vision of most students—interacting with new and emerging technologies in collaborative, inquiry-based learning environments. That will allow adults in the system (including teachers, administrators, and family members) support students in transforming current practices into new knowledge, products, and solutions that increase their learning and motivation to be engaged in lifelong personalized learning that matches their unique talents, interests, and skills. Hobar argues that his research on creating twenty-first century learning communities offers a free e-learning program that can support school leaders achieve learner-centered goals with integrated professional development tools, teams, and social media (see http://www.learningfront.com/Media/LF_TechSchLdr.pdf).

Another post from international researcher Pryor (2012, February 4) who has developed an Australian leadership program in New South Wales (see http://hcweb2.org) emphasizes that all leaders should say "yes" to any learning experiences that facilitate and scaffold learning by access to online spaces and lateral connections between teachers and other learners. Innovative learner- and learning-centered kudos are given those who innovate by sharing and paying it forward as servant leaders and facilitators of learning through collaboration. The system has innovative collaborative online workspaces for scaffolding and supporting learning. All of these efforts on a global scale are helping to transform our current educational paradigm and create the qualities needed to support learning throughout life and careers for new generations of learners and teachers and school leaders.

5 Conclusions and Next Steps

Amazing progress is being made in understanding today's learners. A new edited book by Amsel and Smetana (2011) focus on adolescents and explore research emphasizing the importance of theories that integrate interdisciplinary perspectives. Further, this volume is one that recognizes the central importance of holistic, learner-centered approaches that allow learners to engage in self-directed, personally motivated activities that allow them to develop in positive holistic and unique ways. As it is evident that these approaches are working and the public and media are beginning to see the personal power that results when they battle for what they believe schools should be for individual learners, Cieply (2012) describes how schools are beginning to consider parent and student voices. He writes that a new film showing a parent takeover of a failing public school, being prepared for a September 2012 release, "Won't Back Down," is close to reality across the country and notably in California, Connecticut, Ohio, and Texas. All these signs show what is possible when people know what a transformational learner-centered learning system can do for all learners in the system.

5.1 A New Transformational Learner and Learning Paradigm

Technology frontiers will continue to impact learning systems, particularly advances in cloud computing and collaboration among interdisciplinary researchers from around our globe (e.g., Custom Solutions Group 2012). Research clearly indicates that collaboration and content sharing with cloud computing has changed the nature of collaboration, content sharing, document storage and project management to enable more efficient, faster-acting and cost-effective enterprises. The recent white paper available online through the Web Buyers Guide (see Bibliography) describes a new study by IDG Research, which surveyed more than 260 large-enterprise IT managers. Results indicated that the vast majority of knowledge workers (86 %) placed a very high level of importance on collaborating with internal coworkers and external stakeholders, and having access to the most up-to-date corporate information. With cloud-based delivery models, collaboration happens when information can be easily accessed internally and externally, regardless of where users are, what networks they are on, or what devices they are using. With emerging cloud capabilities, what is happening in industry is also happening in schools accessing cloud technology to enable massively scalable document storage, collaboration, and project management solutions for large enterprises.

Wheatley (2011) has argued that information does not change minds because true change requires a change in perception. With so much information now available in a myriad of forms, her work at the Berkana Institute with a rich diversity of people from around the world has shown that strengthening a community's leadership capacity and self-reliance is the key. When personal relationships, voice, shared leadership, and a focus on meaningful conversations provide a foundation for building trust and empower individuals to be courageous leaders in whatever context they are working. In the context of educational systems and learning, Wheatley argues that information's inability to change minds has many implications for researchers who need to preserve the integrity of their work at a time when science and research in general are so discredited in the eyes of many citizens. In the times we are currently facing, students need to be taught how to engage in rational and responsive discourse with opposing points of view.

Local communities need to become self-determining, and local leaders are real-izing that it is up to them to take responsibility for their own futures and the quality of their educational programs. Wheatley further contends that if more people are active at the local level, they are energized to be creatively engaged in under-standing how large systems work so that information again becomes important and powerful.

As Hargreaves and Fink (2003) describe, sustainable leadership is a shared responsibility of activist engagement based on seven principles: (1) creating and preserving sustaining learning that matters; (2) secures success over time through planning for letting go, moving on, and leadership succession; (3) sustaining the leadership of others by distributing leadership throughout the professional com-munity inside and outside the school; (4) addressing issues of social justice so that all students and adult learners benefit and not just certain individuals or groups at the expense of the rest; (5) developing and not depleting human and material resources through intrinsic rewards and extrinsic incentives that attract and retain the highest quality pool of leaders who know how to sustain themselves; (6) developing environmental diversity and capacity capable of sustaining and stim-ulating continuous improvement across the system and its increasingly complex components, practices, and diversity of individual and team learning processes; and (7) undertaking activist engagement with the environment of standardized reform so that the networked learning community is assertive in influencing transformational change in its learning environment broadly defined. In sum, Hargreaves and Fink contend that sustainability cannot happen in the context of standardization but requires a culture of excellence and cross-fertilizing processes of improvement by a commitment to protect deep learning and to sustain them-selves as lifelong learners and contributors to our expanding world.

5.2 Practice Steps Needed

Research steps to be taken are discussed in the other chapter by the author in this volume. Regarding practice steps, Frakes and Linder (2012) believe that some value of their research lies in recognizing that people's preferences in gathering and processing information (such as with a self-assessment survey like the Myers-Briggs tool) may facilitate or interfere with their ability to embrace systems thinking. When individuals can "naturally" see the world through a systems lens, this awareness can help us and all learners pay special attention to the specific practices that may be outside of their normal preferences. As a result of their research, Frakes and Linder identified tools that trainers and others can use to build familiarity and capacity for each of the systems thinking practices as needed. Knowledge of systems thinking preferences may be equally useful. For example, team members could share their MBTI types and discuss how their preferences might affect their inclination to apply a systems thinking approach. Those with a greater natural inclination toward thinking and acting systemically could assist others as appropriate.

Others like Jourdain (2012, February 4) are suggesting practices that promote interrelationships and systems perspectives through mindful and thoughtful conversational spaces such as World Cafes. The challenge is to move beyond conversations to doing something with appropriate leadership that finds the balance that is invitational for broad-based engagement and shared decision making and that leads to wise action on change initiatives that reshape education and learning. The further challenge is fostering and sustaining the social changes that recreate and transform for the better the shape of the world where we work and live. Jourdain describes work in Brazil with an Art of Hosting model of Circle-Triangle-Square, where the Circle represents social technologies that engage and connect people in deeper and more inclusive ways and meet their longings for meaning, unity, wholeness, and the sacred. The Triangle represents the energy of doing and acting and the structures and hierarchies that are created for doing the decision making and work. The Square represents the physical world as compared with its opposite, the sacred, and the structures that allow new forms of strategic thinking, partnerships, governance, and stewardship. Transparency, clarity, and shared decision making are foundational processes and leadership is flexible and patient as change unfolds over time in predictable and unpredictable ways. The focus on quality relationships and making sure all involved is empowered and engaged.

The payoff for implementing learner-centered practices is that our youth will be better prepared to take their place as team players and servant leaders in the workplace. To influence our young people to be part of a culture of hope, they must be educated to believe that humans can band together to solve great challenges and solve them. As further evidence of this possibility for taking charge and bigger risks, Robertson (2012) has argued we need to understand the new science of *Holacracy* that allows *self-governing* at every level of hierarchy, but not *self-direction.* Teams act in service to the organization and its purpose in the world, and they are taught to be part circles of leaders, and learners were enlightened senior leaders give direction to junior leaders. According to in the Holacracy operating system, teams do not become too self-directed when roles are defined in a coaching culture with accountability and authority to make various decisions and take various actions.

5.3 Policy Steps Needed

Policy suggestions are perhaps the most important steps we can take to address what many of us perceive as an urgency to act on what research on person- and LCM has made abundantly clear. Among those advocating for new approaches to learning and leading, Wheatley and Frieze (2011) describe the basic human need for heroes, particularly in the educational arena. Wheatley and Frieze argue that we make assumptions about leaders as heroes and have learned to revere a command and control model of leadership in organizations and government nationally and globally that include:

- Leaders know what to do, they have the answers.
- People need good plans and instructions, and then they will do what they are told.
- As the complexity and challenges of situations increase, so does the need for high control and a shift of power to the top.

As a result, our human race has surrendered individual autonomy for security. Sadly, however, Wheatley and Frieze (2011) point out that these mistaken assumptions and leadership models lead to the creation of more chaos. With complex and interconnected problems in today's world, there are no simple answers and no individual, however smart and well-educated they might be, who could possibly know what needs to be done. When the leader fails within this model, the argument is that we still do not question our desire for heroes.

With this important argument in mind, the policy suggestions are clear in the context of transforming our educational and new learning systems with learner-centered principles and practices. The suggestions include:

1. Supporting those leaders who know that problems are complex, who know that in order to understand the full complexity of any issue, all parts of the system need to be invited into participate and contribute.
2. Giving our leaders time, patience, forgiveness for mistakes, they may have made for their mistaken assumptions about leaders end their roles; and
3. Being willing to step up and contribute to the transformational tasks that all constituents can share leadership in creating learner-centered learning and schooling practices.

These leaders-as-hosts are candid enough to admit that they do not know what to do and that they can trust in other people's creativity and commitment to get the work done. Wheatley and Frieze argue that host leaders know that, given a caring and respectful invitation, other people, at various levels in the organization's hierarchy, can be as motivated, diligent, and creative as the leader, given the right invitation.

Perhaps most encouraging are what Wheatley and Frieze (2011) contend from their research and experience with host leadership—these enlightened individuals are able to see past the negative dynamics of politics and become curious. Leaders-as-hosts know that people willingly support those things they are involved in creating and they practice meaningful conversations among people from relevant system levels and functions in trusting people to contribute and to find meaning and possibility in their lives and work. Of relevance to the arena of learner-centered education and learning systems, these leaders know that hosting others is the only way to solve complex, intractable problems. Like educators who know the research on engagement, motivation, and self-regulated learners, the new host or servant leaders are willing to empower and facilitate personal growth and individual development. Transformational leaders of the present have a vision and the courage to practice collaborative and meaningful conversations that unlock the power of personal relationships in fostering lifelong learning potential in individual learners.

The practical reality of new leadership roles and their impact is described by Petrucci (2012) in his interview with John Petrucci, a 26-year veteran of the insurance industry. Petrucci emphasized that he believes in *servant leadership* where a leader walks the talk and takes the focus from themselves as leader and becomes a follower who use the word "we" versus the word "I" and share versus dictate visions. Servant leaders are person-centered facilitators who understand that it is about the heart and understanding that everyone can be trusted to do what need to do to be successful if they are built up with interpersonal, communication, and negotiation skills emulated by a servant leader who is available for face-to-face conversations to get to know people for who they are as an individual. They know how to win their hearts and effectively secure and distribute organizational resources; they know how to implement effective training programs and follow-up with individuals to make sure transformational changes are helping all flourish and grow. Servant leaders implement a leadership philosophy that is consistent and accountable.

6 Call to Action

One major conclusion is that educational psychologists and researchers in our field have a responsibility to educate other professionals surrounding the enterprise of education and schooling. Other professionals include researchers and educators as well as the policymakers, parents, and the public in our country and abroad. There is a unique opportunity to join forces with media partners, diverse groups of research collaborators from the ground up and top–down. In addition, there is an opportunity to use our person and learner-centered principles and practices to help others understand new conceptions of learning, motivation, and development. To do so requires not just doing the research but engaging in practices that help others in the learning communities and environments, we serve to understand that learning and change are flip sides of the same social-psychological process—the process of changing one's mind.

A final timely call to action was recently announced by Gertner (2012) relative to what it will take for true innovation in these times of economic turmoil and threatening recessions here in the United States and around the world. Gertner spent 5 years at Bell Labs, one of our country's longstanding innovative research and development laboratories with AT&T, formerly a telephone company monopoly. Bell Labs earned a reputation for having an innovative edge, an edge more comprehensive and ambitious than what is seen today in addressing seemingly intractable problems. What was most noteworthy was the mission and accomplishment of a national communication network that connected all people and all new technologies together. Bell Labs for most of the twenty-first century was the most innovative and practical scientific organization worldwide. For our social science community, Bell Labs contributed new thinking about quality control and statistical methodologies for tackling innovative research on complex human behavior. A culture of creativity was created according to Gertner between 1925 and 1959 by Mervin Kelly who rose from researcher to Chairman of the Board. By traveling around Europe, he was able to attract talented people who fostered a busy exchange of ideas in what they thought of as an "institute of creative technology." This example lingered—a balance between harmony and tension between different groups of hard and soft science researchers and disciplines.

The story of Bell Labs is another visionary example to researchers and practitioners whose aim is to transform new knowledge into new things. Visionary leadership is one that trusts people to be creative and self-motivated to seek understanding when given the freedom to work in teams or individually. What is inspiring to those of us who have been around and knew researchers in the social sciences who were employed by Bell Labs is that their culture of innovation helped us know that person- and learner-centered cultures and contexts support the best in learners, leaders, and producers. Cultures of greed and profit are a thing of the past just as one-size-fits-all models of schooling are no longer serving our children.

We join with others advocating an intensive care unit (ICU) approach to ending apathy—for students and all our learners including ourselves. As advertized in a recent conference on "Ending Study Apathy" (see the discussion on http://www.linkedin.com/groupAnswers?viewQuestionAndAnswers=&discussionID=93505340&gid=2811&trk=eml-anet_dig-b_nd-pst_ttle-cn&ut=1TjB5yF3-g4l81), Hill and Nave (2012, February 7) have been presenting the benefits of ICU to more than 15,000 K-12 educators over the past 3 years. Feedback on the resulting benefits of these learner-centered practices and principles are increased graduation rates and decreased failure rates cf. McCombs, 2008; McCombs & Vakili (2005). It is about time we took our message to the streets, right?

Processes and contexts that support learning are also those that support change. Based on the contributions of others participating in this book and in the field generally, this is also a challenge to help change the future preparation of researchers and educators. Our call to action is to lead and to learn along with our constituents what it takes to transform systems while trusting ourselves and all learners to naturally engage in self-regulated and lifelong learning when supported from the inside out.

References

Ackerman, G. L. (2010). Bridging 21st century gaps: An essay review of Mehlenbacher's *Technology and Instruction. Education Review, 14*(3). Retrieved 3/⁴/11) from http://www.edrev.info/essays/v14n3.pdf.

Adams, J., Khan, H. T. A., Raeside, R., & White, D. (2009). *Research methods for graduate business and social science students.* New Delhi, India and Thousand Oaks, CA: Response Books and Sage Publications (4th printing).

Amsel, E., & Smetana, J. G. (Eds.). (2011). *Adolescent vulnerabilities and opportunities.* New York: Cambridge University Press.

APA Work Group of the Board of Educational Affairs. (1997, November). *Learner-centered psychological principles: A framework for school reform and redesign.* Washington, DC: American Psychological Association.

APA Task Force on Psychology in Education. (1993, January). *Learner-centered psychological principles: Guidelines for school redesign and reform.* Washington, DC: American Psychological Association and Mid-Continent Regional Educational Laboratory.

Barton, P. E., & Coley, R. J. (2010). *The black-white achievement gap: When progress stopped.* Princeton, NJ: Educational Testing Service, Policy Information Center. Downloaded on April 2, 2012 from http://www.ets.org/Media/Research/pdf/PICBWGAP.pdf.

Brady, M. (2011, December 5). When an adult took standardized tests forced on kids. *Washington Post*, "The Answer Sheet" blog by Valerie Strauss—Posted at 04:00 AM ET, 12/05/2011. (Downloaded on December 15, 2011 from http://www.marionbrady.com/articles/2011-Washington%20Post12-5.pdf).

Bransford, J. (2001). *Toward the development of a stronger community of educators: New opportunities made possible by integrating the learning sciences and technology.* Paper prepared for the PT3 Vision Quest on Assessment in e-Learning Cultures. Available at www.pt3.org.

Caine, R. N., & Caine, G. (2011). *Natural learning for a connected world: Education, technology, and the human brain.* New York: Teachers College Press.

Ceci, S. J., & Papierno, P. B. (2005). The rhetoric and reality of gap closing: When the "have-nots" gain but the "haves" gain even more. *American Psychologist, 60*(2), 149–160.

Cieply, M. (2012, February 20). *A battle for schools. The New York Times, Reality and Film.* (Downloaded on February 20, 2012 from http://www.nytimes.com/2012/02/21/movies/viola-davis-and-maggie-gyllenhaal-in-parent-trigger-.

Cornelius-White, J. (2007). Learner-centered teacher-student relationships are effective: A meta-analysis. *Review of Educational Research, 77*(1), 113–143.

Cornelius-White, J.H.D., & Harbaugh, A.P. (2010). *Learner-centered instruction: Building relationships for student success.* Los Angeles, CA: Sage.

Custom Solution Center (2012, February 1). *The cloud: Reinventing enterprise collaboration.* WHITE PAPER: CSO-CIO (downloaded February 7, 2012 from http://www.webbuyersguide.com/Resource/ResourceDetails.aspx?id=20895&category=1178&sitename=webbuyersguide&kc=WBGWPUNL020712&src=WBGWPUNL020712&email=bmccombs%40du.edu).

Darling-Hammond, L. (1996). The quiet revolution: Rethinking teacher development. *Educational Leadership, 53*(6), 4–10.

Darling-Hammond, L. (1997). *The right to learn: A blueprint for creating schools that work.* San Francisco: Jossey-Bass.

Darling-Hammonds, L. (2006). Constructing 21st-century teacher education. *Journal of Teacher Education, 57*(10), 1–15.

Deakin-Crick, R. (2009) Pedagogical challenges for personalisation: integrating the personal with the public through context-driven enquiry. *Curriculum Journal,* 20, 185–189.

Deakin-Crick, R. (2012). Identity, learning power and authentic enquiry (pp. 675–694). In S. Christenson, A. Reschly, & C. Wylie (Eds.), *The handbook of research on student engagement.* New York: Springer Science.

Deakin-Crick, R., McCombs, B., Haddon, A., Broadfoot, P., & Tew, M. (2007). The ecology of learning: Factors contributing to learner-centred classroom cultures. *Research Papers in Education, 22*(3), 267–307.

Deci, E. L., & Ryan, R. M. (1991). A motivational approach to self: Integration in personality. In R. Dienstbier (Ed.), *Nebraska symposium on motivation. Vol. 38. Perspectives on motivation*. Lincoln, NE: University of Nebraska Press.

Dede, C. (2009). Technologies that facilitate generating knowledge and possibly wisdom. *Educational Researcher, 38*(4), 260–263.

Dede, C. (2011, November 5). *Learning through technology*. Thinkfinity Education Speaker Series—a video series for online community of educators. (Downloaded on December 5, 2011 from http://www.readwritethink.org/about/news/learning-through-technology-chris-47.html).

Duffy, T. M., & Kirkley, J. R. (2004). *Learner-centered theory and practice in distance education*. Mahweh, NJ: Lawrence Erlbaum.

Educational Testing Service (ETS). (2011, June 14). *View a statistical profile* (PDF) from ETS's Addressing Achievement Gaps Symposium, Washington, DC, June 14, 2011. (Downloaded on February 15, 2012 from http://www.ets.org/s/achievement_gap/conferences/strong_start/overview.html.

Elias, M. J., Zims, J. E., Weissberg, R. P., Frey, K. DS., Greenberg, M. T., Haynes, N. M.,& Shriver, T. P. (1997). *Promoting social and emotional learning: Guidelines for educators*. Alexandria, VA: Association for Supervision and Curriculum Development.

Engel, A. (2011). *Uniting 4 Kids: Opting out of high-stakes testing – a guide to exercising your parental rights*. Downloaded May 6, 2012 from http://www.angelaengel.com/files/csap/final_parent_guide_u4k.pdf..

Feistritzer, C. E. (1999, November). *The making of a teacher: A report on teacher preparation in the U.S. Website* http://www.ncei.com/MakingTeacher-blts.htm.

Feeding America (2011, September 15). *Virtual town meeting—fighting childhood hunger*. Speakers from the American Federation of Teachers (AFT) and US Department of Agriculture (USDA). Participation from 3–4 pm EST online at www.feedingamerica.org.

Fox, T, (2012, February 8). The science of leading scientists: An interview with national science foundations' Subra Sresh. *The Washington post: On leadership*. (Downloaded on February 10, 2012 from http://www.washingtonpost.com/national/on-leadership/the-science-of-leading-scientists-an-interview-with-the-national-science-foundations-subra-suresh/2012/02/08/gIQAw6iWzQ_story.html).

Frakes, J., & Linder, N. (2012). Posted by Janice Molloy on Wed, Feb 08, 2012 *Systems thinking: A matter of preference?* (Downloaded on February 8, 2012 from Leverage Points Blog http://www.blog.pegasuscom.com/Leverage-Points-Blog/bid/81590/systems-thinking-a-matter-of-preference?source=Blog_Email_[Systems%20Thinking%3A%20A%20).

Fullan. (2010). The big ides beyond whole system reform. *Education Canada*. http://www.michaelfullan.ca/Articles_10/BigIdeas-CEA.pdf.

Hannum, W. H., & McCombs, B. L. (2008). Enhancing distance learning for today's youth with learner-centered principles. *Educational Technology, 48*(3), 11–21.

Gertner, J. (2012, February 25). *True innovation. The New York times—opinion*. (Downloaded on February 26, 2012 from http://www.nytimes.com/2012/02/26/opinion/sunday/innovation-and-the-bell-labs-miracle.html?_r=1&nl=todaysheadlines&emc=thab1).

Goleman, D., Boyatzis, R., & McKee, A. (2002). *Primal leadership: Realizing the power of emotional intelligence*. Boston: Harvard University Press.

Greene, J. A., & Azevedo, R. (2010). The measurement of learners' self-regulated cognitive and metacognitive processes while using computer-based learning environments. *Educational Psychologist, 45*(4), 203–209.

Harper, D. (2012, February 4). *Response to International Society for Technology in Education (ISTE) discussion on "What kind of support should school leaders and administrators give teachers who want to promote digital-age learning environments and the development of 21st century skills in students?"* (Downloaded on February 15, 2012 from http://www.linkedin.com/groupItem?view=&srchtype=discussedNews&gid=2811&item=90198670&type=member&trk=eml-anet_dig-b_pd-ttl-cn&ut=2x7vxntW-bUR41).

Harris, S. (2012, February 20). *Better and better: An interview with Peter Diamandis and Steven Kotler.* (Downloaded on February 20, 2012 from http://www.samharris.org/blog/item/better-than-you-think).

Hill, D., & Nave, J. (2012, February 7). *The power of ICU—The end of student apathy … reviving engagement and responsibility.* Conference (Downloaded on February 15, 2012 from http://www.linkedin.com/company/2311388/614384/product?goback=%2Egde_2811_member_93505340).

Duffy, F. M. (2011a, October). Seizing opportunities at the intersection of anticipatory intentions (planning) and unanticipated events (reality). *The F. M. Duffy Reports, 16*(4), 1–9.

Duffy, F.M. (2011b). *The revolutionaries: A directory of informed critics, creative innovators, and system "architects" and "builders" who are advocates for the transformation of education systems and their component school systems.* Available at www.thefmduffygroup.com.

Fullan, M. (2010b). *The moral imperative realized.* Thousand Oaks, CA: Corwin Press.

Fullan, M. (2010c). *All systems go: The change imperative for whole system reform.* Thousand Oaks, CA: Corwin Press.

Fullan, M. (2011). *Change leader: Learning to do what matters most.* San Francisco, CA: Corwin Press.

Gilboa, I., & Schmeidler, D. (2011, July 3). *Authorization decisions.* (Downloaded on February 16, 2012 from http://itzhakgilboa.weebly.com/uploads/8/3/6/3/8363317/gs_authorization_presentation.pdf).

Graziano, A. M., & Raulin, M. L. (2010). *Research methods: A process of inquiry* (7th ed.). Boston, MA: Allyn & Bacon.

Hargreaves, A. (2011). A *Festschrift* for Andy Hargreaves: 11 papers by leading and emerging scholars celebrating and concentrating on the life work of Andy Hargreaves. *Journal of Educational Change, 12*(2), 131–139.

Hargreaves, A., & Fink, D. (2003). The seven principles of sustainable leadership. *Educational Leadership, 61*(7), 8–13.

Hobar, N. (2012, February 5). Response to International Society for Technology in Education (ISTE) discussion on "What kind of support should school leaders and administrators give teachers who want to promote digital-age learning environments and the development of 21st century skills in students?" (Downloaded on February 15, 2012 from http://www.linkedin.com/groupItem?view=&srchtype=discussedNews&gid=2811&item=90198670&type=member&trk=eml-anet_dig-b_pd-ttl-cn&ut=2x7vxntW-bUR41).

Horwitz, J., & McEwan, P. J. (2011, November 29). *Brookings small reforms report a useful contribution, Says independent review: Report highlights successful education reform efforts largely missed by media and policymakers.* Boulder, CO: National Education Policy Center (NEPC). Available at http://tinyurl.com/6wv43v5.

Jourdain, K. (2012, February 4). *Interrelationship of circle-triangle-square.* Shapeshift blog (Downloaded on February 4, 2012 from https://weboutlook.du.edu/owa/?ae=Item&t=PM.Note&id=RgAAAAB9stQpG7F5RanWqNyebdXLBwBF4uT4gqmJS6ss2kS5YOvyAAAoNCwAACL%2fnH6uwSTT5pxIsg6qaG0AArJR7tKAAAJ&a=Print&cb=0.

Jukes, I., McCain, T., & Crockett, L. (2011). Education and the role of the future educator in the future. *Kappan, 92*(4), 15–21.

Kristjansson, K. (2010). Positive psychology, happiness, and virtue: The troublesome conceptual issues. *Review of General Psychology, 14*(4), 296–310.

Lambert, N., & McCombs, B. L. (Eds.). (1998). *How students learn: Reforming schools through learner-centered education.* Washington, DC: APA Books.

Larson, R. W. (2000). Toward a psychology of positive youth development. *American Psychologist, 55*(1), 170–183.

Lazarus, R. S. (2000). Toward better research on stress and coping. *American Psychologist, 55*(6), 665–673.

Lazarus, R. S. (2003). Does the positive psychology movement have legs? *Psychological Inquiry, 14*, 93–109.

Lee, C. D. (2011). Soaring above the clouds, delving the ocean's depths: Understanding the ecologies of human learning and the challenge for education science. *Educational Researcher, 39*(9), 643–655.

Lee, J., & Shute, V. J. (2010). Personal and social-contextual factors in K-12 academic performance: An integrative perspective on student learning. *Educational Psychologist, 45*(3), 185–202.

Levine, M. (2007). The essential cognitive backpack. *Educational Leadership, 64*(7), 16–22.

McCombs, B. L. (1999). What role does perceptual psychology play in educational reform today? In H. J. Freiberg (Ed.), *Perceiving, behaving, becoming: Lessons learned.* Alexandria, VA: Association for Supervision and Curriculum Development.

McCombs, B. L. (2000). Reducing the achievement gap. *Society, 37*(5), 29–36.

McCombs, B. L. (2001). Self–regulated learning and academic achievement: A phenomenological view. In B. J. Zimmerman & D. H. Schunk (Eds.), *Self-Regulated learning and academic achievement: Theory, Research, and Practice* (2nd ed.) (pp. 67–123). Mahwah, NJ: Lawrence Erlbaum Associates, Publishers.

McCombs, B. L. (2003). Providing a framework for the redesign of K-12 education in the context of current educational reform issues. *Theory Into Practice, 42(2)*, 93–101. *(Special Issue on Learner-Centered Principles—B. L. McCombs, Guest Editor).*

McCombs, B. L. (2004). The learner-centered psychological principles: A framework for balancing a focus on academic achievement with a focus on social and emotional learning needs (pp. 23–39). In J. E. Zins, R. P. Weissberg, M. C. Wang, & H. J. Walberg (Eds.), *Building academic success on social and emotional learning: What does the research say?.* New York: Teachers College Press.

McCombs, B. L. (2007). Balancing accountability demands with research-validated, learner-centered teaching and learning practices (pp. 41–60). In C. E. Sleeter (Ed.), *Educating for democracy and equity in an era of accountability.* New York: Teachers College Press.

McCombs, B. L. (2008, April). From one-size-fits-all to personalized learner-centered learning: The evidence. *The F. M. Duffy Reports, 13*(2), 1–12.

McCombs, B. L. (2009). Commentary: What can we learn from a synthesis of research on teaching, learning, and motivation? (pp. 655–670). In K. R. Wentzel & A. Wigfield (Eds.), *Handbook of motivation at school.* New York: Routledge.

McCombs, B. L. (2010). *Developing responsible and autonomous learners: A key to motivating learners.* An online web-based module for the APA Task Force on the Application of Psychological Science to Teaching and Learning (APS-TL). Washington, DC: American Psychological Association. Available at http://www.apa.org/education/k12/learners.aspx.

McCombs, B. L. (2011). Learner-centered practices: providing the context for positive learner development, motivation, and achievement (chapter 7). In J. Meece & J. Eccles (Eds.), *Handbook of research on schools, schooling, and human development.* Mahwah, NJ: Erlbaum.

McCombs, B. L. (2012). Educational psychology and educational transformation. (Chapter 20, pp. 952-1025). In W. M. Reynolds & G. E. Miller (Eds.), *Comprehensive Handbook of Psychology, Vol. 7. Educational Psychology (2nd ed.).* New York: John Wiley & Sons.

McCombs, B. L. (2013, in press). Chapter 12: Using a 360 degree assessment model to support learning to learn. In Deakin-Crick R. Stringher C. & Small T. (Eds.), *Learning to learn for all: theory, practice and international research: A multidisciplinary and lifelong perspective.* London: Routledge.

McCombs, B. L., & Lauer, P. A. (1997). Development and validation of the learner-centered battery: Self-Assessment tools for teacher reflection and professional development. *The Professional Educator, 20*(1), 1–21.

McCombs, B. L., & Lauer, P. A. (1998, July). *The learner-centered model of seamless professional development: Implications for practice and policy changes in higher education.* Paper presented at the 23rd International Conference on Improving University Teaching, Dublin.

McCombs, B. L., & Miller, L. (2007). *Learner-centered classroom practices and assessments: Maximizing student motivation, learning, and achievement.* Thousand Oaks, CA: Corwin Press.

McCombs, B. L., & Miller, L. (2008). *The school leader's guide to learner-centered education: From complexity to simplicity.* Thousand Oaks, CA: Corwin Press.

McCombs, B., & Vakili, D. (2005). A learner-centered framework for e-learning. *Teachers College Record, 107*(8), 1582–1609.

McCombs, B. L., & Whisler, J. S. (1997). *The learner-centered classroom and school: Strategies for increasing student motivation and achievement.* San Francisco, CA: Jossey-Bass.

Molloy, J. (2010, September 07). Performing beyond expectations: An interview with Andy Hargreaves. *Leverage Points Blog* downloaded on February 20, 2012 from.

Patall, E., Cooper, H., & Wynn, S. P. (2010). The effectiveness and relative importance of choice in the classroom. *Journal of Educational Psychology, 102*(4), 896–915.

Penuel, W. R., & Riel, M. (2007). The 'new' science of networks and the challenge of school change. *Phi Delta Kappan, 88*(8), 611–615.

Petrucci, J. (2012, February 8). *A personal interview with a great leader—*Mike Figliuolo. (Downloaded on February 8, 2012 from http://www.thoughtleadersllc.com/2012/02/a-personal-interview-with-a-great-leader/.

Phelps, R. P. (2011). Teach to the test? *Wilson Quarterly.* (Downloaded on February 16, 2012 from http://www.wilsonquarterly.com/article.cfm?aid=2014).

Phelps, R. P. (2012). The effect of testing on student achievement: 1910-2010. *Nonpartisan education review, 8*(4), 1-34.

Pink, D. H. (2009). *Drive: The surprising truth about what motivates us.* New York: Riverhead Books.

Pink, D. (2011, August 2). *The future of education … 100 years ago.* (Downloaded on August 3, 2011 from http://www.danpink.com/archives/2011/08/the-future-of-education-100-years-ago).

Pryor, R. (2012, February 4). *Response to International Society for Technology in Education (ISTE) discussion on "What kind of support should school leaders and administrators give teachers who want to promote digital-age learning environments and the development of 21st century skills in students?"* (Downloaded on February 15, 2012 from http://www.linkedin.com/groupItem?view=&srchtype=discussedNews&gid=2811&item=90198670&type=member&trk=eml-anet_dig-b_pd-ttl-cn&ut=2x7vxntW-bUR41).

Putnam, R. T., & Borko, H. (2000). What do new views of knowledge and thinking have to say about research on teacher learning? *Educational Researcher, 29*(1), 4–15.

Radel, R., Sarrazin, P., Legrain, P., & Wild, T. C. (2010). Social contagion of motivation between teacher and student: Analyzing underlying processes. *Journal of Educational Psychology, 102*(3), 577–587.

Richardson, W. (2013). Students first, not stuff. *Educational Leadership, 70*(6), 10–14.

Robertson, B. (2012, February 21). *Processing our "shoulds."* Holacracy online post. (Downloaded on February 26, 2012 from http://holacracy.org/blog/processing-our-should-s).

Rogers, C. R. (1942). *Counseling and psychotherapy: Newer concepts in practice.* Boston: Houghton Mifflin.

Rogers, C. R. (1959). A theory of therapy, personality, and interpersonal relationships, as developed in the client-centered framework. In S. Koch (Ed.), *Psychology: A study of a science* (Vol. 3, pp. 184–256)., Formulations of the person and the social context New York: McGraw-Hill.

Rogers, C. R. (1964). Toward a modern approach to values: The valuing process in the mature person. *Journal of Abnormal and Social Psychology, 68*, 160–167.

Rogers, C. R. (1977). *Carl Rogers on personal power.* London: Constable.

Rogers, C. R. (1980). *A way of being.* Boston: Houghton Mifflin.

Rogers, C. R. (1995). *On becoming a person*. Boston: Houghton Mifflin. (Original work published 1951).

Rogers, C. R., Rogers, N., and Cornelius-White, J. H. D. (2012, in press). *Carl Rogers' my trip to China*. LaJolla, CA: Person-Centered Press.

Rosen, L. (2011). Teaching the iGeneration. *Educational Leadership, 68*(5), 10–15.

Ryan, R. M., & Deci, E. L. (2000). Self-determination theory and the facilitation of intrinsic motivation, social development, and well-being. *American Psychologist, 55*(1), 68–78.

Sabelli, N., and C. Dede (2001). *Integrating Educational Research and Practice: Reconceptualizing the Goals and Process of Research to Improve Educational Practice*. (in press). http://www.virtual.gmu.edu/integrating.html and http://h2oproject.law.harvard.edu/educational_funding.pdf.

Scharmer. O. (2011, November). *Leading from the emerging future: Minds for change—future of global development*. Paper prepared for Ceremony to mark the 50th anniversary of the BMZ Federal Ministry for Economic Cooperation and Development, Berlin, Germany.

Seligman, M. E. P., & Csikszentmihalyi, M. (2000). Positive psychology: An introduction. *American Psychologist, 55*(1), 5–14.

Senge, P. (2011, January 11). *Collaborative culture: Insights from Peter Senge on the foundations of organizational learning*. (Downloaded on January 22, 2011 from http://sourcepov.com/2011/01/11/collaborative-culture/).

Sisk, C. W. (2011, November). *Lead: The mobile life coaching and leadership course*. Website and virtual class available at www.chetsisk.com. (Downloaded on November 29, 2011 from http://www.chetsisk.com/index.php?option=com_content&view=article&id=61&Itemid=36).

Sparks, D., & Hirsh, S. (1997). *A new vision for staff development*. Alexandria, VA: Association for Supervision and Curriculum Development.

Stewart, V. (2007). Citizens of the world. *Educational Leadership, 64*(7), 9–14.

Strom, S. (2010, August 6). Nonprofits review technology failures. *New York Times*. (Downloaded on February 10, 2012 from http://www.nytimes.com/2010/08/17/technology/17fail.html?pagewanted=print.

Suarez-Orozco, M. M., & Sattin, C. (2007). Wanted: Global citizens. *Educational Leadership, 64*(7), 58–62.

Tulgan, B. (2009). *It's okay to manage your boss*. San Francisco, CA: Jossey Bass.

Tulgan, B. (2010). *Not everyone gets a trophy—how to manage generation Y*. San Francisco, CA: Jossey Bass.

Walls, T. A., & Little, T. D. (2005). Relations among personal agency, motivation, and school adjustment in early adolescence. *Journal of Educational Psychology, 97*(1), 23–31.

Wheatley, M. (2009). Are we all in this together? (Downloaded on January 19, 2012 from http://www.margaretwheatley.com/articles/All-In-This-Together.pdf).

Wheatley, M. (2010). *Reweaving the web of connections*. originally appeared as a blog on Yes Magazine's site, www.yes.org. (Downloaded on February 11, 2012 from http://www.margaretwheatley.com/articles/Reweaving-the-Web.pdf).

Wheatley. M. (2011, June). *The big learning event*. Park City, UT: Berkana Institute. (Downloaded February 2, 2012 from http://www.margaretwheatley.com/articles/Wheatley-The-Big-Learning-Event.pdf).

Wheatley, M. (2012). *So far from home: Lost and found in our brave new world*. San Francisco, CA: Berrett-Koehler Publishers.

Wheatley, M., & Frieze, D. (2011). *Walk out walk on: A learning journey into communities daring to live the future now*. San Francisco, CA: Berrett-Koehler.

Williams, C. (2011, December). New department of education initiative: Online communities for education professionals. Downloaded on February 18, 2012 from http://www.linkedin.com/groupItem?view=&srchtype=discussedNews&gid=2811&item=80066691&type=member&trk=eml-anet_dig-b_pd-ttl-cn&ut=2ZKSzPqf3e9B81).

Zimmerman, B. J., & Schunk, D. H. (2001) (Eds.). *Self-regulated learning and academic achievement: Theoretical perspectives* (2nd Ed.). Mahwah, NJ: Lawrence Erlbaum Associates.

The Person-Centered Approach in Adult Education

Dorothea Kunze

1 Introduction

In the professional world, C. R. Rogers is known better for his development of psychological counseling and psychotherapy than for his contributions to educational theory and practice. In his autobiographical writings, however, it is evident how much he was preoccupied with issues of educational and learning processes (Cornelius-White 2012; Rogers 1969). From the early 1940s onwards, Rogers began taking what he had learned from the counseling relationship into the interactions with the members of a workshop, into person-centered further education settings, team development, and leadership coaching (1951).

Way ahead of his time, Rogers contributed to a radical paradigm shift to learning and development informed by the concept of person-centered pedagogy. He considers this new approach toward learning as relevant for sustainable learning in comparison with that of expert guidance. Learning achieved through person-centered educational experience is comprehensive, in that it stimulates a growth/development of the entire personality. Rogers calls this learning "significant learning," which means more than collecting facts: "It is learning, which makes a difference—in the individual's behavior, in the course of action he chooses in the future, in his attitudes and in his personality. It is a pervasive learning which is not just an accretion of knowledge, but which interpenetrates with every portion of his existence" (Rogers 1961, p. 280). Person-centered learning is not the same as training or coaching: "Training implies making a person proficient in some trade or art or work which he can then use occupationally. But one cannot 'train' an individual to be a *person*" (Rogers 1970, p. 163).

D. Kunze (✉)
Tulpenstraße 6, 71 093 Weil im Schönbuch, Germany
e-mail: Dorothea.Kunze@institute-facilitate.de
URL: www.pro-firma.de; www.institut-facilitate.de

J. H. D. Cornelius-White et al. (eds.), *Interdisciplinary Applications of the Person-Centered Approach*, DOI: 10.1007/978-1-4614-7144-8_10, © Springer Science+Business Media New York 2013

2 Rogers' Theory of Facilitation of Learning as a Basis for Adult Education

Rogers developed a specific form of facilitating the learning process: The instructor understands himself/herself as a *facilitator*, who encourages a group to take action on their own way of learning, to develop their own solutions, and to decide on their own how to proceed concerning the method or the content. The focus is on the learner/learning group, on their experience and potential and not on their skills and learning deficits in relation to a seminar topic.

With the concept of lifelong learning in adult education, the seemingly distinct differences between learning in childhood and adulthood have become relative. Siebert (2011) argues that "the life phase of adulthood includes the developments that have taken place in childhood and adolescence. In particular, in childhood, a sensitization for learning takes place that is influential for lifelong learning" (p. 12, translation by Renate Motschnig). As a person grows older, however, a wealth of personal and professional experiences will be integrated into the self-concept. Therefore, the learning styles, preferences, and interests of adults are individualized (Arnold et al. 1999; Siebert 2011). Together with their personal history and education, people are generally open to new/further learning opportunities, which will be taken up or discarded.

Person-centered theory is systematic and complex, comprising a personality theory, a theory of interpersonal relationships, and a group theory. This is also the basis of person-centered learning theory (Rogers 1959). These interdependencies are depicted in Fig. 10.1.

Person-centered personality theory describes learning as an autonomous self-monitoring process of exploring our experience. It is assumed that learning cannot be implemented from the outside, but that a person can only learn things, "which he perceives as being involved in the maintenance of, or enhancement of, the structure of self" (Rogers 1951, p. 389). According to Rogers (1969), trying to convey experiences directly turns them into lecturing, thus making the results irrelevant. Sustainable, significant learning is most likely to take place when seminar participants can express their personal concerns, motives, and problems with the seminar topic openly. A genuinely person-centered learning process is self-initiated, self-exploratory, and self-trusting; it is experienced as meaningful to the person. The sense of exploring, of grappling, of grasping, and of understanding comes from within—even if learning opportunities and ideas come from without. Thus, a seminar participant can integrate new experiences into his/her self-concept, thus making the learning sustainable.

This approach requires an attitude of trust in the seminar group and in the individual group member on the part of the adult educator. If the seminar participants experience that they are accepted as persons, and understood in their needs, they can be open to their real problems, professionally, personally, and emotionally. They can turn their attention to the seminar theme and *choose their* way of learning freely. Therefore, it is of overriding importance to provide a

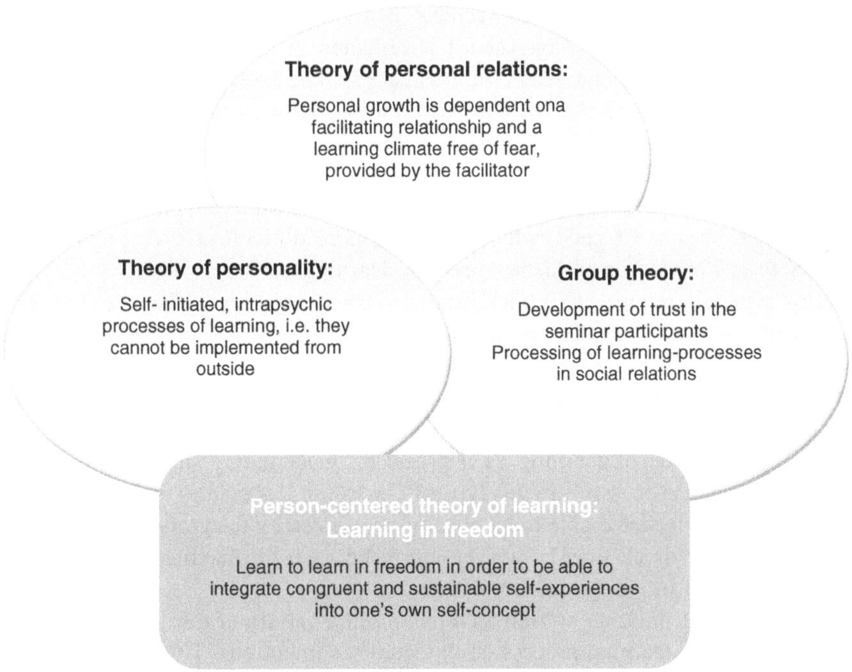

Fig. 10.1 Interdependencies between various contexts/applications of the theory of the person-centered approach

learning climate in which self-determined and creative learning is possible, especially in the initial phase of a seminar. These elements of the facilitation of learning and the theory of relationship and their impact for specific situations of learning are discussed in the following section (see also Kunze 2003; 2008).

3 Conditions for the Facilitation of Person-Centered Learning and Their Practical Implications

Rogers (1961, 1969) described the conditions for the promotion of sustainable learning as attitudinal qualities—not as a method or technique. They are also understood as an offer of a (therapeutic) relationship in adult education.

3.1 Congruence as a Condition for Facilitating Learning

A congruent facilitator is experienced by the group as a genuine, natural, spontaneous, and real person in addition to an expert in the topic at hand. He/she abstains from introducing hidden agendas, goals, tricks, and the establishment of rules for the study group. Congruence is reflected in the ability to be aware of one's own inner experience and communicate it. The facilitator is real, when he shows him/herself as she/he is, without pretense, without defense. A congruent facilitator can admit mistakes or lack of knowledge, concede his/her bias or vulnerability, and just be "human". This experience of a facilitator's genuine credibility promotes confidence in the study group, in contrast to a facilitator behaving behind a professional façade, which makes it more difficult or even prevents the learner from opening up to his/her personal learning needs.

This approach requires an adult educator to be aware of the differences between his/her own planned goals for the seminar and the actual personal objectives of the participants. This further requires the facilitator to include alternatives to methodological proposals in the planning and to be flexible in the handling of his/her designed program. Rogers (1951) describes the extent of the intended flexibility and the importance of learning as a process: "Outstanding in the experiences which have been successful (in this type of classroom leadership) is the concept of flexibility. If the leader is able to let himself be utilized by the group in a variety of ways as their needs change, he will be more successful in facilitating of learning with a minimum of resistance" (p. 401).

The facilitator presents himself as *a person* in a variety of forms, which aim at concentrating the learning process on the learner's intentions. This means that the facilitator will not insist on his/her own seminar design, but that he/she will perceive the learning objectives of the seminar participants and will facilitate their learning activities regarding the process and the topic together constantly with them instead of organizing for them (Rogers 1951). This flexibility also requires the facilitator to be comfortable with open-ended learning processes, since specific outcomes cannot be predicted according to a person-centered view (Rogers 1959).

3.2 Unconditional Positive Regard as a Condition for Facilitating Learning

Unconditional positive regard is evident in the non-judgmental acceptance by the facilitator of the otherness of the learner—including his/her different attitudes, feelings, and ideas. If the learner experiences unconditional positive regard, he/she will increasingly follow his/her learning objectives, needs, and ways of learning in a self-accepting way and judge her/his learning process in a self-responsible way.

As far as his pedagogic ideas are concerned, Rogers refers to the philosophy of John Dewey, an educational reformer (Rogers 1957). For example, in a seminar on supervising assessment interviews, different learning styles among the participants become obvious. The need for exchange is different: One participant declares that he may learn better by a demonstration on the part of the facilitator; another tells him he will learn better by doing it himself. The facilitator is not in favor of any particular learning style—even one possibly preferred by him—but responds to the different needs with unconditional positive regard, respecting different ways of learning equally. He can make various proposals for a modified approach, which exclude an "either–or" to individual learning styles, for example work in three small groups—a "demo group", an exercise group, or a peer supervision group. Thus, the group learns that different learning styles are taken seriously and individual ways of learning are found. This leads to a growing flexibility and mutual respect and acceptance within the group.

3.3 Faith in the Human Organism as a Condition of Facilitating Learning

On the basis of having confidence in the ability of the learner to realize his/her own potential, the facilitator can "provide him with many opportunities and permit him to choose his own way and his own direction in his learning" (Rogers 1969, p. 114). From a person-centered perspective, respect for the (potential) self-determination and for the freedom of choice of learning styles and subjectively meaningful educational content on the seminar theme is the basis for this attitude in adult education (see also Joseph and Linley 2011, p. 93). Rogers (1991c) describes this basic trust in the person as perhaps the sharpest distinction from most institutions in our society. By contrast, in the field of education, administration, and business life, in the family, and in psychotherapy, there is a lot of distrust of the person evident in setting up targets for others, because they are deemed unable to choose appropriate targets for themselves—in contrast to the person-centered approach which expresses trust in the actualizing tendency.

3.4 Empathy as a Condition for Facilitating Learning

Empathy becomes evident in the facilitator's ability to grasp the subjective reality of the learner intellectually and emotionally: If the learner experiences that he/she understood empathically and deeply, he/she will be more likely able to turn to her/his more meaningful issues. He/she can even listen more closely and accurately to himself/herself and will be more willing to accept herself/himself—a condition for moving forward in her/his personal learning process. In a seminar on leadership and presentation for example, I supported a participant empathically to explore her concerns more closely. At first in the initial round, she said that she would like to be able to integrate the method of moderating and presenting into her everyday work of leadership. In the process of being understood empathically, she began to understand her own actual needs, fears, and personal goals, saying, *I would like suggestions on how I introduce the method of moderating in my team—I fear my staff will resist, if I—as a new team leader—invite them to participate more actively in the meetings—which they do not know yet. I don't want to ask too much of them or overrule them. On the one hand I do not want to criticize my predecessor for his style of leadership, but on the other hand I want—gradually—to realize my understanding of leadership and participation.* Through this more accurate self-understanding on the part of this participant, the facilitator can help to structure the issues empathically: her fear of opposition from the team, the need to keep her identity as a leader, how to shape change in leadership, and how to install a new culture of leadership. Frequently, the other participants are preoccupied with similar issues. The facilitator, through interaction and consultation with the group, may then develop with them further ideas and suggestions.

3.5 Getting in Touch with Personal Problems/Incongruence as a Condition for Facilitating Learning

The facilitator helps the learner to become aware of her/his personal problems and individual issues concerning the seminar topic. This experiencing is often associated with anxiety or fear—because it becomes evident that it is not isolated from the person, but the person as such is concerned. You are deeply motivated to learn something, and at the same time, there is a risk of hitting on something disturbing (Rogers 1961). For example, a manager (in a seminar on General Management) experiences his mixed feelings of sadness, anxiety, and confidence: "I have taken over a medium-sized firm from my father. The technological change has come to a standstill for years, the investment into technological development and acquisition has become much more expensive—I had to sack employees, which was very painful for both of us: the employees and myself. In this seminar I want to work on finding ways how to keep my staff committed and how to motivate them in this critical situation." During the seminar, the manager became aware how much energy and time it cost him to manage the technological change. Was it economically worthwhile? Was he thereby neglecting the management of his personnel? After joint analysis and reflection in the group, he said: "I'm looking forward to next week. *I'm much more relaxed. I now know*, which interviews I have to have with the staff and I'm going to be more active in leading, not letting things slide anymore." If a person gets in touch with his/her problem (incongruence), she/he will experience cognitive, physical, and social processes of change *simultaneously*. Crucial for enabling this kind of learning is that the facilitator does not talk *about* leadership and processes of change and that plans for implementation are not designed merely on a cognitive level, but that the participants *experience* themselves as being ready to implement what they have become aware of, what they have sensed, and what they have understood intellectually.

3.6 Offering Resources as a Condition for Facilitating Learning

Apart from the usual resources such as handouts, worksheets, literature, and other didactic methods, the facilitator may offer his/her knowledge and experience in an area when asked, by, for example, presenting cases from his/her own practice. The facilitator offers himself/herself as a resource for learning. If he/she senses, for instance, that a participant is motivated but at the same time is reluctant to commit himself/herself to an approach, he/she can address the participant's feeling of ambivalence in order to support the participant to explore his feelings more deeply in order to be able to arrive at a congruent decision for his method of learning. It is crucial that the learner can sense that it is meant as an offer, which she can accept or turn down (Rogers 1961).

3.7 How the Perception of the Facilitator by the Participants can Facilitate the Learning Process

Rogers (1957) asserts that the relational conditions delineated above have to be perceived and accepted, at least to minimum degree, by the participants in order for learning to occur. This condition is crucial, as the genuine experience of the learning group furthers the growth (or development) of the above-mentioned conditions.

4 Concluding Statements and Participants' Reflections

If this facilitative relationship—even to a small degree—is perceived and accepted by the learner, a communication of trust and security can develop, the fear toward change can decrease, and this promotes sustainable learning. "A climate of mutual trust develops out of this mutual freedom to express real feelings, positive and negative. Each member moves towards greater acceptance of his total being—emotional, intellectual, and physical—as it *is*, including its potential... With this greater freedom and improved communication, new ideas, new concepts, new directions emerge." (Rogers 1970, pp. 14–15).

This strengthening of mutual regard means that the facilitator may become increasingly a learning companion, a member of the group. The potential of the group thus unfolds more and more, with the participants supporting each other in their learning process. To enable such learning means neither being without structure, nor favoring a laissez-faire attitude on the part of the facilitator. It must not be understood as a technique. It is a genuine person-centered approach to adult education or in other words a way of being (Rogers 1980). The group experiences genuine freedom concerning the topic of the seminar: "…freedom of choice, freedom of expression, freedom to be" (Rogers 1970, p. 76). The essential issue, however, is that the freedom that is granted within these limits is real and that learners perceive it as honest and genuine. The following quotes from the final reflections of students in a person-centered counseling class provide concluding ideas and convey an impression of their personal learning experiences. They show the effect of experiencing person-centered learning and demonstrate their changing cognitive and emotional attitudes toward themselves and toward learning:

> The way we are learning here, feels good to me. For the first time I had a different kind of learning, as I have always wanted to. Although I'm 50 years old, I still have a difficult relationship with school. I'm always coming under duress. The more I got to know Rogers' humanistic ideas of man, the more I sometimes felt sad: I keep asking myself: what would have become of me, if I had had different teachers, who had understood my curiosity better? What, if I had attended other schools, in which I would have been more supported and could have unfolded my potential? (Reiner, journalist)
>
> The concept of learning has changed a lot for me. I used to associate learning with school, i.e. with drill and memorizing. Now learning for me means to grow, to be open to new experiences, to appreciate my interests and to have fun doing things, which I experienced here for the first time (Karin, social worker).
>
> For me the group became more and more important. Here, I could risk showing my feelings—which I could never do before—here I was able to be authentic, without running the risk of not being taken seriously. Here performance was not important, here I was valued as a person. I could even risk not achieving anything. I tested it many times. I thank all the members of the group that I was not discounted for this… I felt panic about doing role plays. In this group, they were fun for me. I can learn from them very freely. The experiences that I've had here will be helpful for me in other groups. Today I'm no longer afraid of groups, I find them exciting (Christel, manager of a nursery-school).

Acknowledgments The author thanks Sabine von Levetzow, Germany, and Ian Carty and Colin Lago, England, for their translation help with this chapter.

References

Arnold, R., Krämer-Stürzl, A., & Siebert, H. (1999). *Dozentenleitfaden. Planung und Unterrichtsvorbereitung in Fortbildung und Erwachsenenbildung* [Teacher's guide. Planning and preparation of courses in professional development and adult education]. Berlin: Cornelsen.

Cornelius-White, J. H. D. (2012). *Carl Rogers: The China diary*. Ross-on-Wye: PCCS Books.

Joseph, S., & Linley P. A. (2011). *Positive Therapie. Grundlagen und psychologische Praxis* [*Positive therapy: A meta-theory for positive psychological practice*]. Stuttgart: Klett-Cotta.

Kunze, D. (2003). *Lerntransfer im Kontext einer personzentriert-systemischen Erwachsenenbildung. Wie Wissen zum (nicht) veränderten Handeln führt* [*The transfer of learning in further education within the person-centered systemic approach. How knowledge leads to (no) changed behaviour*]. Köln: GwG.

Kunze, D. (2008). Das Personzentrierte Konzept in Beratung und Pädagogik [*The person-centered approach in counseling and pedagogy*] *Psychodynamische Psychotherapie. Forum der tiefenpsychologisch fundierten Psychotherapie, 2* (8), 179 – 190.

Rogers, C. R. (1951). *Client-centered therapy.* Boston: Houghton Mifflin.

Rogers, C. R. (1961). *On becoming a person: A therapist's view of psychotherapy.* Boston: Houghton Mifflin.

Rogers, C., R. (1969). *Freedom to learn. A view of what education might become.* Columbus, OH: Merrill.

Rogers, C. R. (1980). *A way of being.* Boston: Houghton Mifflin.

Rogers, C. R. (1970). *On encounter groups.* New York: Harper and Row.

Rogers, C., R. (1959). A theory of therapy, personality and interpersonal relationships, as developed in the client-centered framework. In Koch S. (Ed.), *Psychology. A study of science. Vol. III: Formulations of the person and the social context* (pp. 184–256). New York: McGraw Hill.

Rogers, C. R. (1957). The necessary and sufficient conditions of therapeutic personality change. *Journal of Consulting Psychology, 21*(2), 95–103.

Rogers, C. R. (1991c). Ein Klientenzentrierter bzw. Personzentrierter Ansatz in der Psychotherapie [A client-centered or person-centered approach in psychotherapy]. In: C. R. Rogers & P.F. Schmid, *Person-zentriert. Grundlagen von Theorie und Praxis. 7th Edition.* (pp. 238–256). Mainz: Mathias-Gründewald.

Siebert, H. (2011). *Lernen und Bildung Erwachsener [Learning and education of adults].* Bielefeld: Bertelsmann Verlag.

.

Characteristics and Effects of Person-Centered Technology Enhanced Learning

Renate Motschnig-Pitrik

1 Introduction

In this chapter, I draw from a decade of practice and research in person-centered education at the Faculty of Computer Science, University of Vienna, Austria, and the Masaryk University in Brno, Czech Republic. Taking a stepwise incremental approach, my team designed and incorporated web-based, open source technology to support person-centered learning. A pivotal idea was to design the technology to fit the goals of person-centered learning and not vice versa.

According to Rogers (1983), person-centered education aims toward:

- a climate of trust in which curiosity and the natural desire to learn can be nourished and enhanced;
- a participatory mode of decision making in all aspects of learning in which students, teachers, and administrators have their part;
- helping students to achieve results they appreciate and consider worthwhile, to build their self-esteem and confidence;
- uncovering the excitement in intellectual and emotional discovery, which leads students to become lifelong learners;
- developing in teachers the attitudes that research has shown to be most effective in facilitating learning;
- helping teachers to grow as persons finding rich satisfaction in their interactions with learners (Rogers 1983, adapted and shortened).

Clearly, these goals are not achieved by utilizing technology, but, as will be illustrated, are facilitated by a thoughtful integration of learning technology as a smart tool that enables more interaction, more being active, more flexibility and a simpler and wider access to various material resources. Equally, what remains

R. Motschnig-Pitrik (✉)
Computer Science Didactics and Learning Research Center, University of Vienna,
Waehringer Strasse 29/6.41 1090 Vienna, Austria
e-mail: renate.motschnig@univie.ac.at

J. H. D. Cornelius-White et al. (eds.), *Interdisciplinary Applications of the Person-Centered Approach*, DOI: 10.1007/978-1-4614-7144-8_11, © Springer Science+Business Media New York 2013

unchanged by the deployment of technology is the well-established theory that in order to facilitate significant, whole-person learning, "teachers," better facilitators, need to communicate the person-centered core attitudes of congruence, acceptance, and empathic understanding in such a way that learners can perceive them.

So far, numerous studies such as (Aspy 1972; Barrett-Lennard 1998; McCombs 2011; McCombs and Miller 2008; Rogers 1961, 1983) a meta-study (Cornelius-White 2007; Cornelius-White and Harbaugh 2010) have confirmed the effectiveness of the person-centered approach (PCA) in education. But can technology support or even enhance person-centered learning? Can person-centered attitudes be expressed or provided online to such a degree that learners can perceive them?

Before even trying to respond to these questions, let me clarify that the real questions and dynamics lie elsewhere: How can I utilize the computer to help mediating information in a structured, meaningful, and easily understandable way such that more of the face-to-face time in class can be used for communicating in a person-centered way? This can happen in small team work, presentations, and moderations by students, giving constructive feedback, offering students to reflect on their learning or team work, etc. Thus, the challenging task we are facing in technology enhanced education is how Rogers' interpersonal qualities can be included in activities that proceed partly face-to-face and partly in virtual space, supported by computerized tools (Motschnig-Pitrik 2005; Derntl and Motschnig-Pitrik 2005; Derntl 2006).

2 Person-Centered Technology Enhanced Learning in Action

While the subject matter differs from course to course, the following structural elements tend to be included in person-centered technology enhanced learning (PCeL) that essentially hinges on the facilitators' communicating the person-centered attitudes, such that students perceive them and can reciprocate them in their interactions.

- Students' as well as facilitator's goals, expectations, and threats are shared and taken into account.
- There is a flow of open yet respectful communication between participants and facilitator throughout the course, often supported by online communication and written online reaction of students visible to all participants and honored as active participation in the course.
- Students work in small teams to accomplish projects they choose in accordance with the course goals and the instructor's inputs/proposals and feedback. Teamwork at the interpersonal and task-specific level is actively reflected throughout the course.
- Facilitator and students prepare materials for presentation, often related to project milestones or the information necessary to accomplish a milestone.

Materials are available online for easy access; selected parts are presented and discussed in class. Students' projects can be improved after presentation and discussion in class. Results are uploaded and available to all participants, such that they can learn from multiple examples.

- Facilitator and students elaborate and provide resources and links to further information in a course workspace.
- Self-evaluation, typically submitted online, forms part of the grade. Discrepancies between the facilitators and the self-evaluation are discussed with the student. Whenever feasible, peer evaluation, submitted online, is also part of the grade, such that multiple perspectives are taken into account.

However, courses are not the only setting in which PCeL can be facilitated. In the last decade, I have experimented with introducing Significant Learning Communities (SILCs) (Motschnig-Pitrik 2008b). SILCs are communities whose participants aim to significantly learn from each other by meeting in encounter-like settings and by communicating online with the help of computerized tools. Since then, SILCs have been formed to interconnect secondary-level teachers, research groups, and researchers cooperating with industry. In Brazil, a highly influential project, projeto CASa (Cavalcante 2009), implemented a conceptual cousin of SILCs to provide for lifelong learning among all academic lecturers at the University of Fortaleza, Ceara.

3 Research Results and Students' Reactions

The research summarized below shows beneficial effects on several measured outcomes. Direct statements from students provide qualitative support and are intended to expose to readers the meaning students infer from their experiences.

Effects on interpersonal relationships. In PCeL style courses, the majority of students indicate that their interpersonal relationships improve as a result of attending the course. This is not only the case for relationships with classmates but also with family, partners, and work colleagues (Figl and Motschnig-Pitrik 2007; Motschnig-Pitrik 2008a).

Figure 1 provides an example from one study (Motschnig-Pitrik and Standl 2012) that showed the vast majority of respondents attributed rather positive or very positive effects on interpersonal relationships to courses conducted in a person-centered way. Those very few (1–2 persons) who indicated a rather negative effect on working colleagues, superiors, friends, and companions explained that they felt they were misunderstood by the other person but later the misunderstanding was clarified. We conclude that person-centered courses tend to have sustainable constructive long-term effects on interpersonal relationships in a vast majority of cases.

Learning on three levels. Across various PCeL courses, students indicate that— compared to traditional courses—they tend to learn about the same at the level of

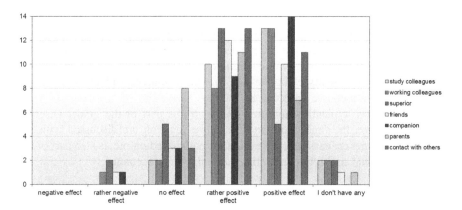

Fig. 1 Long-term effects of person-centered courses on interpersonal relationships (n = 27)

intellect, but significantly more at the level of skills and the level of attitudes (Derntl and Motschnig-Pitrik 2007; Motschnig-Pitrik and Derntl 2008).

Motivation. Empirical evaluations indicate that facilitators, who are perceived as highly congruent, respectful, empathically understanding and competent in the subject area, can motivate students more strongly than educators who are rated lower on these dimensions (Motschnig-Pitrik and Mallich 2004).

Profitable elements. From 24 features, those that students indicated to benefit most from and that were rated to be present in PCeL classrooms significantly more strongly than in traditional courses were: active participation in the course; exchange and discussion with peers and instructor; the opportunity of bringing in personal interests and contributions; and the support via a web-based platform (Derntl and Motschnig-Pitrik 2007; Motschnig-Pitrik 2006; Motschnig-Pitrik and Derntl 2008).

Online-learning contracts. When asked how much they learned from employing learning contracts, the vast majority of students responded that they had learned more or much more than through learning for traditional examinations (Derntl 2006; Derntl and Motschnig-Pitrik 2005).

Feeling of community. From the 14 features of Barrett-Lennard's community questionnaire (Barrett-Lennard 2005), the most significant increases tended to happen in: "Attentive listening to others," "climate of respect, caring, trust," and "experience of connectedness and community," across all PCeL courses (Motschnig-Pitrik and Figl 2008).

Team competencies, team orientation. Although students experience a significant rise in team skills, their team orientation and team attitudes do not change statistically significantly as the result of attending one person-centered course (Figl 2009; Figl and Motschnig-Pitrik 2008; Motschnig-Pitrik 2006; Figl and Motschnig-Pitrik 2007).

The students' voice. In the following, I share a sample of students' reactions taken from the most a recent PCeL course on "Communication and Soft Skills" conducted by the author at the Masaryk University in Brno, Czech Republic, in

2011. These excerpts are intended to illustrate the versatile kinds of learning students reflect.

> The most important lesson for me is that teaching should not be done in an authoritative way, but the teacher should instead be a motivator and moderator and just connect the crowd and point them in the right direction. [..] I learned other opinions on the same problem and also gained neat slides that I can look into when I need a solution to a problem. Thanks for the Course!
>
> The most important thing that I learned from this course was my opinion about this country and local people according to the impression I had in the beginning. Maybe someone will think that this is not something that has to do with this course, but for me it is! Because, I will stay, live and study in this place for two years, and I had the chance to be and to communicate with local people, now I have an idea how they are, and how can I communicate with them, and I have a good and a positive feeling being in this country.
>
> The discussions were probably one of the things I learned the most from, because it is interesting to hear various opinions. [..] Also, we were discussing topics that I don't talk about on a daily basis. Information can be found in books, but this is the kind of abstract knowledge that is hard to gain.
>
> I think of myself as a more of a quiet, unassertive and sometimes passive. I was surprised how I felt free to participate in discussions. Maybe it was thanks to the friendly and relaxed atmosphere.
>
> I also downloaded materials for further reference, so my learning has not stopped, yet. Yes. What I liked most was the way this course was organized and executed - interactively.
>
> I learnt mostly how to listen actively and how to express my opinions in a way that doesn't insult others.
>
> Even though I often wasn't at the same wave with my colleagues, it was nice to discuss all the different opinions. I've learned that with the specific approach you can discuss and come to terms with almost anyone.
>
> Last but not least I'm also going to take with me the 3 Core Conditions for Personal Development by Carl Rogers.

4 Conclusions and Open Questions

As in pure face-to-face settings, person-centered attitudes are essential in technology enhanced environments. Using web-based technology as an ally to providing resourceful learning environments has proved highly worthwhile if the integration provides a "healthy" mix of face-to-face and online elements, such that the advantages of *each medium* enhance the potentialities of person-centered learning.

Further research should explore the personal and work-related effects of the experienced added value of PCeL courses by conducting more long-term studies. We could ask: "How does attending such courses affect partnerships, families, and relationships with co-workers?" I envisage that *long-term perceptions* are likely to capture the sustained, meaningful learning outcomes unfolding from person-centered courses clearly. Furthermore, the effectiveness of person-centered learning across cultures and in *multi-cultural environments*—as often reflected by international students—needs to be confirmed. In brief, PCeL seems to lie at the heart of whole-person, democratic, culture-transcending learning that enhances us as learners—whether students or facilitators—in a perceivably constructive direction.

References

Aspy, D. N. (1972). *Toward a technology for humanizing education*. Champaign, Illinois: Research Press Company.

Barrett-Lennard, G. T. (1998). *Carl Rogers' helping system: Journey and substance*. London: Sage Publications.

Barrett-Lennard, G. T. (2005). *Relationship at the centre: Healing in a troubled world*. Philadelphia, PA: Whurr Publishers.

Cavalcante, F. (2009). *Projeto CASa*. Austria: Presentation at the University of Vienna.

Cornelius-White, J. H. (2007). Learner-centered teacher-student relationships are effective: A meta-analysis. *Review of Educational Research, 77*, 113–143.

Cornelius-White, J. H., & Harbaugh, A. P. (2010). *Learner-centered instruction: Building relationships for student success*. Thousand Oaks, California: Sage Publications.

Derntl, M. (2006). *Patterns for person-centered e-Learning*. Berlin: Aka Verlag.

Derntl, M., & Motschnig-Pitrik, R. (2005). The role of structure, patterns, and people in blended learning. *The Internet and Higher Education, 8*(2), 111–130. Elsevier Publishers.

Derntl, M., & Motschnig-Pitrik, R. (2007). Inclusive Universal Access in Engineering Education. *Proceedings of 37th Frontiers in Education Conference (FIE)*: Milwaukee, WI: IEEE.

Figl, K. (2009). *Team and media competences in information systems*. München: Oldenbourg.

Figl, K., & Motschnig-Pitrik, R. (2007). Developing Team Competence in technology enhanced courses. *Proceedings of World Conference on Educational Multimedia, Hypermedia and Telecommunications (ED-MEDIA)*. Vancouver: AACE.

Figl, K., & Motschnig-Pitrik, R. (2008). Researching the Development of Team Competencies in Computer Science Courses. *Proceedings of 38th ASEE/IEEE Frontiers in Education Conference, Saratoga Springs, NY* (pp. S3F-1–S3F-6). IEEE: NY.

McCombs, B. L. (2011). Learner-centered practices: Providing the context for positive learner development, motivation, and achievement (Chapter 7). In J. Meece & J. Eccles (Eds.), *Handbook of research on schools, schooling, and human development*. Mahwah, NJ: Erlbaum.

McCombs, B. L., & Miller, L. (2008). *The school leader's guide to learner-centered education: From complexity to simplicity*. Thousand Oaks, CA: Corwin Press.

Motschnig-Pitrik, R. (2005). Person-centered e-learning in action: Can technology help to manifest person-centered values in academic environments? *Journal of Humanistic Psychology:SAGE, 45*(4), 503–530.

Motschnig-Pitrik, R. (2006). Two technology-enhanced courses aimed at developing interpersonal attitudes and soft skills in project management. In W. Neijdl & K. Tochtermann (Eds.), *Innovative Approaches for Learning and Knowledge Sharing. Proceedings of the 1st European Conference on Technology Enhanced Learning, EC-TEL 2006*, Crete, Greece, LNCS 4227 (pp. 331–346). Berlin: Springer.

Motschnig-Pitrik, R. (2008). Can person centered encounter groups contribute to improve relationships and learning in academic environments? In M. Behr & J. H. D. Cornelius-White (Eds.), *Development and Interpersonal Relation—Person-Centered Work*, PCCS Books.

Motschnig-Pitrik, R. (2008b). Significant learning communities as environments for actualising human potentials. *International Journal of Knowledge and Learning (IJKL), 4*(4), 383–397.

Motschnig-Pitrik, R., & Derntl, M. (2008). Three scenarios on enhancing learning by providing universal access. *Universal Access in the Information Society, 7*(4).

Motschnig-Pitrik, R., & Figl, K. (2008). The effects of person centered education on communication and community building. *Proceedings of World Conference on Educational Multimedia, Hypermedia and Telecommunications, Austria* (pp. 3843–3852). Vienna, Austria: AACE.

Motschnig-Pitrik, R., & Mallich, K. (2004). Effects of person-centered attitudes on professional and social competence in a blended learning paradigm. *Journal of Educational Technology and Society, 7*(4), 176–192.

Motschnig-Pitrik, R., & Standl, B. (2012). Person-centered technology enhanced learning: Dimensions of added value. Manuscript submitted for publication.

Rogers, C. R. (1961). *On becoming a person: A psychotherapists view of psychotherapy*. London: Constable.

Rogers, C. R. (1983). *Freedom to Learn for the 80's*. Columbus, Ohio: Charles E. Merrill Publishing Company.

Ubiquitous Educational Computing and Learner-Centered Instruction: A Likely Pair

Adam P. Harbaugh and Jeffrey Cornelius-White

> *Education either functions as an instrument which is used to facilitate integration of the younger generation into the logic of the present system and bring about conformity or it becomes the practice of freedom, the means by which men and women deal critically and creatively with reality and discover how to participate in the transformation of their world.*
>
> —Paulo Freire.

1 Overview of Ubiquitous Computing and Learner-Centered Instruction

Ubiquitous computing can be defined as an environment where computers are thoroughly integrated into our lives and daily activities. From laptops to smartphones to tablet PCs, more people than ever before have constant access to computers and the Internet. Although access to these technologies is limited by financial resources, the cost of being "connected" has fallen in recent years to make ubiquitous computing a reality for a quickly growing number of people.

As public interest in and acceptance of the benefits of technology for improving our lives increase, schools are beginning to follow, by increasing the amount of advanced technologies available for students and teachers. Many schools are striving for a more ubiquitous computing environment through one-to-one (1:1) computing, which refers to an environment where all students have or are provided computers for their own personal use. A 1:1 environment holds promise as an environment to support a learner-centered instructional approach (Cornelius-White et al.2012; Fleischer 2012).

Learner-centered instruction refers to trusting and empathizing with students, having high expectations, believing teachers are facilitators more than direct imparters of information, fostering collaboration more often than individual and competitive work, supporting differentiated (developmentally appropriate) and self-directed student learning (Cornelius-White and Harbaugh 2010). It is essentially the practice of sharing choice and control with learners (McCombs and

A. P. Harbaugh (✉) · J. Cornelius-White
Missouri State University, 901 S. National Ave, Springfield MO 65897, US
e-mail: jcornelius-white@missouristate.edu

J. H. D. Cornelius-White et al. (eds.), *Interdisciplinary Applications of the Person-Centered Approach*, DOI: 10.1007/978-1-4614-7144-8_12,
© Springer Science+Business Media New York 2013

Whisler 1997), so that they have the freedom to learn (Rogers 1969). In an effective 1:1 environment, students are using technology to create, synthesize, and evaluate and other activities that require them to be active, hands-on learners. An effective 1:1 environment requires that teachers are facilitators, providing and guiding students through opportunities to attain and master knowledge and skills necessary for interdependence in the twenty-first century.

Some have raised concerns about accepting a philosophy that having more technology in schools leads to a better education (Weston and Bain 2010). There are also several issues with choosing which technology best suits the students' needs and then implementing that technology. Other problematic issues raised through a goal of ubiquitous computing related to access (Rockman et al. 2000). Not all students have access to computers or the Internet outside of the school building. Another concern of particular importance is that technology was not intended to and cannot replace teachers. Teachers still, regardless of the amount or types of technology in the school, need to maintain facilitative relationships with students, guiding them through the learning process. Indeed, research by Motschnig and colleagues has shown how technology-enhanced environments can leave space for even richer in person interactions and encounters (Motschnig-Pitrik and Mallich 2004; Motschnig-Pitrik 2005). Regardless of a teacher's expertise with a particular technology, the teacher has an opportunity and responsibility to guide a student's learning experiences in an ethical and responsible way using the technology as a means to the end that is the student's development. Each of these and other emerging issues needs to be considered when incorporating new technology into the school.

One of the most pressing questions facing educators today is the efficacy of the "flipped classroom" model (cf. Zappe et al. 2009). In this instructional model, a traditional, transmission model of instruction is flipped or inverted. In the traditional, transmission model, the student passively receives instruction in the classroom, while the teacher delivers instruction through lecture, demonstration, or some other teacher-centered means, followed by the student going home to become active with a homework assignment in an environment devoid of the teacher. In the flipped version of this instructional delivery method, the student is asked to receive instruction outside the classroom, often with the help of technology, and when the student returns to the classroom, she has the benefit of the teacher as facilitator for the active portion of instruction. The flipped classroom model has increased in popularity over recent years. However, educational researchers need to be careful to continue to have a voice in determining the efficacy of this model.

Another concept revolutionary to education is the increased accessibility and omnipresence of online courses. This phenomenon, combined with the flipped classroom or other models of blended instruction, provides researchers and practitioners challenges to find and support best learner-centered instructional practices. What is the role of the teacher in the flipped classroom model when the teacher's responses are intentionally omitted from the conversation, for example, during the lecture or demonstration phase of the model where the student is unable to ask a live and present teacher for clarification or further explanation? Derntl and Motschnig-Pitrik (2005, p. 128) suggest that "technological advances must go hand in hand with improved interpersonal skills and attitudes of educators." Do teachers' instructional choices in technology-rich environments build bridges between students and facilitators of learning within the community and, if not, then how can we, as educational leaders, offer choices that do build these important bridges? As a start to answer these and many other questions emerging around ubiquitous computing and students' usage of computers for learning, we need to look to what the research community is already doing. The synthesis of this research described in the remainder of this chapter begins that important work.

2 A Meta-Synthesis of the Research on Ubiquitous Computing in Education

The Ozarks educational research initiative (OERI), a collaborative partnership between 16 member school districts in the state of Missouri, requested that the Institute for School Improvement at Missouri State University conduct a "meta-analysis" of research on 1:1 technology initiatives to inform member districts and to help guide related research activities for the project (Cornelius-White et al. 2012). The authors identified and analyzed four systematic reviews of research, which included 131 total unduplicated studies, focused on 1:1 educational technology; five additional systematic reviews of research that included but went beyond 1:1 educational technology; and 24 other reviews of 1:1 technology initiatives in elementary and secondary education. Findings and conclusions of these selected reviews were coded and analyzed according to their strength of evidence. Those reviews with findings coded as moderately or strongly supported came almost exclusively from the group of four focused, systematic reviews (Penuel et al. 2002; Penuel 2005; Bethel et al. 2008; Fleischer 2012).

Generally, laptops, rather than other kinds of computing devices, have been the focus for systematic reviews of 1:1 technology research through 2011. These reviews show that writing is the area of student achievement with the largest and most consistent positive impact in 1:1 initiatives compared to other student outcomes. A small to medium, but consistent, effect size ($g = 0.30-0.35$) for writing improvement was found across multiple studies. Additionally, computer usage and literacy are clearly improved in environments where students have generous access to computers. Although this finding was clearly supported across studies, inconsistent reporting made determining an effect size impossible. The most consistent findings for implementation impact in 1:1 educational technology initiatives include provision of thorough, staged professional development, infrastructure and technical support, district–school–teacher leadership and collaboration and the need for ongoing research and evaluation of 1:1 initiatives. Again, although these findings were consistently supported across studies, inconsistent reporting prevented us from providing a magnitude of effect. Very little information, none of it systematic or experimental, was found with regard to cost-benefit analysis or other funding concerns.

3 Research Focused on Ubiquitous Computing and Learner-Centered Instruction

Results of the meta-synthesis further showed that 1:1 implementation (one computer for each child) was more successful when the teacher employed learner-centered strategies, such as fostering cooperative and self-directed projects, inviting questions, and other co-regulated learning endeavors, which, in turn, then led to a more learner-centered climate. The synthesis found support that professional development will be more successful if it addresses teacher beliefs about instruction and technology, includes relevant hands-on training, and involves collaborative or cooperative learning among teachers and is accompanied by sufficient technical support and collegial assistance when needed. We also found that through effective professional development, teachers' beliefs tend to change toward those that might be considered more learner-centered.

Employing learner-centered strategies during 1:1 implementation can also lead to twenty-first century skills, such as the ability to work independently, think critically, complete large and/or complex ventures, and work collaboratively with peers. These domains have traditionally been goals for learner-centered instruction, representing a more holistic and progressive view as compared to a focus on traditional achievement alone (Rogers 1969; Motschnig-Pitrik and Mallich 2004; Cornelius-White 2007). Although the meta-synthesis found that research in these areas is characterized by less clarity, rigor, and consistency of findings, these claims have been consistently supported at moderate levels.

For example, it was shown in several studies that students' collaboration with teachers, other students, and/or people in the community was improved through 1:1 initiatives. Similarly shown is that students conduct more research, maintain attention on longer-term projects, know more available resources for consultation, and improve their organizational skills as a few studies have supported these outcomes.

When in ubiquitous computing environments paired with facilitative teachers utilizing learner-centered instructional practices, students learn how to learn, perhaps the most important outcome from Rogers' (1969) original perspective. These students are developing critical and creative thinking skills that are important in career development. When students are presented with both authentic problems to solve and the tools to solve them, from the computing resources to the skills of how to effectively use these resources, the students are deeply engaged in important experiential learning (Rogers 1969). The information literacy skills that students develop in effective ubiquitous computing environments will be invaluable in and out of the work place. As an additional result and benefit for teachers and students, working with computer-skilled students may lead to situations of mutual learning and co-actualization for learners of all ages and levels.

4 Conclusion

Initiatives for a 1:1 technology-enhanced learning environment have become increasingly common in K-12 education. A meta-synthesis of research on 1:1 technology initiatives aimed to address learning issues, synthesizing available literature while attending to the quality of research for each of the three broad domains: student outcomes, implementation, and funding issues. This meta-synthesis identified and analyzed four systematic reviews of research, which included 131 total unduplicated studies, focused on 1:1 educational technology. Results of the analysis showed that 1:1 implementation was improved when learner-centered strategies were employed, which, in turn, can lead to a more learner-centered climate. Likewise, the research found that employing learner-centered strategies during implementation of 1:1 computer initiatives leads to improved twenty-first century outcomes or skills.

The person-centered community, including counselors, educators, and researchers, can establish their position in the field of ubiquitous educational computing by finding ways to support implementation of ubiquitous educational computing consistent with the Learner-Centered Psychological Principles (American Psychological Association 1997). Specifically, research needs to investigate the roles of school personnel empathy, unconditional regard, challenge, and other key learner-centered relational variables (Cornelius-White 2007) in such technology-rich environments. Additional research should also answer practical concerns such as how to provide a sustainable infrastructure as technology is constantly advancing. With these and similar issues being addressed by researchers, the person-centered community will be in a strong position to manage the inevitable increase in technology in our schools in ways that are consistent with the values of the community.

References

American Psychological Association. (1997). *Learner-centered psychological principles: A framework for school reform and redesign.* Retrieved June 25, 2012 from http://www.apa.org/ed/governance/bea/learner-centered.pdf.

Bethel, E.C., Bernard, R.M., Abrami, P.C., and Wade, A.C. (2008). Ubiquitous Computing in K-12 Classrooms: A Systematic Review. The Eighth Annual Campbell Collaboration Colloquium, Vancouver, BC. 12–14 May 2008.

Cornelius-White, J. H. D. (2007). Learner-centered teacher-student relationships are effective: A meta-analysis. *Review of Educational Research, 77*(1), 113–143.

Cornelius-White, J. H. D., & Harbaugh, A. P. (2010). *Learner-centered instruction: Building relationships for student success.* Thousand Oaks: Sage.

Cornelus-White, J. H. D., Sell, G. R., Chang, C., Mclean, A., and Roworth, R. (2012). A meta-synthesis of research on 1:1 technology initiatives in K-12 education. Technical report for Ozarks Educational Research Initiative. Institute for School Improvement, Missouri State University.

Derntl, M., & Motschnig-Pitrik, R. (2005). The role of structure, patterns, and people in blended learning. *Internet and Higher Education, 8,* 111–130.

Fleischer, H. (2012). What is our current understanding of one-to-one computer projects: A systematic narrative research review. *Educational Research Review, 7*(2), 107–122.

McCombs, B., & Whisler, J. (1997). *The learner-centered classroom and school.* San Francisco: Jossey Bass.

Motschnig-Pitrik, R. (2005). Person-centered e-learning in action: Can technology help to manifest person-centered values in academic environments? *Journal of Humanistic Psychology, 45,* 503–530.

Motschnig-Pitrik, R., & Mallich, K. (2004). Effects of person-centered attitudes on professional and social competence in a blended learning paradigm. *Educational Technology and Society, 7*(4), 176–192.

Penuel, W. R. (2005). *Research: What it says about 1 to 1 learning.* Sponsored by Apple Computer, Inc. Available from http://ubiqcomputing.org/Apple_1-to-1_Research.pdf.

Penuel, W. R., Kim, D. Y., Michalchik, V., Lewis, S., Means, B., Murphy, B., et al. (2002). *Using technology to enhance connections between home and school: A research synthesis.* Menlo Park, CA: SRI International. Available from http://ctl.sri.com/publications/downloads/Task1_FinalReport3.pdf.

Rockman et al. (2000). *A more complex picture: Laptop use and impact in the context of changing home and school access.* San Francisco: Author. Available from http://www.rockman.com/projects/126.micro.aal/yr3_report.pdf.

Rogers, C. R. (1969). *Freedom to learn: A view of what education might become.* Columbus: Charles E. Merrill.

Weston, M. E., & Bain, A. (2010). End of techno-critique: The naked truth about 1:1 laptop initiatives and educational change. *Journal of Technology, Learning, and Assessment, 9*(6), 5–25.

Zappe, S., Leicht, R., Messner, J., Litzinger, T., & Lee, H.W. (2009). *'Flipping' the classroom to explore active learning in a large undergraduate course.* In *Proceedings, American Society for Engineering Education Annual Conference and Exhibition.*

Part IV
Children and Family

Foundational Oppression: Families and Schools

Bert Rice

Speaking generally, oppression seems to be regarded as a bad thing. From what, then, does this badness arise? A common view is that it comes from the unjust or cruel use of power one person has over another (Merriam-Webster 1975). Power is abused if the person over whom it is exercised suffers harm as at least a reasonably foreseeable consequence of the abuser's use of that power. It is that harm which stamps oppression as evil.

But, does this perspective really capture what we mean when we talk about oppression? Slavery is a paradigmatic example of a system of oppression: Masters oppress slaves. Does the existence of oppression hinge upon whether the master treats slaves well or poorly? If a slave is treated with kindness and not harmed by her master, is she not oppressed? If she is oppressed, it follows that oppression does not rest on harm done but on freedom denied. For one person to oppress another, no abuse or misuse of power is required, only the exercise of power over. Oppression, then, involves the taking away of choice and opportunity, the substitution of one's own judgment for that of another. A person who is free, that is, not oppressed, may choose wisely and benefit herself or may choose foolishly to her own detriment. Therefore, a person who is not oppressed may, on account of the choices she makes, suffer more than an oppressed person, whose choices are being made for her. Oppression is defined not by degree of harm but by the exercise of power over others, which lessens their freedom.

Oppression is one type of relationship between human beings, and it is common parlance to speak of one person oppressing another. Usually, however, one refers to a group of people oppressing another. One racial group is said to oppress others, or a gender, a religion, or those who share a romantic preference are seen as oppressors relative to those outside the group. Persons from different groups may disagree about what form of oppression is the most serious and fundamental.

B. Rice (✉)
5530 South Shore Drive, Chicago, IL 60637, United States
e-mail: moonrice@earthlink.net

J. H. D. Cornelius-White et al. (eds.), *Interdisciplinary Applications*
of the Person-Centered Approach, DOI: 10.1007/978-1-4614-7144-8_13,
© Springer Science+Business Media New York 2013

Another group often regarded as victims of oppression is children and young people, who in some contexts are said to be oppressed by adults (New York Times 1988). Oft stated examples of such oppression include the use of children as workers in factories, fields, mines, and other places (Child Labor 2012), the physical and sexual abuse of children (Child Abuse 2012), and the use of children as soldiers (Military Use of Children 2012). Notice, however, that in each of these examples, the crux of the oppression or exploitation is seen to be the harm done to the child, not the child's loss of freedom. Child labor is viewed as oppressive because of the harm done to young bodies that are not up to the physical demands of the jobs. Physical abuse is seen as direct harm. Sexual activity is thought to be inherently abusive because of the psychological and emotional harm it brings, as well as physical harm. Acting as soldiers in wars is acknowledged as both physically dangerous and emotionally traumatic.

Therefore, the oppression of children is looked at differently from the oppression of adults: The former is based on harm, while the latter is based on the denial of freedom. Our society views child labor, with its potential for harm to the child, as unacceptable, but schooling, which is intended to benefit the child, is mandatory. It is not seen as oppressive to forbid child labor, nor to require schooling, but both take away a child's freedom of choice.

That denying children freedom, far from being wrongful, is actually an essential part of their development is such an accepted concept that it has been used throughout history to justify other denials of freedom. The Negro slave was said to be in a childlike state and, therefore, need the protection and guidance of the white master (Fitzhugh 1854). Women, like children, needed the protection and support of men, who took power over them (Futrelle 2010). Christianity was needed to supplant the childish rituals and mores of "pagan" religions (Wolff and Cipolloni 2007). Being attracted to persons of the same sex is a stage every child goes through on the pathway to the development of adult sexuality, which is characterized by opposite sex attraction (Born Gay 2009).

The person-centered approach to certain human relationships, as described by Carl Rogers (Rogers 1977), is, at its core, a rejection of oppression as an inappropriate form of human relationship. That approach was first developed in the context of individual therapy (Rogers 1942, 1951): The therapist inevitably possesses power over the client, but person-centered therapy (also known as client-centered therapy) instructs the therapist not to use that power over but to create an environment in which the client has the greatest possible freedom of action (Brodley 2011). Freedom is viewed as foundation for growth of the person: How can I become a better person if the very essence of what it means to be a person, the ability to make meaningful choices, is denied me?

The evil of oppression, then, comes from its denial of the humanity of the oppressed. Surely, this basic evil is not altered by the age of the victim. A person of 17 years, no less than one of 18, who is denied meaningful choice, is oppressed. Even an infant makes choices of behavior: crying at times, cooing at others, sleeping, drooling, and moving. The infant is communicating her judgment about what she needs, and the parent who ignores those communications and substitutes parental judgment for that of the infant is acting as an oppressor.

Our readiness to draw a line between, on the one hand, oppression of the young and, on the other hand, oppression of any category of adults is unprincipled. Our need to draw this line stems from love for our children, which produces in us an intense desire to protect them from harm and to do for them what is best. It is very difficult to see that in substituting our judgment for theirs, we are acting as their oppressors.

I am a parent and a teacher, so I have plenty of experience with the oppression of children. I started life as a child and was also a student, so I have had the opportunity, as well, to experience oppression from the other side. Most of you, as well, have had or will have similar opportunities to experience this oppression from both sides. Being or having been both oppressor and oppressed gives us a chance to understand oppression in a more complex and universal way than we could if limited to a single role.

Examples of my role as oppressor abound. When my son had graduated from grade school (the one at which I taught) and was beginning high school, he decided, with encouragement from me, to try out for the soccer (football) team. I was motivated, at least in part, by a desire to see him get into better shape, as he had, in my view, spent his summer avoiding exercise and getting out of shape. Football practice was very grueling, with conditioning drills being predominant. He hated it and wanted to quit. He was practicing with players ranging in age up to 3 years older, and he was, by far, the smallest person on the team. I insisted he stay, "for his own good," so he could get into shape. I decided I knew what was best for him and substituted my judgment for his. I was his oppressor.

It is, perhaps, even easier as a teacher to slip into the role of oppressor. In my classroom, I assist a head teacher, and it is often my task to roam around the room, making sure that students are "on task." Every time I redirect a student's attention away from her interest of the moment to the current "work," I have committed an act of oppression. From homework and classroom assignments through implementing a system of discipline based, in part, on the assumption that students cannot be trusted to discipline themselves, we teachers deny freedom to students.

The institutions of families and schools are foundationally oppressive. Neither institution is likely to disappear or be overthrown soon. Those of us who are parents and teachers are not likely to stop substituting our judgments for the judgments of our children and students. There will still be situations in which we believe we know better than the young people in our lives what is best for them. Other values, besides our valuing of human freedom, can come into play and push us away from liberating the young. Nevertheless, it is possible and, I believe, desirable to look without blinkers at what we are doing when we take away freedom, to understand that this is oppression, and to carefully weigh the importance of competing values before we decide whether or not to exercise power over others, no matter what their age.

References

Born Gay. (2009). Is same-sex attraction a passing phase some young people go through? ProCon.org http://borngay.procon.org/view.answers.php?questionID=000015 Accessed 22 January 2012.

Brodley, B. T. (2011) The nondirective attitude. In K. A. Moon, M. Witty, B. Grant, & B. Rice (Eds.), *Practicing client-centered therapy: Selected writings of Barbara Temaner Brodley* (pp. 47–62). Ross-on-Wye, UK: PCCS Books.

Child abuse. (2012). *Wikipedia.* http://en.wikipedia.org/wiki/Child_abuse Accessed 22 January 2012.

Child labor. (2012). *Wikipedia.* http://en.wikipedia.org/wiki/Child_labour Accessed 22 January 2012.

Fitzhugh, G. (1854). *Sociology for the south, or, the failure of free society.* Richmond: A. Morris.

Futrelle, D. (2010) Women are... part 4: retarded children edition. Web post. Man Boobz Misogyny. http://manboobz.com/2010/12/11/women-are-part-4-retarded-children-edition/ Accessed 22 January 2012.

The Merriam-Webster Dictionary for Large Print Users. (1975). *Springfield.* MA: G & C Merriam Co.

Military use of children. (2012). *Wikipedia.* http://en.wikipedia.org/wiki/Military_use_of_children Accessed 22 January 2012.

The New York Times. (1988). Rights group tells of oppression of children, citing 18 countries. http://www.nytimes.com/1988/01/06/world/rights-group-tells-of-oppression-of-children-citing-18-countries-html?pageswanted=print&src=pm Accessed 22 January 2012.

Rogers, C. R. (1942). *Counseling and Psychotherapy.* Cambridge: Riverside.

Rogers, C. R. (1951). *Client-centered therapy.* Cambridge: Riverside.

Rogers, C. R. (1977). *On personal power.* New York: Delacorte.

Wolff, L., & Cipolloni, M. (2007). *The anthropology of the Enlightenment.* Stanford: Stanford University.

The Person-Centered Approach in Family Education

Dagmar Nuding and Dorothea Hüsson

1 Learning in Freedom: The Person-Centered Approach in Schools

Rogers developed his approach first as a therapeutic approach. Then, he broadened the approach to create principles for fostering facilitative relationships, which were applied in education (Rogers 1969, 1983). These principles serve as the basis for person-centered family education. The positive influence of an acknowledging low authoritarian teacher's personality on the students' performance was researched and replicated by Tausch and Tausch (1998). Their numerous studies proved the high influence of the teacher behavior on the constructive and creative development of personality of young people. The book "Educational Psychology" influenced and changed the predominant authoritative and directive education style in German schools and families. Jef Cornelius-White and Renate Motschnig-Pitrik (2010) summarized over 100 studies from several countries, most prominently the USA, Germany, and Austria. They estimated the effectiveness of person-centered learning and got an overall effect size of Cohen's $d = 0.65$,[1] which represents a medium to large effect of person-centered elements on students' behavior, affects, and cognitive outcomes.

Over 20 years ago, Behr (1989) began to compare the concept of person-centered pedagogy with progressive education approaches. Lux (2007) and Schmid (2008) took the basics of the person-centered approach and brought them in relation to more modern theories. The central statement especially in the field of early education "no education without attachment" (Fröhlich-Gildhoff 2010) is

---

[1] Cohen's d, an often-used measure for effect sizes, expresses the amount of difference between two groups on some variable relative to the amount of variation within the groups. A d of 0.2 is interpreted as a "small" effect, a d of 0.5 is interpreted as a "medium" effect, and a d of 0.8 is considered as a "large" effect.

D. Nuding (✉) · D. Hüsson
University of Education, Oberbettringer Straße 200 73525 Schwäbisch Gmünd, Germany
e-mail: dagmar.hoelldampf@ph-gmuend.de

J. H. D. Cornelius-White et al. (eds.), *Interdisciplinary Applications of the Person-Centered Approach*, DOI: 10.1007/978-1-4614-7144-8_14, © Springer Science+Business Media New York 2013

more and more supported by the results of modern brain and attachment research (Ahnert 2004; Großmann and Großmann 2004; Hüther 2004, 2005). Thus, the person-centered approach with its central element of the relationship gets more and more importance also in the educational field. Learning processes are no longer reduced to only cognitive learning of facts; a person-centered learning culture based on the pupils' needs is created, and developmental processes of young people are facilitated in a holistic way.

Teachers are supported to communicate in a more effective way and to create student-centered lessons. Student-centered lessons reflect teachers' personalities and focus on a good pupil–teacher relationship (Gordon 1974; Miller 1999; Schmitz-Schretzmair 2011). Besides teacher–student interaction patterns, applying the person-centered approach is also helpful in parent–teacher dialogues (Nuding et al. 2008; Mühlhäuser-Link et al. 2008; Aich 2011). The task force school of the GwG—Gesellschaft für Personzentrierte Psychotherapie und Beratung e.V. [German Association for Person-Centered Therapy]—offers trainings for teachers and schools to facilitate them on their way to a person-centered school and learning culture. This way of being serves as the foundation for person-centered approaches to family education.

2 The Person-Centered Approach in Early Education

Coinciding with Rogers' statements, infant research states that the human being is competent, initiative, differentiated, and able to go into relationships from birth on and that as a human being, the self is configured within relationships (Stern 1985). Babies are in need of unconditional regard and empathic attachment figures, who are direct and responsive in their reaction. Core elements of the person-centered paradigm can be found in the actual discussions of a modern early education, without being declared as such. But they are part of the trainings in (early) education, and it would be unthinkable without them (Fröhlich-Gildhoff 2010). Professional creation of relationships belongs to the training of childhood educators at all universities in Baden-Württemberg (Robert-Bosch-Stiftung 2008). Students studying childhood education at the Schwäbisch Gmünd University of Education are trained in person-centered play therapy and communication as part of their studies. The curriculum for kindergartens in Baden-Württemberg fosters a person-centered attitude, even if not specifically declared as such: "The pedagogic action is based on respect, positive regard toward the child. The pedagogic worker takes every child as he or she is." (Ministerium für Kultur, Jugend und Sport Baden-Württemberg 2011, p. 16, own translation). In practice, this child-centered way uses child conferences or a slow "getting used to" going to kindergarten by the children. Person-centered elements are used also in cooperation with parents: Through unconditional positive regard and a respectful attitude toward the parents, they are seen as experts for their children and education is lived as a partnership approach.

3 The Person-Centered Approach in Families

One of the seminal parent trainings as a primary-preventive support was initiated by Gordon's (1970) parent effectiveness training. In the meantime, a large number of various parents' trainings can be found on the market. With the exception of the positive parenting program (Triple P®), which rests on cognitive-behavioral concepts, almost all the others rest on humanistic concepts (for an overview, see Tschöpe-Scheffler 2006). In this section, three popular person-centered approaches to parent trainings and one approach of child training will be presented.

3.1 Gordon's Parent Effectiveness Training: Family Effectiveness Training

Thomas Gordon, a student of Carl Rogers in the early 1960s developed the parent effectiveness training (1970). This approach struck great interest with parents. At that time, many parents were looking for methods of education which were not characterized by exertion of power, by punitive measures, by disciplining actions, and by violence, but by a relationship-oriented unconditioned accepting contact between parents and children.

Realizing that the effective therapeutic factors are not constrained to therapy, Gordon developed a model for positive constructive performance of human relationships, and in this way, he implemented the essential contents of the person-centered approach into family education. The approach is preventive and practice-oriented to help parents achieve positive successful relationships inside the family in everyday life. It includes parental empathy, acceptance, being real, and democratic interactions with a focus on active listening, I-messages, and negotiations in conflict resolution.

The efficacy of the Gordon's parents' training is proved by many research studies and two meta-analyses (Cedar and Levant 1990; Müller et al. 2001). The 26 primary studies used by Cedar and Levant (1990) showed a general effect excellence of $d = 0.33$; the 15 primary studies used by Müller (2001) showed an excellent mean effect size of $d = 1.47$. Both meta-analyses showed a higher efficacy of the trainings within children between 7 and 12 years, $d = 1.3$, in comparison with parents of children between 3 and 7 years $d = 0.92$ (Cornelius-White and Motsching-Pitrik 2010).

3.2 The Person-Centered Parents' School "Living Together"

The GwG (2008) tried to improve social development which seemed to be formed by parental precariousness and loss of orientation in education using the concept of the person-centered parents' school. The person-centered parents' school aims at the self-experience of educating and enlargement of the parental self-concept to construct an appreciating, empathic, and confidential relationship with their child.

Beyond that, parents are taught basic theories of development, communication, and systemic aspects in eight steps:

1. Critical reflection of their own role as parent.
2. Attentive identification of the needs of children.
3. Taking their own needs seriously.
4. Facilitating the understanding by active listening.
5. Being authentical by I-messages.
6. Limit setting.
7. Negotiating rules by means of family counseling.
8. Gathering ideas for a better living together.

In the parents' school, it is important that these contents will not be distantly approached, like a stock training program, but instead that parents experience and internalize the person-centered tenor and the importance of a good relationship using dialogues, role-play, and self-reflection.

3.3 Filial Therapy: Child–Parent Relationship Therapy

Filial therapy was developed by the Guerneys (Guerney 1964). A parent trained by a therapist as "therapeutic agent" independently practices at home with his or her own child, facilitating cohesiveness and connection through play, which becomes reflected in weekly supervision with the therapist and within a group of participating parents attending the same program (Landreth and Bratton 2006).

With other means than traditional education models, filial therapy puts the focus on the parent–child relationship, where the cause for a potentially problematic behavior of the child is seen. The parents are trained in basic "child-centered skills" such as active listening, empathic understanding, realizing the needs of the child, limit setting, and the construction of the child's self-regard.

In this way, parents learn to build up a therapeutically efficient relationship with their children within which both of them experience change (Landreth and Bratton 2006). Bratton and colleagues (Bratton et al. 2005) confirm the high benefit of this intervention with different therapeutic agents in their meta-analysis using 26 primary studies with a mean effect size of $d = 1.05$. For the studies which explored settings in which no therapists were involved but parents were the therapeutic agents, a mean effect size of $d = 1.15$ was calculated.

A recent meta-analysis (Nuding et al. 2012) shows a mean effect size of Hedges' $g = 0.847$[2] (p = 0.000) for children at risk using fourteen primary

---

[2] The effect size measure Hedges' g is suggested by Larry Hedges to calculate effect sizes for small groups. Similar to Cohen's d in its intent and interpretation, it is based on a standardized difference, but is computed slightly differently from Cohen's d.

studies. This value confirms the high efficacy elaborated by Bratton and colleagues (2005). For parental empathy and acceptance measured by the Measurement of Empathy in Adult–Child Interactions Scale (MEACI), Nuding and colleagues (2012) calculated a high significant effect size of Hedges' $g = 2.560$ (p = 0.000).

3.4 Kids' Workshop^{TM}

Barbara Williams, a consultant and psychotherapist for children, developed the Kids' Workshop^{TM} (Rogers 1980; http://www.kids-workshop.com). Barbara Williams is delivering her workshop as Co-Director of Communication Trainings Seminars for the Person-Centered Approach Institute in Italy since 1994 and in France since 2003. Her unique workshop is designed to sustain children recognizing their own person-centered qualities in order to develop characteristics like trust, empathy, and congruency necessary for creating a higher self-image. The workshop, which is a combination of theory and experiential exercises, is based on Rogers' theories and the theory of V. Satir. The exercises involve role-playing, storytelling, working with puppets, and other figures.

4 Summary

The person-centered approach is used beyond psychotherapy in various fields of family education. New concepts were developed and proved to be highly effective such as Gordon's parent effectiveness training (PET)—family effectiveness training (FET), and filial therapy. Likewise, core elements of the person-centered approach are integrated in standard pedagogical trainings without specific acknowledgement.

References

Ahnert, L. (Ed.), (2004). *Frühe Bindung. Entstehung und Entwicklung.* [Early attachment. Accruement and development.] München: Reinhardt.

Aich, G. (2011). *Professionalisierung von Lehrenden im Eltern-Lehrer-Gespräch. Entwicklung und Evaluation eines Trainings.* [Professionalization of teachers in parent-teacher-dialogues. Development and evaluation of a training program]. Hohengehren: Schneider.

Behr, M. (1989). Wesensgrundlagen einer an der Person des Kindes und der Person des Pädagogen orientierten Erziehung. [Elements of an education oriented on the person of the child and teacher]. In M. Behr, F. Petermann, W. M. Pfeiffer & C. Seewald (Hrsg.), *Jahrbuch für personenzentrierte Psychologie und Psychotherapie, Bd. 1* (pp. 152–181). Salzburg: Otto Müller.

Bratton, S., Ray, D., Rhine, T., & Jones, L. (2005). The efficacy of play therapy with children: A meta-analytic review of the outcome research. *Professional Psychology: Research and Practice, 36*(4), 376–390.

Cedar, B., & Levant, R. F. (1990). A meta-analysis of the effects of parent effectiveness training. *The American Journal of Family Therapy, 18*, 373–384.

Cornelius-White, J.H.D., & Motschnig-Pitrik, R. (2010). Effectiveness beyond psychotherapy. The person-centered and experiential paradigm in education, parenting, and management. In M. Cooper, J. Watson & D. Nuding (Eds.), *Person-centered and experiential therapies work. A review of the research on counseling, psychotherapy and related practices* (pp. 45–64). Ross-on-Wye: PCCS-Books.

Fröhlich-Gildhoff, K. (2010). Die Bedeutung des Personzentrierten Ansatzes für eine moderne Frühpädagogik. [The importance of the person-centered approach in early childhood education.]. *Person, 14*(1), 43–53.

Gordon, T. (1970). *P. E. T.: Parent effectiveness training.* New York: Peter H. Wyden.

Gordon, T. (1974). *T.E.T.: Teacher effectiveness training: The program proven to help teachers bring out the best in students of all ages.* New York: Peter H. Wyden.

Guerney, B. G. (1964). Filial therapy: Description and rationale. *Journal of Consulting Psychology, 28*(4), 376–390.

GwG—Gesellschaft für Personzentrierte Psychotherapie und Beratung (Ed.). (2008). *Person-zentrierte Elternschule—Miteinander leben.* [*The person-centered parents' school "Living Together"*] Köln: GwG-Verlag.

Großmann, K. & Großmann, K.E. (2004). *Bindungen—das Gefüge psychischer Sicherheit.* [Attachment—the arrangement of psychological safety.] Stuttgart: Klett-Cotta.

Hüther, G. (2004). Die neurobiologische Verankerung von Erfahrungen und ihre Auswirkungen auf das spätere Verhalten. [Neurobiological memories of experiences and their effects on later behavior]. *Gesprächspsychotherapie und Personzentrierte Beratung, 35*(4), 246–252.

Hüther, G. (2005). *Die Macht der inneren Bilder. Wie Visionen das Gehirn, den Menschen und die Welt verändern.*[The influence of internal images. How vision change the brain, the people and the world.] Göttingen: Vandenhoeck & Ruprecht.

Landreth, G. L., & Bratton, S. C. (2006). *Child-parent-relationship therapy (CPRT): A 10-session filial therapy model.* New York: Brunner Routledge.

Lux, M. (2007). *Der Personzentrierte Ansatz und die Neurowissenschaften.* [The person-centered approach and neurosciences.] München: Reinhardt.

Miller, R. (1999). *Beziehungsdidaktik.* [Didactics of relationship.] Weinheim: Beltz.

Ministerium für Kultur, Jugend und Sport. Baden-Württemberg (Hrsg)., (2011). *Orientierungs-plan für Bildung und Erziehung in baden-württembergischen Kindergärten und weiteren Kindertageseinrichtungen.* [Orientation for education in kindergartens and other pre-schools in Baden-Württemberg] Retrieved July 13, 2012, from http://www.kultusportalbw.de/servlet/PB/show/1285728/KM_KIGA_Orientierungsplan_2011.pdf.

Mühlhäuser-Link, S., Aich, G., Wetzel, S., Kormann, G. & Behr, M. (2008). The dialogue between teachers and parents: Concepts and outcomes of communication training. In M. Behr & J.H.D. Cornelius-White (Eds.), *Facilitating young people's development. International perspectives on person-centered theory and practice,* (pp. 176–197). Ross-on-Wye: PCCS Books.

Müller, C. T., Hager, W. & Heise, E. (2001). Zur Effektivität des Gordon-Eltern-Trainings (PET)—eine Meta Evaluation [Effectiveness of Gordon's parent effectiveness training (PET)—a meta-analysis.] Gruppendynamik und Organisationsberatung, *32*, 339–364.

Nuding, D., Aich, G., Jakob, T., & Behr, M. (2008). The use of the person-centred approach for parent-teacher communication: A qualitative study. In M. Behr & J. Cornelius-White (Eds.), *Person-centred work with children, adolescents and parents* (pp. 164–175). Ross-on-Wye: PCCS Books.

Nuding, D., Crawford, I, Härtel, J. & Behr, M. (2012). Wirksamkeit filialtherapeutischer Elterntrainings bei Eltern von Risikokindern. [Effectiveness of filialtherpeutic parent trainings for parents of children at risk]. In S. Kägi & U. Stenger (Hrsg.) *Forschung in Feldern der Frühpädagogik. Grundlagen-, Professionalisierungs- und Evaluationsforschung* (pp. 302–320). Hohengehren: Schneider.

Robert-Bosch-Stiftung (Hrsg.), (2008). *Frühpädagogik Studieren—ein Orientierungsrahmen für Hochschulen.* [Study early childhood education—an orientation for universities.] Retrieved July

13, 2012, from http://www.bosch-stiftung.de/content/language1/downloads/PiK_orientierungs rahmen_druckversion.pdf.13.07.2012.

Rogers, C. R. (1969). *Freedom to learn. A view of what education might become*. Columbus: Merill.

Rogers, C. R. (1980). *A way of being*. Boston: Houghton Mifflin.

Rogers, C. R. (1983). *Freedom to learn for the 80's*. Columbus: Merill.

Schmid, P. F. (2008). Eine zu stille Revolution? Zur Identität und Zukunft des Personzentrierten Ansatzes. [A revolution too quiet? About identity and future of the person-centered approach]. *Gesprächspsychotherapie und Personzentrierte Beratung, 39*(3), 124–130.

Schmitz-Schretzmair, R. (2011). Personzentrierte Kommunikation, Kooperation und Konfliktlö-sung—in Schulen werden diese drei Kompetenzen mehr denn je gebraucht. [Person-centered communication, cooperation and conflict resolution—basic necessity for schools.] Ges-prächspsychotherapie und Personzentrierte Beratung, 42(2), 77–80.

Stern, D. (1985). *The interpersonal world of the infant: A view form psychoanalysis and developmental psychology*. New York: Basic Books.

Tausch, R. & Tausch, A.-M. (1998). *Erziehungspsychologie: Begegnung von Person zu Person.* [Educational psychology. Encounter from person to person.] Göttingen: Hogrefe.

Tschöpe-Scheffler, S. (Ed.). (2006). *Konzepte der Elternbildung—eine kritische Übersicht.* [Concepts for parents training—a critical overview.] Opladen: Budrich.

Part V
Business and Leadership

Successful Management with the Person-Centered Approach: Building the Bridge to Business

David Ryback and Renate Motschnig-Pitrik

1 Being with Carl Rogers

Renate:
David, what made you interested in the person-centered approach (PCA) as such and what caused you to consider the PCA in management? How, then, did your interest evolve?

David:
I first met Carl Rogers at a psychology class during my Masters studies at San Diego State University. He came to give a presentation on his approach and to say that I found him fascinating would be an understatement.

I walked with him to his car and I recall asking him about Romeo and Juliet. I don't recall exactly how I asked the question—it had something to do with unconditional love and the dynamic of unrequited romance. Nor do I recall exactly how he responded to my question (after all these years), but I do remember being extremely impressed with his openness to the whole issue. That small interaction, walking with him to his car, had a very big impact on my life. As I began to read more and more about the PCA and about Carl's take on openness and authenticity, my interactions with others began to change dramatically. I was quite shy and now I was able to open up significantly as I *focused on others' needs* rather than my own.

My world changed. There was so much more to communicate about with those with whom I chose to interact. I became socially involved with a purpose, *to be of service to others* as I could learn of their perspective and needs.

D. Ryback (✉)
EQ Associates International, 1534 N. Decatur Road NE, Suite 201,
Atlanta, GA 30307-1020, USA
e-mail: David@EQassociates.com

R. Motschnig-Pitrik
Computer Science Didactics and Learning Research Center, University of Vienna,
Waehringer Strasse 29/6.41, 1090 Vienna, Austria
e-mail: renate.motschnig@univie.ac.at

J. H. D. Cornelius-White et al. (eds.), *Interdisciplinary Applications
of the Person-Centered Approach*, DOI: 10.1007/978-1-4614-7144-8_15,
© Springer Science+Business Media New York 2013

Years later, when I had my first academic job as an assistant professor, I was given the mission of initiating a conference on humanistic education at the University of West Georgia's Department of Psychology. My first impulse was to invite Carl to be the keynote speaker.

During some free time at the conference site, I asked Carl if he would take some time with me to talk about some of the issues in my own life. He agreed, and we went to his hotel room where we relaxed in chairs and I tried to open up about how I felt about myself. When I shared with him how I often felt marginalized or misunderstood because I found it hard to express myself openly, he responded: "Kind of apart from others, as if they don't like you … or respect or appreciate you?"

This simple reflection struck me like a bolt of lightning. In a few words, Carl opened my eyes to recognize how much I needed respect and appreciation. This was in sharp contrast to my superficial veneer of appearing independent and self-reliant. Of course I was independent and self-reliant—always had been, having left home at the age of 17 to be totally on my own in a new country. But a deeper part of me, which I chose to ignore, was actually dependent on others "appreciating" me. This was a second major shift in my life because of a simple interaction with Carl Rogers.

2 Bringing the PCA into the Business World: A "Safe Place" to Deal with Differences

Renate:
David, "hearing" you say this fascinates me on multiple levels: The way you're sharing yourself so transparently and expressing how influential Carl Rogers was in your life touches me. I find it hard to hold back from adding something personal at this point too. I've experienced what I'd call a similar revelation on my path when reading and re-reading Carl Rogers' books. This, I think, inspired me to look at how the wisdom of the PCA that was, and is, so precious to me could be made accessible to a wider range of persons than clients in therapy. Now, coming back to the context of this chapter, I'm wondering how important it might be for managers and their employees to be mutually "appreciated" as fully as possible, regardless of how self-reliant they already were. How much more motivation this would enhance, and foster improved results in all spheres, personal and work related. Now I'm most curious about how and why you started consulting enterprises.
David:
Renate, there's no doubt in my mind that exploring the more transparent aspects of personality might make the members of a team or organization more powerful in their business dealings. Perhaps it all comes down to allowing each individual to

explore his/her own unique abilities and potential talents to emerge so as to make their best contributions to the challenges at hand.

As the years passed, I found myself getting more involved in consulting with business enterprises in addition to my clinical practice. Of course, my approach was heavily influenced by Carl's principles (Rogers and Ryback 1984). I thought a book making this unexpected integration of the PCA and good business needed to be written. My contention was that if managers and directors were honest about their feelings in their interactions with one another, then they could not but be more efficient and more successful with the business at hand. How to get beyond the competitive ego competition and buckle down to work together in harmony was my focus. Wouldn't teams that worked together, just as did the PCA groups I'd experienced at retreats and conferences, be much more powerful and effective?

One of the most enlightening lessons I learned from Carl during one such experience was that *a group could not reach its peak of potential until the members were allowed to explore their differences in a* "safe space," *allowing them to more readily learn about each member's unique needs and attributes, so they could be better motivated.* What was unique about each individual so that they could offer the best of their skills? The formal organization chart was just a beginning. The real, natural hierarchy of power could be fluid and shifting, depending on the needs of a particular job and the dynamics of the interpersonal relationships. What a powerful concept! Leadership, at its best, is a shifting dynamic—and that was clearly a tremendous discovery that I wanted to share in my book.

Ten years after Carl's passing, I decided to write such a book about applying the PCA to the world of business leadership. As I was completing the first draft in 1995, Daniel Goleman came out with his best seller, *emotional intelligence* (EI). I realized this concept was powerful and carried the potential to influence our culture. I also saw incredible similarity to the PCA—knowing your own feeling and empathy for others' feelings being the highlights. I decided to integrate Carl's ideas with those of EI and the title of my book ended up being *Putting* EI *to Work* (1998), in which I included some of the dialogue I had with Carl during my visit to his home a decade or so earlier, a dialogue that took place as we enjoyed afternoon walks along the beach behind his home in La Jolla. My mission of being of service to Carl Rogers had been finally completed.

3 Hard Facts and Open Emotions: A Universal Struggle

Renate:
I feel somewhat different about this. I see your mission as realized or kind of accomplished, yet I also see you *still acting* on that mission. The whole potential of the job isn't maximized yet, is it? Just wanted to share my feelings here. How

would you describe the effect of Carl Rogers on yourself and did it change you throughout the years?

David:

Of course, Carl Rogers affected me by making me *more sensitive to the emotional dynamics of those in my world,* whether that was in my clinical office, or with corporate clients, or in my social network in general. But more than that, his influence deeply affected my writing. I had always been a bottom-line advocate, trying to cut trough the superficial and trivial and getting to the essence of things. Before meeting Carl, I had done research on mind-set—how we understood the world based on our expectations. I also worked extensively with autistic children, training mute echolalic patients to begin the new adventure of speech acquisition. Even before earning my doctoral degree, I had some publications to my credit on these topics. I spent some time at UCLA in California, learning the behavioral techniques to train these very "disturbed" children. I was successful enough to be invited to offer workshops to parents of autistic children across the U.S. and Canada. In other words, I was doing the work of a staunch behaviorist.

So when I had the opportunity to apply Carl's PCA principles to the problems of the world, I was faced with a dilemma. How could behaviorism, which I knew worked where other approaches failed, and Carl's humanistic approach both be "the answer"? I set out to try and resolve this conflict with a paper titled, *The Dilemma of Initiative*, in which I looked at both applications in the world of psychotherapy.

One of the stark differences between the two approaches is how the behaviorists traditionally had diminished the importance of consciousness and self-awareness, and how the PCA emphasized that very same concept. So the answer had to do with whether one chose to emphasize therapy as a technique or as a process in living. Clearly, the PCA was more attractive in that it held a strong respect for the dignity of the individual rather just on bottom-line results. But the dilemma remained—did the PCA have a clear victory over the more technical behavioral approach to human challenges?

My conclusion aimed at fairness to both sides: "Stereotypes aside, both are humanistically responding to a person's need for help. The main difference is in vocabulary. The existentialist's vocabulary is semantically 'warmer' than that of the behaviorist. But can we blame the behaviorists for poor public relations?"

Unable to uncover a victor in this ideological battle between Rogerian and behaviorist values, I decided to declare a truce. In an article in the *Canadian Psychologist*, I formulated a new philosophical approach which I called Existential Behaviorism. I justified this bizarre combination with the realization that both sides believed they had a monopoly on the truth. I wrote: "'Truth' is nothing more than a concept describing majority consensus of valued peers."

I decided that both systems have their relevant points and that a resolution inculcates the best of both—appreciation of bottom-line results, including technical know-how, as well as respect for individual free will and self-determination. Comparing the basic philosophies of free will vs. behavioral determinism, I concluded that both were real—we could accept that we live in a cause-and-effect world explained by science and, at the same time, give "equal significance to the alternative that existential decisions (spontaneous and unpredictable) allow for the complete freedom of movement and choice." More recently, I've changed the title of my "compromise" to Existential Determination, characterized as a "combined paradigm" for choosing freely yet logically (Ryback 2012).

4 Deep Empathy: A "Tendency to Grow"

Renate:
This reminds of Carl Rogers' inner disputes that he captured in his intriguing chapter, "Persons or Science" (Rogers 1961). I'm glad he shared the divergent voices in himself as well as his path to reconciliation so clearly. Again, David, your exploration on behaviorism and (consciously not using the word "versus") the PCA lets me find a parallel in my experience in facilitating students' learning. I feel and know (from my research) that I'm most effective and resourceful if I use a mix of didactic elements on top of what is primary to me in all endeavors— building a threat-free, trusting atmosphere, based on genuine, person-centered values and inviting collaborative learning among all persons involved.

David:
Yes, perhaps many like-minded people have had a similar struggle—to integrate their more conventional education with Rogers' "revolutionary" approach. Over the years, this dilemma between the philosophies associated with Rogers and Skinner continued for me. But, as time passed, I became more immersed in trying to understand the "technology" of empathy. I kept experimenting on my own use of empathy in my private practice. What worked best for me, and for my clients? What kept me involved, seeing client after client, day after day? More than that, what would excite me in my practice of empathy?

I realized, over time, that there was a way of doing client-centered empathy that engaged me most thoroughly, so that I looked forward to each session, to "going to work" each day, expecting more excitement in my helping others. I also noticed that, as I did this emerging style (for me), my clients would, toward the end of the session, utter words like: "Yeah, that's it. That's exactly how I feel." And a very satisfied smile would cover their face. "Those aren't the words I'd use," some would say, "but it's exactly how I feel. You've got it!"

Attempting to put this new (for me) experience in a larger context, I reviewed the writings of Rogers, Rollo May, Sidney Jourard, and Abraham Maslow. I perused Eugene Gendlin's book, *Focusing*, in which he wrote about shared felt meanings, and Jerold Bozarth's book, *Person-Centered Therapy*, where he discussed reflection and empathy.

I saw how the flow of reflective empathy could be compared to jazz, as both involved the invitation to improvise, "free to choose any direction," as Rogers put it. Entrainment in body and mind could occur both among jazz musicians as well as between therapist and client, "being sensitive, moment to moment, to the changing felt meanings which flow in this other person," according to Rogers. An openness leading to togetherness exists in both. And, finally, an openness to, and mutual respect for ongoing process leading to something new rather than mere repetition exist in both good jazz as well as client-centered empathy, "a tendency to grow, to develop, to realize its full potential," in Rogers' words again.

I began to read about the neuroscience of empathy to better understand how empathy worked. There was something that Carl Rogers had initiated many decades ago that was very special and extremely effective, and now I was trying to figure out the "why" of it. As I culled over the emerging research on deep forms of empathy, I began to become aware that there were others who tried to describe it as well, using such terms as transcendental empathy, authentic knowing, linking, embodied counter-transference, and self-empathy. Tobin Hart wrote about experiencing "the other's feelings directly in my own body." A friend of mine, Maureen O'Hara, put it so well: "It is the meeting—the relationship in which two or more sovereign and sacred 'I's meet as a 'we' to engage with significant questions of existence." Rogers characterized this deep form of empathy as "entering the private perceptual world of the other." Jerold Bozarth went a step further, "entering the world of the client 'as if' the therapist were the client."

Coming back to my path of development along PCA lines, I realize that, over the years, that first meeting, walking Carl to his car after his presentation to my class at San Diego State University, continued to have its influence on me. My life continued to change as I battled with the contrast between the PCA and behaviorism, as I tried to understand the neuroscience of that special process of empathy that became so precious in my life, as I began to discern the difference between "ordinary" empathy and deeper empathy, emerging in the literature with nuanced characteristics. Toward the end of his life, Rogers expressed the following hope: "We're always on the move, to a new theory, new ways of being, to new areas of dealing with situations, new ways of being with persons. I hope that we're always a part of the 'growing edge.' "

So Carl Rogers and his associates had a great influence on me over time. And that influence had a continuing effect on my development as a professional and as a person. I learned to emphasize the importance of human connection early on. I grew increasingly interested in the process of empathy, particularly the deeper form which I naturally fell into and which emerged in the literature over the decades, I was relieved to discover. Carl Rogers, Rollo May, Abraham Maslow and others were all there at the beginning and some gave it their particular brands—Fromm's "art of loving," Buber's I-Thou connection, Jourard's "transparent self," Bugental's "search for authenticity." But whatever terms we choose to use, the PCA has had a tremendous effect on my life and that of so many others. Few people, especially among the younger generation, realize what a powerful, though subtle, influence Carl Rogers had on all our lives.

Empathy: More Powerful than Pills, Training Manuals or Reward and Punishment

Paula was a strong leader, always confident, sure of her decisions and arrogant toward those who showed any signs of weakness, such as sharing any need for emotional support. She considered herself an emotionally sensitive person, yet those who worked for her walked on eggshells for fear of her verbal diatribes. Tension danced around her like moths around a flame.

One day, her image of indestructible self-reliance shattered completely. She was juggling a project, and the deadline was missed. This was not her style. Just as she was unforgiving to others' mistakes, she was equally unforgiving to herself. During my consult with her, as she was sharing this story, she broke down in heavy sobbing, beating her forehead with her closed hands. "I'm a failure," she kept repeating through sobs. "I deserve to die."

As I tried to comfort her, her story poured out. Born in Beijing, Paula was a child when her parents and older siblings were sent to the countryside to serve the Cultural Revolution sweeping China, leaving her alone at home. She had to fend for herself, getting her own food, and the necessities for life at the tender age of 11. She had no fear, she told me, and was able to take care of herself. After the Cultural Revolution, she emigrated to the U.S. and began her education here in the States with no help from her family. She was determined to succeed, even if there was no one to help her.

Paula was strong, all right, and determined, and self-sufficient. But there was no place for her tender side, though it resided deep within her, hidden not only from society, but from her own self-awareness. With a series of PCA-trainings in her department, Paula was able to share her personal story that she had never shared before. Others saw her tender, hidden side and began to understand her decision to be such a tough fighter. With this sharing, as others empathized with her, Paula changed dramatically. She turned out to be as warm and nurturing in her style now as she was mean and demanding before. More than anyone else, she'd go out of her way and spend extra time offering assistance at the slightest need. She still did an excellent job, but now her whole team was doing a great job, rather than holding back for fear of public criticism. Her department became outstanding in terms of productivity. She now had the experience of empathy, something she was totally devoid of before. Her personality was amazingly different and this changed all her relationships. What was it about the experience of empathy, this made me wonder, that could cause such a change for the better? Why did empathy work better than pills, than training manuals, than reward and punishment?

5 Openness and Transparency in Today's Global Business World: Leadership with Vulnerability Equals Integrity

Renate:

Thank you for sharing so richly and deeply about yourself in relationship to Carl Rogers and his heritage, as well as your making sense of it and building bridges to new ideas, the realms of business and behaviorism! It feels nice to know you a bit better now. And it calls for more, if you are willing to continue?

David:

Sure, I enjoy this dialoguing. Usually, writing is quite a lonely experience, but this form of communication is different. Which of the many questions you brought up initially do you want to pursue next?

Renate:

Okay, great! Let me resume briefly. While exploring your path, we've already encountered empathic understanding and scratched transparency and openness. Let's share more on openness since it's key to our theme here. And, in the business context, it has several aspects and levels, like the strategic level, the (inter-)personal level, the impact of the Internet, etc. I'm very interested to hear your view on any of these and whether you think there is more openness at work in our time than, say, a decade ago? If so, what effect does it have?

David:

There's so much that comes to mind here. I'll explore the context first since it is essential to understanding the various intertwined levels. Business is primarily human interaction with a focus on exchange of money for goods and services. People want what business offers, or the business goes out of business. So *the focus is on people, their needs and their wants. The more a business can focus on this and convey an interest in serving the customer, the more successful it should be, other things being equal.* That's why customer service is becoming so important, as competition becomes keener in a difficult economy. The PCA is exactly what business needs to offer the best customer service. So there are at least two aspects of the PCA in business—one is the focus on service to the customer; the other is how people in business can explore their own personalities to become better communicators among themselves as they compete for the customers' attention and loyalty. So let's focus on that second aspect for now.

The myth used to be that business people have to be hard-nosed and cut-throat, leaving no stone unturned in the quest for success, even if this means deception and strategic manipulation. The metaphor was survival of the fittest, in the sense of physical superiority, a la Darwin. But even in Darwin's framework there was an error. It turns out that those species that survived did so not as much because of superior physical strength, but rather because of the ability to adapt to existing circumstances. Wilson (2012), arguably Darwin's heir, maintains in his recent book that adapting to the challenges of social grouping, not biology, has determined human evolution. Similarly, business competition is not so much size and monetary power (though that may help) but rather, the ability to adapt to emerging challenges.

Renate:

To me, what you say about the need to adapt, to stay flexible, appears to match the developmental targets of the PCA so well that I just can't hold back from jumping in here with a quote from Rogers: "The only man who is educated is the man who has learned how to learn … how to adapt and change … Change, a reliance on process rather than upon static knowledge, is the only thing that makes any sense as a goal for education in the modern world" ((Rogers 1983 p. 120). But you wanted to say more …

David:

Well, what I was thinking was that, with the emergence of electronic communication, the world became, as McLuhan (1968) predicted, a global entity with seamless connections across geographical boundaries. There is now less opportunity for hidden strategies. Not only are geographical boundaries eliminated, but so are the advantages of secrecy. Since virtually everything can be found online (including Twitter, YouTube, apps, assorted social media), aided by hackers legitimate or otherwise, there is little room for secrecy.

My point in this little trip into business mythology is that, with much less secrecy in the world of business, personal transparency becomes more de rigeur, even more advantageous. Within a functioning team, it is more acceptable to explore honest feelings among members. *What makes for the most powerful team efficiency is when its members have dealt with personal and personality differences so thoroughly that the members are freed up to express themselves with fewer defenses and therefore with a greater likelihood that any hidden talents will be more easily shared.* And, with more honest feedback from teammates (because of shared transparency), the emerging "talents" can only grow more efficient over time.

In a nutshell, my point is that openness is becoming more apparent in part because of advances in electronic communication, leading to greater openness both systemically in business organizations and therefore more "doable" in departments or teams—first the macrocosm, then the microcosm. According to the highly successful CEO of Salesforce.com, "There's also a level of openness and transparency that we're not used to … Organizations and governments who don't move to that speed and with that transparency will rapidly become obsolete" (Benioff 2011). Ironically, technological advances have paved the path for greater application of the PCA in business.

So where the image of strong self-reliance at the expense of transparency existed, there is now no longer a need for such a defensive posture. People who are quite self-reliant, such as myself, also have aspects of themselves that occasionally need nurturing. Business leaders who are self-reliant (as most are) can be free to share their need for support and nurturing occasionally within a framework of personal integrity, where they openly share their desire to be close to others and appreciated not only for their strength, but also for their basic humanity. One excellent example of that is Alan Mulally, CEO of Ford, about whom I will share more later.

6 Corporate Drift Toward the PCA: From Vindictive, Greed-Oriented Groupthink to a Diplomatic, Open-Minded, Consensus-Building Culture

Renate:
I'd also say that self-reliant people can grow through sharing and listening in the sense of extending their perspective and facilitating the growth of others while growing themselves. I like such situations and refer to them in my writings as "co-actualizing" (Motschnig-Pitrik and Barrett-Lennard 2010). For example, I can imagine that your dialogues with Carl Rogers in (Ryback 1998) were such an opportunity for mutual enrichment, even though you both were self-reliant.

David:
Yes, that's a very good point. People who are very self-reliant also have needs for human contact, though such needs are often overshadowed by their high degree of productivity. Carl Rogers was such a person—quite self-reliant, almost to a fault— yet uniquely transparent about the flow of his emotional experience, and with the refreshing ability to *communicate his feelings in a nurturing, selfless manner.*

Back to your questions on openness, there is no doubt in my mind that there is a drift to more openness at the workplace in our time, at least in a number of prominent and successful corporations. By the same token, we must be clear that there has been a number of flagrantly unsuccessful corporations that have been driven by greed rather than openness and public awareness. This kind of greed-oriented groupthink, once it convinces the top level of management, then filters down the corporate hierarchy and affects every aspect of the company's business style. *This is exactly what the PCA has to combat in terms of humanistic values versus greed.* "Wall Street is its own worst enemy," says Reich (2011), former Secretary of Labor under President Clinton. "With all its expensive lawyers and 'hired-gun "experts,"' Wall Street has a 'huge tactical advantage' for getting the rule [of government regulation] thrown out."

Business Drift to the PCA: From Domineering to Diplomatic Consensus-Building

Certain successful companies over time show clear movement toward the PCA. For example, the Disney corporation shifted from Michael Eisner's domineering style to the more consensus-building style of Robert Iger. Hewlett-Packard chose low-key Mark Hurd over the self-promoting Carly Fiorina. Intel moved to the more diplomatic Paul Otellini and away from the

---

rough-and-tumble Andy Grove. A *Business Week* article pointed out the drift toward the PCA, not mentioning that term, of course, but describing Intel as displaying "more of an open mind-set than in years past."

The clear success of automaker Ford over its American competitors is in no small part due to its drift toward PCA values. This shift began when Bill Ford, Jr. took over from the aggressive, rigid style of his predecessor. A student of Buddhist philosophy and an avid naturalist, Bill Ford was much more people-oriented. Putting the success of his legacy ahead of personal gain, Ford then turned the reins over to former Boeing executive, Alan Mulally, whom the *Wall Street Journal* characterized as a "gregarious man ... an executive with a strong track record for building teamwork in a large organization," with his desire for "a teamwork-oriented, collegial management culture." How can the PCA be manifested in such a large organization? By being aware of needs and aspirations from all sides, no small task. In Mulally's own words, "You talk to customers, dealers, Ford employees, UAW, your suppliers, your investors—everybody ... I need to network with these groups."

In Germany, a similar drift toward PCA values was occurring among the management of the most distinguished auto brand, Daimler-Benz in early 2005. When it joined with an American partner, Chrysler, Daimler-Chrysler shifted from the personality-driven Jurgen Schrempp to the more PCA style of Dr. Dieter Zetsche, much more laid back and people-oriented.

Renate:
Let me interrupt you just for one remark. My colleague-friend, Helmuth Beutel, worked as a coach for Daimler-Benz at that time. He promoted the motto: P-P-P in the order: Person, then Product, then Profit! This sounds very consistent with what you're bringing up here.

David:
Yes, I like that. It puts the person at the top of the priority list, even for a company so intensely focused on technology. There are some indications that a trend toward humanistic values characterized by the PCA is evident across the globe. Back in America, in Atlanta, Georgia, Home Depot was also making a shift toward the PCA. Robert Nardelli, characterized by the business community as number-oriented and autocratic, was, in early 2007, replaced by Frank Blake, a people-oriented, PCA-type person. Bernie Marcus, one of the two founders of Home Depot, characterized Blake as "a great listener and a good people person." The chief of the big utility firm, Southern Company, said: "He will listen twice as much as he speaks." When I met with Blake, I found him to be courtly and a good listener. He said, "You'll see the associates and customers at the top, and me as CEO at the bottom."

Though not all companies are going in this direction, it does appear that there is a trend to PCA values in many successful corporations. In her book, *The DNA of Leadership*, Glaser (2006) sees companies remaining autocratic as creating a vindictive, politicized atmosphere leading to competitive conflict within the organization. Legendary leader Jack Welch maintains that "lack of candor permeates almost all aspects of business." There is clearly a need for more movement toward PCA values. Candor, a mainstay of the PCA, is one of the strengths of the modern corporation dealing with increasing challenges in a troubled global economy.

So, to answer your question about whether there is more openness in business these days as opposed to a decade ago, I would answer a tentative yes. But I can say with certainty that there is more *awareness* of the need for what we know as PCA values in business, and I've tried to give some examples that have worked for certain corporations who have managed to continue to prevail in this troubled economy.

7 Handling the Truth, Leading with Openness and Ensuring a "Safe Space" to Explore Differences

Renate:
I like your exploration on a broader, strategic level and how these impactful developments are sparked by persons holding respective values and acting on them. David, one other question on openness on a more personal level is still on my mind. You know, Rogers had emphasized openness, if appropriate. Now, I've often been told that with some superiors you can't be open or otherwise you'd risk your job. Do you have any responses to those who'd like to be more open, authentic, but can't afford to lose their job?

David:
Well, as for risking one's job by being too open with the boss, my response would be that openness, in the true spirit of the PCA, is not a matter of spitting out everything that comes to mind, but rather a discriminating attitude. Carl himself explained that he might share one of his provocative thoughts only if it remained in his consciousness for a while, allowing ephemeral reactions to remain more private.

My own take on this is that PCA-honesty is as much an acquired attribute as it is a moral quality. PCA-openness involves three components, in my estimation:

1. Your *inner truth* about the matter at hand,
2. *Awareness of the audience* or hearer of your "truth," and his/her/their sensibility about the matter at hand, and
3. A consideration for the *relevance of your* "truth" to the matter at hand.
   With these three components in mind, I believe speaking honestly to your boss is to be commended.

Renate:

This makes a lot of sense to me, David, and is definitely something one can consciously try. Even if the real situation might be much more complex and you won't be sure about the relevance. What helped me a lot, once I had read your book on *"Putting* EI *to Work,"* was to prepare for meetings by clarifying my "inner truth." This allowed me to "listen for inner resonances and dissonances" with the situation at hand and thus provided valuable information. Often I could experience what Rogers had already found and expressed so persuasively and which also plays a central role in your book, namely that the "wisdom" of the whole organism with feelings and meanings, thought, logic exceeds that of "pure reason" as well as that of pure emotions.

Now, let's see where this can take us in the realm of teamwork, something that is becoming ever more essential in our intertwined and complex world. If each person in a team was aware of their "inner truth" and its relationship to the situation at hand, couldn't such a team perform better than one under the leadership of one person? In other words, what do you think about self-organizing or self-managed teams as one other innovative aspect in management that you illuminated so vividly in your 1998 book?

David:

As for self-organizing teams, that is a complex issue. All businesses start off with structure, very early with a business plan, and later with a plan to structure the organization with assigned responsibilities. There is very little research on self-managed teams. My own experience is that it works best when the "players" are responsible individuals to begin with. Self-organized teams work best when each individual can be counted on to use his/her initiative and sense of integrity without needing structure from others. It also works best when there is at least *one strong personality to provide* "safe harbor" *for the inevitable conflicts* that arise when individuals struggle to solve problems with different approaches. Carl Rogers himself was the best model for such interaction that I have ever witnessed. These struggles need to be resolved in an open manner where all are privy to the dynamics involved. It is then that the team becomes a powerful force of productivity.

It certainly helps if all participants are highly caring, empathic and congruent in order to ensure the team's effectiveness, but the team could still be effective if the major thrust of the combined personality of the group has these characteristics. In other words, the "strong personality" (and this could be a shared quality between two or among three or four "leaders") has a powerful effect on the group's personality.

Renate:

So it seems there are multiple ways in which teams can be effective. And, more research on self-organizing team is definitely needed. I'd fully subscribe to that. I guess Jef, Michael and I could start researching our self-organizing cooperation in editing this book. I sense we're a truly self-organized team and I enjoy learning a lot in a highly constructive way through that work. We have fun too, of course. And what about you, David, would you like to share any personal experience you had in a self-organizing team or group? How about another example?

David:
Sure. And, you know, much of this is subtle. So here's an example, which you asked for, from my experience with self-organizing groups: During my early years, I was in a very large group and the assigned leaders decided to test this principle. They made an announcement that they were yielding their leadership status completely and would just be on the sidelines in case of emergency. They were leaving their leadership roles completely.

Almost immediately, I stepped in to fill the leadership vacuum and began asking questions of the group. Another individual also appeared in a quest to be in a leadership position. There was absolutely no conflict between the two of us. I was not intending to become the leader; rather I was wanting to *help the group reach the decisions as to what direction it wanted to go in.* My leading "partner" and I immediately blended in our "personality style." My aim was to allow as much emotional openness as possible. Very quickly, individuals began to utter what their needs were and teams began to form almost seamlessly according to mutually shared objectives. I had never experienced such a strong dynamic in terms of self-organization until that experience.

My point is that *the qualities of the* "leader" *or* "strong personality" *(or* "soft personality" *in terms of softly spoken) or, to use a PCA term, facilitator, is of utmost importance. That individual bears a strong responsibility to ensure a sense of safety for unconventional openness.* And that person's influence is more important than the PCA qualities of the team members involved, though they are important as well.

Let George Do It: The Subtle Power of a "Safe Place" for Open Questions

At one point, a committee I was part of was looking for the right leader for a long-term project. The one we all thought would be the right one, George, decided that the challenge was more than he wanted to take on. I continued to ask George what about the project was too much. Without going into unnecessary detail, as we explored his fears, it turned out that George was really OK with the project after all and has continued as its successful leader for years. What made this dramatic turn in his life and in the success of the organization? Looking back, I'd have to say it must have been the gentle support in creating a "safe place" to share his concerns. Without that, everyone would have accepted his denying the position and his life possibly might have been much less satisfying, in terms of his career. I guess a lot of this process had to do with the perseverance to create that "safe space" to open up about his concerns which, once shared, were easily dealt with and overcome.

8 Person-Centered Teams: From Personal Development to Bottom-Line Business

Renate:
So, if I understand you correctly, the "strong/soft personality" is vital, a facilitative leader, so to speak. This can be one individual or a shared quality among members. This is exciting for me, to look out for shared leadership qualities. Sure, I agree leadership is pivotal in traditional structures, but I haven't thought it to be so important in self-managed teams. I thought relevant, vision-related competencies and, essentially interpersonal qualities in the sense of PCA values would be primary. In other words, strength in relating to others while cooperating toward shared objectives would come first. When I think about this more deeply, I get a sense that a strong, shared vision (e.g., Senge 2006), paired with close and effective collaboration, could "substitute" for the leader in a small team. At least, this is something that worked in my experience and I thought it was consistent with the "New Team Ethic" chapter in your 1998 book. Is my understanding of it inaccurate or did you move on to a different stance on this?

In any case, I also have some experiences from (not only) person-centered encounter groups that confirm your view: Decision-making can take endlessly long and this full democracy, as we might call it, surely wouldn't be effective in business. So you see, I've not yet found my full "inner truth" on that and would be curious whether my exploration sparked any further ideas in you?

David:
Your thinking is razor-sharp. What you're detecting is the different ideologies between "leaderless" groups on the one hand and, on the other, PCA-type groups led by effective leaders. So here's my thinking on that as of this moment. For starters, most groups would need a "strong/soft" leader to begin the process of trusting the "safe place" to open up. Of course, that leadership could be shared between or among compatible leaders.

On the other hand, there are groups of individuals who already share most of the PCA values who might be able to move ahead forming their own leaderless group because no one in the group is resisting the PCA values. You, Michael and Jef are one good example. You already share the PCA values so you go ahead and complete the project without having to battle about the principles by which you work together.

There is little doubt in my mind that team members involved in such an experience are very highly affected in a very positive manner. *They develop a balance between self-confidence or "new" assertiveness and sensitivity to others' feelings.*

Renate:
From my own experience, I fully subscribe to what you just said. I'd describe working in such a team as highly experiential, enriching, truly challenging at times and also fun. In your view, all in all, does it make sense to delineate the notion of a

person-centered team, in particular? How would you characterize a person-centered team and how would it exist in business?

David:
Based on all this, I would describe the notion of a person-centered team as one characterized primarily by a priority on emotional sensitivity to all members, at the expense of any originally designed hierarchy based on status, and hearing all voices, no matter how soft or hesitant. The term "person-centered" in business has a strange sound to it. Of course, everyone in business would accept that wording, as business is about people, as I mentioned previously. So there would be no question about the acceptance of that term. The term "brainstorming" might help, as that refers to people sharing their ideas without prior judgment or criticism. Perhaps the emphasis, in the business world, might be on that blameless type of communication where everybody can speak freely, and *the criterion for acceptance is that it supports productivity, or some other bottom line* of a particular business. So relevance becomes important. Now we can see more clearly why the PCA finds difficulty in finding a comfortable seat in the world of business.

In therapy or counseling, the end point being sought is personal growth and development. In business, it's a bottom line of some sort—productivity, profit, etc. Personal development is part of the process in business, but the primary focus is more materialistic. So that's where the challenge is.

In both counseling and business, however, the PCA value system puts the responsibility of being heard on both the person having something to say and the other members of the group. Thus, decisions become much more consensual rather than based on competitive personalities and end up as what the group considers most important, once all voices have been heard. In a sense, this is democracy in its most primal form.

9 Savvy Leadership: How to Compete Without Losing Sight of Humanistic Values

Renate:
As you might imagine, I like what you say about the PCA being "democracy in its most primal form" and "going PCA" although it means taking a risk. This is because, much too often, I've heard otherwise. For example, when presenting research results, like students' improvement in team competences after participating in a course based on the PCA, I tend to hear: "Nice, but this approach wouldn't work with organizations; it's too individualistic!" To me this sounds unfair and ignorant of all that has been done on interpersonal relationships and encounter groups. So I see there's still a lot to do, and who knows how open people are toward revising their beliefs.

David:

The question whether Rogers' theory is too individualistic is difficult to answer satisfactorily. I strongly believe that the relatively recent concept of EI (yet already over 15 years old as popularized by Daniel Goleman) has been fairly successful in bringing PCA values to the corporate world. Research focusing on bottom-line financial figures has been very convincing as to the benefits of PCA values—such as empathy and emotional awareness—to financial success. And there appears to be a "second wind" or resurgence of interest in EI, particularly as evidenced by the recent success of such books as *Primal Leadership, Building* EI, *Social Intelligence,* EI *2.0, The Brain and* EI, *Go Suck a Lemon, Leadership* and others.

Renate:

So David, at this point, would you like to share your idea about what's most important for EI and PCA values to get into the realm of management?

David:

I have been thinking about how challenging it is to apply the PCA to the business environment. I think it can be done more easily with groups of people who are already committed to the PCA. Otherwise, there may be too much "static." Though I think there is a movement in that direction, there is still the competition in the marketplace for financial goals as primary and that seems contrary to the PCA.

Renate:

Sure, working with persons who already have internalized some or rather much of the PCA value base would come first. Then, I'd like to better understand what you mean by: "too much 'static.' " Is it like there may be too much profit motive learned and rigidly imposed from a traditional business culture so that it's hard for people to "unlearn" and open up to values such as open-mindedness, honesty, listening to the other for real understanding, etc?

David:

I think that the values of the traditional business world are first of all highly competitive. The PCA can only be approached from a flexible value system. A business cannot succeed without competing with other similar businesses. The dilemma is to combine the PCA with such values. I think it can be done, though not in a naive, innocent way but rather in a way that stays competitive along with values that are more humanistic. *It requires a very special type of leadership that is savvy—understands the needs to compete and how to do so successfully—but also humanistic in its values.* That's why I mentioned those corporations such as Hewlett-Packard, Home Depot and Ford that seem to be going in that direction. Their CEOs are not naive or "innocent," but rather very skilled in working with people. It's that very special skill of working well with people that can make the PCA work in business, at least to some extent, or maybe to a larger extent if the leader is skilled and committed to the PCA.

10 Emotional Intelligence: The Gateway for Translating PCA Language to Business

Renate:

As I read this, it strikes me that what you're writing, using words that would resonate with business representatives, make me immediately recall the person-centered value base, although relating to a whole field, rather than a person. Let me clarify by trying to "translate" and I hope I'm not overstretching Rogers' ideas here, but this is how they exist in me: Your expression, "the values of the business world are first of all competitive and then the PCA can be approached," can be read to mean accepting and respecting the needs of the other (the business context here) first. Then, David, your words, "It requires a … leadership that is savvy … understands the needs to compete and how to do so successfully," underlines the need for empathic understanding in a wider sense—to the organization as an entity—than empathizing with the inner world of a customer. Although that would be a central part, it calls for understanding the whole situation with all its complexity. However, all this respect and extended empathic understanding would be based on your realness or congruence, in your words—"with values that are more humanistic"—as a basic precondition, a "sine qua non condition."

I agree it's essential to use the customers' terminology if you want to be heard at all. And I fully agree that combining the PCA with business values creates a dilemma, a real challenge. And, as you can imagine, I do appreciate you not only thinking the combination can be achieved but actually investing yourself in acting on the challenge in your own way!

David:

Yes, Renate, you're on target here—*the challenge is to* "translate," *as you say, from the counseling culture to the business culture*—exactly! How do we translate the PCA from person-centered to business-centered without losing the values of the humanistic person? That's where EI becomes so helpful. In the framework of EI, two things happen that are crucial:

1. The humanistic values are "translated" into the business culture. Of the four components of EI, three of them have to do with emotions—two with emotional awareness (of self and of others) and one with emotional self-management (of anger or stress, in particular).
2. The principles having to do with emotions are proposed as helpful toward the bottom line and ongoing research confirms this. There is no reason to apologize for the focus on emotional awareness and authenticity. If anything, companies now often feel apologetic for not being cognizant of EI in their business practices.

That's why I think EI is such a strong move in that direction. It takes the PCA values of emotional honesty, altruism, authenticity, nurturing style and applies it to business in a very straightforward manner. And it seems to be increasing in popularity and acceptance over the years. Even the highly successful business author, Stephen Covey, "translates" Rogers' concept of mutual understanding into another best seller, *The 3rd Alternative* (2011), in which he encourages empathy between entities in conflict, packaging Rogers' classic ideas in a new bottle. Can you understand now why I used that as a framework for my book which is really about Carl Rogers' values?

11 Carl Rogers' Values in Business: "The Perfect Client Experience"

Renate:

I can understand, David, and I smile now as I understood immediately when I read your book over a decade ago. To me, the PCA value base shines through brilliantly and I know that Carl Rogers wasn't particular about how follow-up approaches would call themselves, as long as the core values would be passed on. Furthermore, in my perception, you express your derivation of core values from Carl Rogers and your deep sympathy to him and his ideas in a way that speaks to me deeply, then and now, and each time again as I turn to your book.

Yes, I understand that the path for the future must not be a naïve one but rather one that combines business-oriented and PCA values, and one that doesn't neglect leadership competence but is strong in a democratic sense of facilitation where humanness including emotions count.

Let me once again get back to what you said before. One other immediate and very strong reaction that your sentence, "I think it (PCA in management) can be done more easily with groups of people who are already committed to the PCA," raises in me: YES; and that's why it is so vital that at schools and universities we embody and pass on these values. This insight, of course, doesn't provide a quick fix for current problems but, to me, seems to be the way for the future to enable the change we want to see. Any reaction to this?

David:

Here's my brief response: First of all, I very much appreciate your recognition of my respect, and even love, for Carl Rogers. My appreciation for him has grown over the years since his passing, as I struggle with the application of his ideas, as well as his personhood, to the world of business. He was always a joy to be with, in my experience, but now I also see the richness and the unique and special quality that he brought forth wherever he was, whenever he spoke in public, and whenever he published his ideas. Yet I've always avoided expressing my feelings about him, focusing only on his contributions. So I thank you for facilitating my feeling for him and allowing them to come to the surface. (I guess that says something about your sensitivity and emotional awareness!)

Second, your comments make me realize something new—that *Rogers himself had that capacity to make his humanistic approach work for different cultures:*

from counseling to education, then on to international conflict, but not yet business. Possibly, had he lived longer, he might have accomplished more in that area with which we are now struggling.

Carl made us aware how much teachers needed the PCA. He alluded to the fact that even educational administrators and leaders might benefit. Certainly, warring nations and groups benefited from Carl's intervention with his approach, e.g., his work in Northern Ireland (bringing Catholics and Protestants together) and other areas, his and my research (1984) on international negotiations (between Israel and Egypt). So, bottom line is that education and politics would be far greater in aiding people develop and survive with the application of the PCA. And yet the struggle between the PCA and more conventional, competitive approaches persists. So our work is cut out for us. And, yes, I agree with you that it could best start in the educational process in our schools and universities.

Renate:
So far, for the mid-term strategy, and for the shorter term, do you have any idea on how we can address management and invite them to listen more openly?

David:
The best way to convince management to spend more on the development of empathy and emotional awareness is to share with them the research done by the advocates of EI. The data reveal that such development results in greater merit increases and job satisfaction, less turnover (63 % in one study), increased sales figures (an increase of over $2,000,000 at L'Oreal), improved leadership skills, and overall job success and team performance (saving the U.S. Air Force $3,000,000 a year, according to the U.S. Government Accounting Office).

So, over time, there is more awareness of the need for what we know as the PCA. Whether or not there is more at the executive level is quite difficult to estimate, but, clearly, executives and managers are learning more and more about PCA values. The increasing focus on customer relations and customer service makes clear that we are indeed moving in that direction. We can feel it as customers—clerks and service providers typically come closer to being person-centered than they have in the past. Just this morning, I went to open up a bank account and, in the process, the bank agent handed me a card which he signed. On it were four promises to be reliable, responsive, competent, and empathetic. Next to this last item was the statement: "I listen to you and am sensitive to your feelings." The motto on the side of the card read: "The Perfect Client Experience."

Ultimately, in this highly competitive world of business, those with PCA sensibilities will prevail. And, as I've tried to illustrate, businesses that are comfortable with the PCA seem to succeed more often than their autocratic competitors. As Brown (2011/2012), former director of the famed Xerox PARC R&D lab, puts it: "If you can't empathize with others, it's very hard to solve their problems."

The PCA, engendered by Carl Rogers over a half-century ago, is certainly finding its place in the sun, not necessarily by that name, but certainly by the values it espouses. And the Internet, with all its faults, has given unprecedented voice to these values, not only in business, but in other arenas as well.

Thank you, Carl Rogers, for building bridges to many areas, and now, business.

Renate:

No doubt … and as a consequence there is clearly a need to adapt the classical model of the PCA more sensitively to make it accessible and even desirable to managers and employees in businesses and a multitude of arenas, as you're saying. Personally, I strongly believe that more of the PCA values could drift into the workplace and higher effectiveness could be accomplished if more of the colleagues in the PCA community became excited about this vision and were received by management, then their offering of the core conditions—adapted to the management context, as you illustrated—could be reciprocated, at least to a modest degree. So, if our readers can take some inspiration from our sharing, and even follow up on some of these ideas, then this chapter may leave its mark on the course of the PCA in the world of business.

David:

I certainly agree completely with your perspective, Renate. That's what this chapter is all about—an important step in that direction. Bringing the PCA to the world of business is a challenge, and you and I have tackled that challenge, hopefully in a way that others can relate to and bring to the marketplace. The PCA is making its way into management, and there's no turning back. If Carl could know this, he'd be smiling with a sense of great fulfillment.

References

Benioff, M. (2011). Charlie Rose talks to Marc Benioff. *Bloomberg Businessweek,* Dec. 5, p. 52.

Brown, J. S. Quoted in Stone, B. (2011/2012). Meanwhile, in silicon valley. *Bloomberg Businessweek, 8,* 60–64.

Covey, S. R. (2011). *The 3rd alternative*. New York: Free Press.

Glaser, J. (2006). *The DNA of leadership*. Cincinnati: Platinum Press.

McLuhan, M. (1968). *War and peace in the global village*. New York: Bantam.

Motschnig-Pitrik, R., & Barrett-Lennard, G. T. (2010). Co-actualization: A new construct for understanding well-functioning relationships. *Journal of Humanistic Psychology, 50*(3), 374–398.

Reich, R. (2011). Wall street has only itself to blame. *The Week,* Dec. 30, p. 46.

Rogers, C. R. (1961). *On becoming a person: A psychotherapist's view of psychotherapy*. London: Constable.

Rogers, C. R. (1983). *Freedom to learn for the 80's*. Columbus: C. E. Merrill.

Rogers, C. R., & Ryback, D. (1984). One alternative to nuclear planetary suicide. In R. F. Levant & J. M. Shlien (Eds.), *Client-centered therapy and the person-centered approach*. New York: Praeger.

Ryback, D. (1998). *Putting emotional intelligence to work*. Boston: Butterworth-Heinemann.

Ryback, D. (2012). Humanism and behaviorism. In L. L'Abate (Ed.), *Paradigms in theory construction*. New York: Springer.

Senge, P. M. (2006). *The fifth discipline: The art and practice of the learning organization.* New York: Crown Business.
Wilson, O. W. (2012). *The social conquest of earth.* New York: Norton.

Author Biographies

David Ryback received his Ph.D. from the University of Hawaii and then travelled through Europe and Asia for a couple of years to further his education in human nature. He returned to Georgia to direct a conference on humanistic education to which he invited Carl Rogers, as keynote speaker, and then a working friendship ensued, resulting in a co-authored paper, "One alternative to nuclear planetary suicide." After years as associate editor of the *Journal of Humanistic Psychology*, David settled into consulting with business and government organizations on applying the principles that Rogers engendered to make bottom-line success more easily attainable. He is the author of *Putting Emotional Intelligence to Work* (Butterworth-Heinemann) and *ConnectAbility: 8 Keys to Building Strong Partnerships with Your Colleagues* (McGraw-Hill) and is book review editor for *The American Journal of Family Therapy*. With fiction writing as his hobby, David is under contract with Tiger Iron Press to publish his first novel, *Beethoven in Love,* due out in 2013.

Renate Motschnig born in Ostrava, Czech Republic, is a professor of computer science and head of the Computer Science Didactics and Learning Research Center at the University of Vienna, Austria. Renate held positions at the RWTH Aachen in Germany, the University of Toronto, Canada, and teaches and cooperates with at the Masaryk University in Brno, Czech Republic. She participated in encounter groups and several events based on the person-centered approach. She is deeply interested in the multiple ways in which mutual understanding and whole-person learning happen. She is an author of more than 130 scientific articles, one book, and is determined to foster a style in education that is based on person-centered attitudes, our co-actualizing potential and thoughtful support by web-based technology. She appreciates synergies between presence and distance, and a multitude of (scientific) disciplines and cultures.

Person-Centred Approach: Theory and Practice in a Non-therapeutic Context

Eva Sollárová and Tomáš Sollár

1 Position of the PCA in the Context of Humanistic and Mainstream Psychology

There are attempts to advance humanistic psychology and psychotherapy in the twenty-first century. Among these, Cain (2003) identifies and comments on problems and challenges faced by humanistic psychology: humanistic psychology's minimal representation in American universities, declining membership in humanistic organisations, a lack of a coherent and shared vision, a plan for future development and strategies to enhance the growth and impact of humanistic psychology and psychotherapy. He offers concrete proposals to address these challenges facing humanistic psychology and to stimulate action.

Among those, Cain asks *whether humanistic psychology addresses relevant issues* with potential to make a meaningful contribution to psychology and the public. He thinks that humanistic psychologists "have fallen short in addressing relevant issues... and do not appear to be addressing adequately the major areas of importance of mainstream academic or clinical/applied psychology... the domain of humanistic psychology should not be limited to only those areas where it has tended to focus (e.g. human relations, personal growth)" (Cain 2003, p. 16). On the other side, he can see the unlimited potential of humanistic psychology in contributing to any area of psychology.

The aim of the Old Saybrook 2 Conference that took place in 2000 was to reassess and re-envisage contemporary humanistic psychology. Warmoth (2001) reflects on an authentic sense of the unfulfilled potential of humanistic psychology

E. Sollárová (✉) · T. Sollár
Faculty of Social Sciences and Health Care, Institute of Applied Psychology,
Constantine the Philosopher University, Kraskova 1, 949 74 Nitra, Slovakia
e-mail: esollarova@ukf.sk

T. Sollár
e-mail: tsollar@ukf.sk

J. H. D. Cornelius-White et al. (eds.), *Interdisciplinary Applications*
of the Person-Centered Approach, DOI: 10.1007/978-1-4614-7144-8_16,
© Springer Science+Business Media New York 2013

as well as discussions and work done to expand the professional applications of the field beyond the area of psychotherapy.

Humanistic psychologists agree that there are plenty of situations in which traditional humanistic thoughts, values and skills are applicable. Facilitating situations and conversations focused on conflict resolution or cooperative problem-solving, willingness to take personal risks, or active listening, which can all be useful in a wide variety of organisational and community settings.

The idea of developing optimal human functioning and well-being was an inherent focus on humanistic psychology theory and practice from its beginnings in the 1960s; although these ideas were primarily applied within humanistic psychotherapy, they became clearly articulated and a part of psychological mainstream approaches under the heading of positive psychology, thanks to Seligman's initiatives and work in 2000 and 2008 (Seligman 2000, 2008)..

Among humanistic psychologists, there are two standpoints visible—either blaming Seligman for not giving humanistic psychology the role it deserved and claiming that positive psychology has usurped what already had been established in humanistic psychology (Taylor and Martin 2001; Cain 2003) or accepting the fact that the emergence of positive psychology "has provided a conceptual home for researchers and practitioners interested in all aspects of optimal human functioning…" (Linley and Joseph 2004, p. 3).

We totally agree with this evaluation of the potential of humanistic psychology and present our understanding of the potential of the person-centred approach (PCA) in addressing some important areas beyond psychotherapy that we consider important for the academic and applied psychology mainstream. We also reconsider the topic presented in the perspective of historical inputs of the PCA as the base for our present understanding, experience and proposals for future developments.

2 Core Thoughts of the PCA Influential for Non-therapeutic Contexts

Among many historical inputs of PCA that have a great potential for its further development beyond the area of psychotherapy, we will mention selected thoughts and values of humanistic psychotherapy, the concept of the fully functioning person and the process of developing optimal personality functioning. The overview will help find the answer whether or how new the topic of PCA beyond the psychotherapeutic context is.

2.1 Thoughts and Values of Humanistic Psychotherapy

Seeman (2002), in his understanding of the link between humanistic thoughts and values and humanistic psychotherapy, stresses the "emphasis on the positive value of helping people to maximize their optimal human potentialities" (p. 617). He points out four major themes or major characteristics that represent a *unifying framework for humanistic psychotherapy:*

- *Whole-Person Perspective* as the dominant aspect of the therapist's approach that involves the emphasis on the theme of *self.*
- *Strong Emphasis on Optimal Personality and Positive Functioning* that fits in with an interest in human potentialities and with a positive view of human nature. Rogers (1961) description of "the fully functioning person" or Seeman's (1983, 2008) research on positive health is an example illustrating the accent on optimal functioning.
- *Accent on Whole-Person Communication* and on "Presentness" and "Experiencing" in Therapeutic Practice "implemented" in and through the therapeutic relationship.
- *Emphasis on Relationship and Connectedness*—also supported by the research on empathy helping to recognise its central role in the therapeutic process.

The aforementioned characteristics are not limited to psychotherapeutic context, even though; they have been predominantly applied and verified within it. As early as in 1951, Rogers presented in his book client-centred psychotherapy (Rogers 1951) not only his revolutionary ("current") view of the client-centred therapy but also its applications beyond psychotherapy (group-centred leadership and student-centred teaching) and implications for psychological theory of personality and behaviour. Later, in 1959, in his work "Theory of Therapy, Personality and Interpersonal Relationships, as developed in the Client-Centred Framework", Rogers (1959) differentiated between applications of the theory and the approach which the therapy is based on. He proposed a general philosophy of life and relationships. Thus, the concept of the fully functioning person and the conditions facilitating the development towards such an optimally developed personality are readily available within the PCA, extending its potential far beyond psychotherapy.

2.2 The Concept of the Fully Functioning Person

Seeman (2002), in exploring possibilities for further development of humanistic psychotherapy, stresses *the potential of the concept of the fully functioning person in providing directions of development.* The concept according to Seeman encompasses both the whole-person idea and the fulfilment of personal potentialities that mark the goals of humanistic psychotherapy.

The concept has been quite intensively studied in the context of humanistic psychology. It represents one of top emphases in the content of the Journal of Humanistic Psychology since its beginning in 1961 (Taylor and Martin 2001) or almost 30 years of its empirical verifications carried out by Seeman and his team

(Seeman 1983, 2008). The concept of optimal human functioning is also high on the agenda of positive psychology (Linley and Joseph 2004).

Rogers originally wrote the paper on the concept of the fully functioning person in 1952–1953, and he published it in its original form in 1963 (Rogers 1963).

Rogers presents "speculations" on the general characteristics of the person who has completed psychotherapy. He presented the picture of the fully functioning person after he had formed a picture from his experience with his clients. It is his picture of what constitutes personal or psychological health.

According to Rogers (1962, p. 32), such a person is

> *sensitively open to all of his experience* – sensitive to what is going on in his environment, sensitive to other individuals with whom he is in a relationship, and sensitive to the feelings, reactions, and emergent meanings which he discovers in himself. The fear of some aspects of his own experience continues to diminish, so that more and more of his life is available to him. Such a person *experiences in the present*, with immediacy. He is able to live in his feelings and reactions to the moment... He lives freely, subjectively, in an existential confrontation of this moment in life. Such a person is *trusting*ly able to permit *his* total *organism* to function freely in all its complexity in selecting that behavior which in that moment of time will be most generally and genuinely satisfying. (p. 33)

The trends Rogers has presented describe an individual who is *becoming integrated*. He is unified within himself from the surface level to the level of depth. He is becoming "all of one piece". The distinctions between "role self" and "real self", between defensive façade and real feelings and between conscious and unconscious are all growing less the further these trends continue. All that the individual experiences and is, within the envelope of his organism, is increasingly available to his conscious self, to himself as a person. There is a continuing growth of good communication between all the different aspects and facets of his or herself. Such a person is a *creative person*. With his sensitive openness to his world, and his trust in his own ability to form new relationships with his environment, he is the type of person from whom creative products and creative living emerge.

Finally, such a person lives a life which involves a wider range, a greater richness, than the constricted living in which most people find themselves..., and the reason they can thus live fully in a wider range is that they have this underlying *confidence in themselves as trustworthy* instruments for encountering life.

Rogers sees every person as having the potential to grow and to fully function if specified conditions are present. "A way of being" based on PCA qualities is open to anybody regardless of his/her profession or role. Becoming fully functioning is an implicit goal not just for therapy but for self-actualised life in general. Describing "the world of tomorrow" and "the person of tomorrow" in A Way of Being (Rogers 1980) or On Personal Power (Rogers 1977) he presents his view of a radically new world with such a kind of person—those who decided to develop in fuller correspondence with their own integrity, as a consequence of their decision made either in therapy or at work. The impact of such people on society and how Rogers describes his vision fully meets the criteria of a citizen that corresponds with the present agenda of positive psychology. Rogers' visions used to be criticised as naïve while the same agenda under the heading of positive psychology is accepted as a legitimate psychological mainstream theme.

2.3 The Development of an Optimally Functioning Personality

Rogers' observations are made from a background of client-centred therapy. He assumes that all successful psychotherapy has a similar personality outcome. The answer to the question *what conditions are necessary so a person can become fully functioning* is expressed in the central hypothesis of client-centred therapy, according to which a person has enormous potential inside himself/herself to understand himself/herself or to change the self-image of his or her attitudes and self-managing behaviour, and that it is possible to get to these sources only when a certain definable atmosphere is provided to facilitate psychological attitudes or qualities—emphatic understanding, congruence, and unconditional positive acceptance (Rogers 1951). These conditions create the basis for the process of a client that facilitates his or her own personal development.

Seeman (2002) in his description of psychotherapy according to the human system model, specifies that "psychotherapy is a process in which the therapist helps the client to explore his or her modes of communication, enhance communication clarity and effectiveness, and foster maximal organismic connectedness and integration"... while the fully functioning person is characterised by an optimal level of organismic connectedness and integration (p. 629).

These conditions or characteristics of the process are applicable not only for the relationship between therapist and a client but according to Rogers (1980) between a parent and a child, a leader and a group, a teacher and a pupil or the superior and the subordinate. These conditions are applicable for every situation where the development of personality is involved. The characteristics valid for psychotherapy according to Rogers are applicable also to all of the abovementioned relationships.

Related to our research and practical experience, we would like to concentrate on one of potential application of PCA beyond psychotherapy—PCA in organisations.

2.4 PCA Beyond the Psychotherapeutic Context: Is it New?

Ten years after introducing client-centred psychotherapy, Rogers comments on its development from a method of counselling to an approach to human relationships applicable to a variety of activities, some of them very distinct from psychotherapy itself (Rogers 1951, p. 12). Tom Gordon in the same book presents a definition of a social therapeutic approach—a group-centred approach—in group leadership and organisational administration as well as experiences from application of the principles and philosophy of client-centred psychotherapy to supervision and administration of groups. Those experiences stimulated thinking about "therapeutic group leadership" with a new concept of leadership, where a leader would "facilitate the distribution of leadership, and would accelerate the development of a group toward the maximum utilization of its potential" (Rogers 1951, p. 333). The primary concern of the "group-centred" leader is to facilitate the group's development, help the group clarify and achieve its goals and help the group to actualise itself. The group's development is facilitated when a group-centred leader tries to create the same conditions which in client-centred therapy have been found necessary for releasing the constructive forces within the client: the members of the group have the opportunity to participate and freedom to communicate, in a non-threatening psychological climate.

In the 1960s, the encounter and "T-group" movement preceded organisational development theory and practice. For both the PCA and the whole of humanistic psychology, it is valid to say that since the 1970s, their impact on organisational development and management theory has lessened. As Montuori and Purser (2001) comment, managers in a changed socio-economic environment during and after the 1970s—turbulent and unpredictable—preferred practical tools and result-oriented interventions leading to pragmatic results and outcomes to "touchy-feely" group process-type interventions, which was how humanistic approaches were viewed.

We have shown that the field beyond therapy was articulated by Rogers and his team as early as the early 1950s (Rogers 1951), in proposing the PCA as the application of client-centred therapy in others—non-therapeutic settings. The approach has been validated since then in the practice of various caring professions, education, organisations and the public in general.

What has been an implicit goal of all the work in all these settings or, with the "non-client" participants of these activities, was to facilitate the development of optimal human functioning and well-being regardless of how the "content" of work was specified or became specified. How the work was done was by employing the qualities of facilitators that correspond with the conditions Rogers proclaimed as necessary and sufficient for personality change.

In practice, it means that PCA, with its theory specifying where, what and how to work and live, is fully compatible with what at present is articulated under the heading of positive psychology, more specifically applied positive psychology: the following 3 themes are aimed to contribute to the discussion of what and how to increase the impact of humanistic psychology within psychology as a science as well as in practice.

3 The Process of Developing Optimal Personality Functioning in the Therapeutic Versus Non-therapeutic Context

There is a large applicability of the findings based on the way one's own capacities can be released to change one's personality and the way in which relationships (mainly) can reinforce such a self-oriented change.

One of the applications is also in *education/training, facilitating and interventions*, which have been, in a theoretical and practical way, dealt with by Rogers (e.g. Rogers 1951, 1983). This approach is fully relevant to the many types of effective education for children, students and adults. The meta-analysis of Cornelius-White (2007) synthesising 119 studies from 1948 to 2002 evaluating person-centred education as an educational psychology model showed effectiveness of learner-centred teacher–student relationships. Another example of recent studies applying PCA into education is represented by numerous studies carried out by Motschnig-Pitrik and her team (Motschnig-Pitrik 2008; Motschnig-Pitrik and Figl 2007; Motschnig-Pitrik and Mallich 2004).

Our own experiences cover PCA teaching of English to preschool children (Sollárová 2000), psychology courses and social skills training for university students (Sollárová 2005), training communication skills for adults, helping professionals (Sollárová and Sollár 2007) and PCA skills for managing work relationships (Sollárová et al. 2011). We will point out two elements relevant to the issue of the paper—the process of teaching (and learning) and results or outcomes that can be generalised from our educational experiences with adults.

3.1 The Process of Learning in PCA Skills Training

PCA skills training contains analogical elements to what Rogers (1951) and Seeman (1983, 2008) state as the elements in the process of therapy towards the integration of the client:

- *Exploration of one's own feelings and experience in the state of anxiety*
  When the participants select and deal with authentic situations that they perceive as problematic, stressful or conflicting, their re-experiencing during their exploration is negatively charged, which is also typical for an explored situation in a real context; the facilitation of exploration, for example support in an emphatic and accepting atmosphere, strengthens the ability of participants to explore this experience even in a state of anxiety.

- *Experiencing the whole range of one's own attitudes*
  In role-play situations, participants play out situations that are the causes of their discomfort; they also experience feelings towards the other participants of a situation as they would in a real situation
- *Symbolisation of one's own actual experience*
  When a participant, for example during self-exploration supported by the emphatic understanding of a facilitator, names what his/her experience is about ("...I am angry and terrified when I imagine that my clients (=unemployed) will think that I am such an incompetent and unwilling creature like my colleague ...")
- *Assimilation of the new experience into one's own self-image*
  When a participant acknowledges and accepts the facets of one's self so far unacknowledged or unaccepted ("... It is important for me to be perceived as a polite and competent social worker...")
- *Development of an internal centre of evaluation and the acceptance of the self and others*
  In situations when the participant is not able to accept that a significant person evaluates him/her negatively ("...I know that my mother is not satisfied with what my husband is like; I feel that in spite of that it doesn't influence my satisfaction with my husband...").

The direct results or outcomes of participants acquiring PCA skills in interpersonal interactions at work are mainly:

- skills in communicating clearly and congruently
- skills in understanding the communication of the other person in an interaction
- skills in facilitating clarity of communication with a person with a different standpoint
- skills in improving team communication when members differ in their understanding and experience
- skills in managing stressful, conflicting and emotionally charged situations (more details in Sollárová 2005, 2008).

3.2 Coaching

Another area in facilitating the development of the healthy functioning of a person beyond the psychotherapeutic context is represented by *coaching*. Person-centred coaching psychology is, according to Joseph and Bryant-Jefferies (2009) and Stober (2006), a way of working with people based on a meta-theoretical supposition that people have the potential to develop and grow and that when internal potential is released, they can move on and become more autonomous, socially constructive and optimally functioning. It requires a social environment with specified qualities and attitudes. These core attitudinal qualities create the necessary conditions posited by Rogers (1957), or a social environment that facilitates constructive unfolding of the actualising tendency (of a client).

A person-centred coaching psychologist provides a client with an accepting and authentic relationship where he/she does not feel judged or pressured. Then, the client will move the locus of evaluation within his/her self and be motivated towards optimum functioning. According to Joseph et al. (2009), the essential role of the person-centred psychologist, regardless of the fact where the client is situated from a perspective of psychological functioning, is to facilitate the self-determination of the client in such a way that he/she would move towards a more optimal functioning.

In an environment where a person does not feel to be judged and pressured, he/she does not feel the need to defend himself/herself and self-actualisation can happen. The application of the abovementioned attitudinal qualities in coaching work represents, according to Stober (2006), the core conditions for effective coaching practice. The recognition of key conditions as necessary for a change in the person coached is similarly applicable to coaching as to psychotherapy.

The psychology of coaching is the same activity requiring the same theoretical background and the same practical skills as work with people who are in distress and dysfunctional. Therefore, within a person-centred perspective, there is no theoretical difference between counselling and coaching. It is not important where one starts.

Thus, on a theoretical level, the role of the person-centred psychologist is always the same whether he/she works as a coach or a consultant or a clinical psychologist, but on a practical level, the content of sessions will be different as clients usually bring different material to consultancy than to coaching (more details in Sollárová 2011). Based on the ideas regarding the process of developing optimal personality functioning, we propose the following conclusions:

- The process of learning and developing optimal personality functioning beyond the psychotherapeutic context is articulated in PCA theory and practice, based on the theory and practice of the process of change in client-centred therapy, and as such it is applicable to education, trainings and coaching.
- The conditions necessary for facilitating learning and developing optimal personality functioning beyond the psychotherapeutic context are derived from client-centred therapy, articulated in PCA theory and practice and applicable in education, trainings and coaching.

4 The "Fully-Functioning Person" Beyond Therapy, and the Measurement of Optimal Personality Functioning in PCA Growth-Oriented Interventions

It is clear that the interest in the optimal functioning of a person exceeds the boundaries of psychotherapy both within the PCA and within the positive psychology. The question is in what way both can benefit from theory, research and practice in client-centred therapy.

The results of many years of empirical work within client-centred psycho-therapy have indicated that there are consistent patterns of behaviour that characterise optimal personal organisation and that could thus serve in the development of *criterion measures for assessing psychotherapy outcome* (studies in Rogers 1951; Seeman 1983, 2008).

If we accept that the specified characteristics of an effectively functioning human system can serve as measures for assessing psychotherapy outcome, could the same measures be used for assessing outcomes of PCA growth-oriented interventions beyond therapeutic settings, too? We argue in the affirmative.

If we accept that there are measures differentiating the level of integration of a person empirically validated in studies of the process of client-centred psycho-therapy (Rogers 1951), can those measures identify the level of personality integration in non-therapeutic settings? If we accept the universal validity of the idea of the natural process of the self-actualisation of a person, it means that the process of personality integration happens not only in therapy and that a person at a certain point of his/her existence is on a certain level of integration, we can propose to apply those measures of personality integration conceptualised and empirically verified within client-centred theory and research in psychological theory and research beyond therapy. Will the measures of personality integration show similar relations to characteristics specified as predictable consequences of high person-ality integration, as an outcome of successful client-centred therapy, in non-ther-apeutic context—with non-clinical population? We argue, yes.

In our study (Sollárová and Sollár 2010) of the parameters of a psychologically integrated person conducted on a sample of care professionals (social workers), we used the discrepancy between the "real self" and the "ideal self" as a measure of personality integration, in accordance with Rogers' proposal and findings that low discrepancy between the real self and the ideal self is characteristic for an inte-grated person; further, we verified relationships between the integration of an individual represented by the level of congruence between real self and ideal self and specified parameters of optimal personality functioning—proactive coping, self-evaluation, neuroticism and openness to experience—found by Rogers (1951, 1962) and Seeman (2008) within the psychotherapeutic context. We found that the more an individual is integrated, the more he/she is proactive, less neurotic and evaluates him/herself more positively. The correlations showed moderate rela-tionships between the studied variable pairs. Proactive coping stresses the aspect of future orientation in solving everyday situations. The result found supports Rogers' (1962) finding that a fully functioning person will take more satisfactory decisions and actions, thanks to his/her trust in their own organism as the source of experiential data.

Higher and more positive self-esteem in highly integrated persons corresponds with those parts of changed self-concept that Rogers (1951) states as changes in an organised configuration of perceptions of a person's own characteristics and abilities and images of him/herself in relation to other people and the environment, as a consequence of increased self-acceptance as a valuable person.

The relationship between integration and neuroticism (in the direction of a lower level of neuroticism in more integrated persons) corresponds with the character of changes in the basal structure of personality that Rogers (1951) states as characteristics of a changed personality as a consequence of a successful therapy—decreased neurotic tendency and decreased level of anxiety.

Based on our study and findings, we would summarise the previous ideas and comments and propose the following conclusions:

- The concepts of a "fully functioning person" and a "psychologically integrated person" as synonymous with optimal personality functioning are based on the general theoretical concepts of humanistic psychology and theory of personality (mainly self-actualisation and actualising tendency); thus, they are not limited to the psychotherapeutic context and are valid in a non-therapeutic context as well.
- The characteristics of an effectively functioning human system as proposed and verified as a successful psychotherapy outcome can be applied in assessing outcomes of PCA growth-oriented interventions beyond therapeutic settings.
- The measures differentiating the level of integration of a person empirically validated in studies of the process of CCT can be applied as measures identifying the level of personality integration in non-therapeutic settings.
- The measures of personality integration show similar/analogical relationships to characteristics specified as predictable consequences of high personality integration, as an outcome of successful CCT, and in a non-therapeutic context, too.

5 Perspectives of PCA Managerial Competence

Until now, we have stressed ideas that can serve as a basis for asserting the legitimacy of applying the PCA in non-therapeutic settings.

What implication for the managerial role does a PCA way of being represent—that is, developing PCA thoughts, qualities, attitudes and skills? Below, we share some of our experience and insight.

The perspective of a PCA coaching managerial "style" is quite analogical to the therapeutic way of "offering" conditions that are necessary (and sufficient) for a change in the other person in the relationship, with the consequence of a more fully functioning of the person whatever it might mean for a specific person in a specific context or situation. This perspective is theoretically and practically ready to be applied, and we consider the PCA coaching model (Joseph and Bryant-Jeffries 2009; Sollárová 2011) (applied by coaches and managers), one of top potential areas where PCA can gain significant impact in applied psychology fields. The role of a PCA facilitator/group-centred leader is typically understood and dismissed with the critique or trivialisation of viewing PCA as too "touchy-feely" a therapeutic way of being with others. Does this perspective cover the whole potential of PCA in the organisational context? We propose there are other perspectives where PCA can offer its theoretical and practical potential in building organisational effectiveness. We will discuss one of them.

In the organisational context, focus on objectives, results, assessment and evaluation, crisis and (managing) change is typical for the present economic situation worldwide, and probably, most typical is competition among companies. It all creates pressure in the work environment, especially for managers. The question is whether a PCA primarily focused on interpersonal relationships can compete with different approaches that are typically result-oriented. Is the PCA philosophy in discrepancy with orientation towards results? Is focus on interpersonal relationships the aim (in) itself? Or can it also lead to good, even excellent results within the organisation? Most definitely, it can. And what consequences can a PCA way of being (or PCA competence) have for a manager? In situations that are not primarily focused on facilitation of the growth of others but focused on decision-making, problem-solving, managing change, conflict resolution, task assignment or performance evaluation, it means situations where managerial integrity and autonomy have a significant role. PCA can serve on his/her behalf as well! Both in

- building and managing effective work relationships as a means to good results and
- being effective in a difficult, crisis or even hostile environment as a means to decide and function according to one's integrity and to achieve one's aims, as well.

We first met with the idea of building and managing effective work relationships via PCA at the ADPCA 2000 conference, in a presentation by Ernie Meadows. After participating in his workshops and trainings, we started to apply and develop PCA within our own managerial roles and trainings for managers as well.

"Becoming" more and more "persons" in accordance with the PCA "way of being", we naturally started to be person-centred in all the roles, contexts and situations we found ourselves. Maybe because psychotherapy has not been our primary professional context, we became sensitive to where and how Rogers's ideas are especially applicable beyond therapy, and together we have had exciting conversations, discussions, attempts, as well as experiences and results that have had a significant impact on our lives. We both have rich experience with managing change, managing unsuccessful organisations or organisations in crisis. It might have focused our attention towards those types of managerial roles and situations that were primarily derived from difficult contexts, high demands on building goals, strategy, standards, performance and results that created a lot of pressure, resistance and conflicts in the process of change. Our belief in the "power" of PCA brought results.

We have presented more detailed comments and experiences elsewhere (e.g. Sollárová 2005, 2008; Sollárová et al. 2011). For the purpose of this article, we will stress the concept of being effective in a difficult, crisis or hostile environment as a means making decisions and functioning according to one's own integrity and also to achieve one's aims.

In managerial roles and situations where a manager's task is to manage new, usually highly demanding or unpopular tasks or goals, to make difficult decisions or to assert high standards, his/her focus on their own integrity and a congruent way of communication is primary. In situations when he/she faces resistance, conflict, disagreement, critique, his/her attitude demonstrating empathic listening and unconditional positive regard will create conditions for constructive dialogue. Together with a congruent manner of communication on the manager's side, it creates the correct ingredients to arrive at conclusions legitimate and acceptable to both sides.

A summary of the complexity and universality of PCA in the non-therapeutic context, as we specified for the role of a manager, is then as follows:

The PCA way of being equips managers (and anybody in another role, of course, too) with competence to facilitate the other person(s) to become more effective in communication and interactions; build and manage effective communication and interactions within his/her own work team and with his/her colleagues; and be effective in one's own communication and interactions (especially in difficult or hostile conditions) (Sollárová 2005).

Instead of a final note, we will present an extract from a reference from a manager (we will call him John) written after a five-day training in a PCA model in coaching:

Quite a long while before I participated in the training, I identified two main problems in my work as a division director of our company:

Firstly, I was not able to increase the motivation of my subordinates (colleagues) not just to do their jobs mechanically but also to use their initiative, and to be interested in achieving better results.

Second, I am highly perfectionist and believe that I am the one who can do the work best. The consequence is that I usually leave meetings with a large number of new tasks that I have given myself, as a result of my conclusion that nobody would do them as I would expect.

Both these problems became clear in the process of working on a recent task, which was to forecast production of one specified product where my division depends on data from other divisions in the company. To be able to forecast with high accuracy we need complete and exact data and that was a problem. The same problems repeated themselves and I was not able to find a way out of deadlock.

During our first day of the training you showed me a different way of managing people. I plucked up the courage and at the next meeting with my colleagues I reversed the roles. Asking questions, I tried to identify the real source of the problem and then to find the way out of the deadlock. My colleagues of course repeated their arguments on poor data. Thanks to my questions based on careful listening they themselves identified that it was in their own interest to have good data and that they should take more initiative and be more proactive (instead of passively waiting and being uncomfortable with bad data). From this very first "new-style" meeting it was them who left the meeting with tasks not me. I started to use such conversations almost every day. First I carefully listened where they had arrived at with the problem, and then we discussed the present state of affairs and delegated new tasks. I quite anxiously tried not to take on any task and I also tried to listen more and left my colleagues to come up with ideas. This is how I understood what I learnt.

I would describe the results of my changed managerial style as follows:

1. Three weeks later we got further than the previous two months and I did almost nothing.
2. My colleagues easily accepted new rules that I implemented without any introduction. They definitely identified a radical change in my attitude. I even felt uncertainty from their side—they did not know what was going on but they accepted tasks and solved them without comment.
3. Two weeks later I realised that they themselves started to do things that I had previously had to order them to do before.
4. They started to come up with new ideas and they worked on them (were developing them).

I realised that their previous low level of activity was a consequence of my high level of activity. I took on everything myself and they had no space. When I started to coach them more new perspectives opened up in front of them. Together with the pressure that it's them who are responsible for their results, they woke up, took on the problem as theirs and started to really solve it. ...

I believe that it all sounds like a fairy tale. It is exactly how I feel when I realise how easy and simply it happened. I appreciate this experience highly.

I realised the power of listening and asking questions that do not manipulate; they just straight and simply go to the core of the problem. As a coachee remains in his answers and following resolutions free, he himself finds out "what the problem is about" and he himself finds an optimal solution and then easily accepts his share of the responsibility. Higher responsibility leads to higher activity because tasks are not commanded but because he them upon himself and thus wants to do his best in fulfilling the task.

The experience of John demonstrates all three of the perspectives that we presented as PCA applications in the workplace: in his role of coaching his colleagues, he demonstrated the first presented role of a facilitator of the growth of the other; in his role as a member of the team, he showed how to build and manage effectively interactions in the team, and how he was effective in changing the originally passive and resistant attitudes of his colleagues to pro-active, responsible attitudes and autonomous functioning of the team as his own goal. John's experience of developing a PCA way of being demonstrates the application of PCA in the organisational context with its potential towards organisational effectiveness. As such, both theory and our experience confirm that PCA is able to facilitate it.

References

Cain, D. J. (2003). Advancing humanistic psychology and psychotherapy: Some challenges and proposed solutions. *Journal of Humanistic Psychology, 43*(3), 10–41.

Cornelius-White, J. (2007). Learner-centered teacher-student relationships are effective: A meta-analysis. *Review of Educational Research, 77*(1), 113–143.

Joseph, S., & Bryant-Jefferies, R. (2009). Person-centred coaching psychology. In S. Palmer & A. Whybrow (Eds.), *Handbook of Coaching Psychology* (pp. 211–228). London: Routledge.

Linley, P. A., & Joseph, S. (2004). Applied positive psychology: A new perspective for professional practice. In P. A. Linley & S. Joseph (Eds.), *Positive psychology in practice* (pp. 3–12). Hooken, NJ: Wiley.

Montuori, A., & Purser, R. (2001). Humanistic psychology in the workplace. In K. J. Schneider, J. F. T. Bugental & J. F. Pierson (Eds.), *The Handbook of Humanistic Psychology. Leading Edges in Theory, Research, and Practice* (pp. 635–646). Beverly Hills: Sage.

Motschnig-Pitrik, R. (2008). Significant learning communities as environments for actualising human potentials. *International Journal of Knowledge and Learning (IJKL), 4*(4), 383–397.

Motschnig-Pitrik, R., & Figl, K. (2007). Developing team competence as part of a person centered learning course on communication and soft skills in project management. *Conference on Frontiers in Education—FECS* (pp. F2G-15–F2G-21).

Motschnig-Pitrik, R., & Mallich, K. (2004). Effects of person-centered attitudes on professional and social competence in a blended learning paradigm. *Educational Technology & Society, 7*(4), 176–192.

Rogers, C. R. (1951). *Client-Centered Therapy*. London: Constable.

Rogers, C. R. (1957). The necessary and sufficient conditions of therapeutic personality change. *Journal of Consulting Psychology, 21*(2), 95–103.

Rogers, C. R. (1959). A theory of therapy, personality, and interpersonal relationships, as developed in the client-centered framework. In S. Koch (Ed.), *Psychology: A Study of a Science* (Vol. 3, pp. 184–256)., Formulations of the Person and the Social Context New York: McGraw-Hill.

Rogers, C. R. (1961). *On Becoming a Person*. Boston: Houghton-Mifflin.

Rogers, C. R. (1962). Toward becoming a fully functioning person. In A. W. Combs (Ed.), *Perceiving, Behaving, and Becoming: A New Focus for Education* (pp. 21–33). Washington, DC: Association for Supervision and Curriculum Development. http://www.centerfortheperson.org/1962_Toward_Becoming_a_Fully_Functioning_Person.doc. Accessed 8 Jan 2009.

Rogers, C. R. (1963). The concept of the fully functioning person. *Psychotherapy: Theory, Research, and Practice, 1*(1), 17–26.

Rogers, C. R. (1977). *Carl Rogers on personal power*. New York: Delacorte Press.

Rogers, C. R. (1980). *A Way of Being*. Boston: Houghton Mifflin Co.

Rogers, C. R. (1983). *Freedom to Learn for the 80th*. New York: MacMillan Publ.

Seeman, J. (1983). *Personality Integration: Studies and Reflections*. New York: Human Sciences Press.

Seeman, J. (2002). Looking back, looking ahead: A synthesis. In D. J. Cain & J. Seeman (Eds.), *Humanistic Psychotherapies: Handbook of Research and Practice*. Washington: APA.

Seeman, J. (2008). *Psychotherapy and the Fully Functioning Person*. Bloomington: AuthorHouse.

Seligman, M. E. P. (2008). Positive Health. *Applied Psychology: An International Review, 57*, 3–18.

Seligman, M. E. P., & Csikszentmihalyi, M. (2000). Positive psychology: An introduction. *American Psychologist, 55*, 5–14.

Sollárová, E. (2000). PCE as a teaching style—Its potential in facilitating creativity. Paper, 15th ADPCA Conference, La Jolla, CA, USA, Aug. 9–13.

Sollárová, E. (2005). *Aplikácie prístupu zameraného na človeka (PCA) vo vzťahoch*. Bratislava: Ikar.

Sollárová, E. (2008). Optimálne fungovanie osobnosti. Aplikácia prístupu zameraného na človeka na rozvojové tréningy. In I. Ruisel a kol. (Eds.), *Myslenie—osobnosť—múdrosť* (pp. 237–252). Bratislava: UEP.

Sollárová, E. (2011). Koučing. In T. Kollárik, J. Výrost & E. Letovancová a kol. (Eds.), *Organizačná psychológia* (pp. 280–298). Bratislava: UK.

Sollárová, E., & Sollár, T. (2007). Charakteristika zmien interpersonálneho správania v rôznych typoch výcvikov. In E. Sollárová, M. Popelková, & M. Pohánka (Eds.), *Zážitkové učenie a podpora rozvoja osobnosti* (pp. 116–123). Nitra: FSVaZ.

Sollárová, E., & Sollár, T. (2010). The psychologically integrated person and the parameters of optimal functioning. *Studia Psychologica, 52*(4), 333–338.

Sollárová, E., Sollár, T., & Romanová, M. (2011). *The Potential of the Person-Centered Approach in Non-therapeutic Setting*. Presentation at the ADPCA 2011 Conference, Chicago, July 27–31.

Stober, D. R. (2006). Coaching from the humanistic perspective. In D. R. Stober & A. M. Grant. (Eds.), *Evidence Based Coaching Handbook. Putting Best Practices to Work for Your Clients* (pp. 17–50).Hoboken NJ: Wiley.

Taylor, E. I., & Martin, F. (2001). Humanistic Psychology at the Crossroads. In K. J. Schneider, J. F. T. Bugental & J. F. Pierson (Eds.), *The Handbook of Humanistic Psychology. Leading Edges in Theory, Research, and Practice* (pp. 21–27). Beverly Hills: Sage.

Warmoth, A. (2001). The Old Saybrook 2 report and the outlook for the future. In K. J. Schneider, J. F. T. Bugental & J. F. Pierson (Eds.), *The Handbook of Humanistic Psychology. Leading Edges in Theory, Research, and Practice* (pp. 649–666). Beverly Hills: Sage.

A Person-Centered Approach to Innovation Management: Experiences and Learnings

Klaus Haasis

1 Introduction "Speaking Personally"

"Communication—creativity—innovation" describe and encapsulate the focus of my professional life. For the last 16 years, I have worked as CEO of a public regional development agency to improve competitiveness and regional, national and international collaboration. Moving from the private to the public sector requires a certain adjustment. Step by step I grew into the business of managing innovation, networks, and relationships—building on my extensive private sector experience and along the way developing new competences and insights. The offer, 5 years ago, to participate in a training course for a Person-Centered Approach (PCA) to counseling was a turning point for me. Today, PCA is a very important part of my professional and private life. Here, I would like to share with you some of the experiences of my professional work.

The first challenge is "to share." I feel a bit like Rogers (1961) in the chapter "Speaking Personally" in his book "On Becoming a Person" where he points out:

> I would like to make it very plain that these are learnings which have significance for me. I do not know whether they would hold true for you. I have no desire to present them as a guide for anyone else. Yet I have found that when another person has been willing to tell me something of his inner direction this has been of value to me, if only in sharpening my realization that my directions are different. So it is in that spirit that I offer the learnings which follow (p. 17).

Adopting this attitude as an author is very relieving for me. Thus, the following need not be right or wrong, good or bad, it is just "my experience."

K. Haasis (✉)
Rebhalde 7 70191 Stuttgart, Germany
e-mail: klaushaasis@web.de

J. H. D. Cornelius-White et al. (eds.), *Interdisciplinary Applications of the Person-Centered Approach*, DOI: 10.1007/978-1-4614-7144-8_17, © Springer Science+Business Media New York 2013

2 Linking the Concept of Creativity by Carl Rogers to Innovation

In the first half of the last century, the Austrian economist Josef Schumpeter came up with the term "creative destruction" to link innovation and creativity and to illustrate the disruptive process of transformation that accompanies innovative entrepreneurs as change makers.

In the 1950s, Carl Rogers as a psychotherapist presented a completely different approach talking about "constructive creativity." And at the end of his book "On Becoming a Person" (Rogers 1961), he describes his view of a theory of creativity (p. 353). He writes: "It has been found that when the individual is 'open' to all of his experience... then his behavior will be creative, and his creativity may be trusted to be essentially constructive" (p. 352). For Rogers, the outcome of creativity "has to be something observable, some product of creation ... symbolized in words, or written in a poem, or translated into a work of art, or fashioned into an invention. These products must be novel constructions" (p. 349). Rogers defines the "creative process" as "the emergence in action of a novel relational product, growing out of the uniqueness of the individual on the one hand, and the material, events, people or circumstances of his life on the other" (p. 350).

Reading this first I was both surprised and impressed because I realized that Rogers was also an avant-garde thinker in the field of creativity and the "relational" dimension of creativity which today is more and more called "social innovation." And he was avant-garde in describing the crucial aspect of reducing anxiety and insecurity to create openness for new and trusted ideas, which is the first step in a successful innovation process.

3 My Model for the Innovation Process

I find it useful to have my own models. They help me to symbolize my experiences. So, how do I see the innovation process today? Even if the so-called linear model of innovation has been surpassed by other models, in my opinion, there is a creative development process in the beginning and an implementation process at the end. Particularly, there is a dialog process in the middle to bridge the gap between research and development on the one side and application and implementation on the other. It is not a simple transfer. As seen in Fig. 1, I call it a "transfer dialog" because it is a learning process and not a one-way action.

Fig. 1 The idea to value innovation model. © Klaus Haasis, Stuttgart 2012

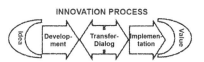

In every step of the innovation process, we have to deal with "action," and since actions always have the potential to concern people, we have to deal with people relationships. People taking part in any innovation process have to change, adapt and to adopt it. They have to change perspectives to get new ideas, they have to leave their comfort zone to believe in something new, and they have to change their former habits to use a new product, service, or process. This can cause anxiety and lead to resistance and conflicts.

According to Thom and Etienne (2000), there are four characteristics of "innovation tasks," which I like a lot:

- degree of novelty,
- complexity,
- uncertainty and risk,
- possible conflicts.

Being in relationships as a member of a network, a business community or a cluster initiative can reduce this anxiety and uncertainties. My experience is that today being innovative is more and more about being social. Being social means being connected with others, working in teams, collaborating and sharing. Where do we have to be innovative and social today? Everywhere—at our place of work, in business partnerships, in networks, communities and cluster initiatives. Networks can have a positive impact on the innovation process. I see a three-step value chain for successful and innovative networking in teams, organizations, and communities:

- Building up relationships and linking to each other.
- Sharing knowledge and learning from each other.
- Open collaboration and developing common projects.

But what are fruitful conditions for change and collaboration? I would like to define collaboration culture and innovation climate as the crucial conditions to achieve a fruitful atmosphere for successful innovation processes.

4 A Short View on Collaboration Culture and Innovation Climate

The view on innovation and collaboration is normally directed toward enterprises and their employees. I would like to expand the perspective to "systems" like organizations, communities and networks and even regions. For my PCA to innovation management, I focus on the concept of "innovation climate" and "collaboration culture" as depicted in Fig. 2.

Based on the idea of organizational culture by Svyantek/Bott, the *collaboration culture* can also be defined as "a set of shared values and norms ... that guide ... interactions with peers, management and clients" (Patterson et al. 2005, pp. 380–381). The *innovation climate* could be defined as the relation between the

Fig. 2 The idea to value
innovation model. ©Klaus
Haasis, Stuttgart 2012

context of a system and the behavior of its members including how the members
experience the system (Patterson et al. 2005). Indicators for a fruitful innovation
climate could be innovation competence (I can.) and innovation readiness (I want!)
(Thom and Etienne 2000). This framework is a good tool to handle innovation
tasks and to navigate through innovation processes.

5 The Role of the Innovation Manager Seen from a Person-Centered Perspective

My role in dealing with complexity, novelty, uncertainties, risk and possible
conflicts brought by innovation could be defined as being an "innovation manager." In the last four years, this role has led me in understanding that being
innovative and managing innovation nearly always means breaking some rules;
and that breaking rules often leads to severe conflicts. I learned that conflicts are
part of my professional role as an innovator, change maker, and "rule breaker" and
that these conflicts have nothing to do with me as a person but with my role in the
innovation process. So, I started to develop a concept of my professional role as a
"person-centered rule breaker."

For me, it was very relieving to understand that resistance is part of my professional role. It prepared me for possible conflicts in the innovation process and
enabled me to search for solutions in a stress-free way. I was able to look at the
collaboration partners in an empathic way conscious of the anxieties my ideas,
proposals, and actions were causing. Even in these controversial situations I, as a
"person-centered rule breaker," was able to show positive regard to people
involved in the innovation process and at the same time feel completely congruent
with the process.

I would like to share some concrete experiences:

- I have found in meeting discussions that it is helpful for the innovation and
  collaboration process to actually write down the concerns and complaints of
  others on a wall or flipchart, even if these concerns and complaints have to do
  with me in my role as an innovator—and even if I feel attacked and criticized as
  a rule breaker. It improves the atmosphere and the energy in the room if this is
  articulated and visible, that is, written large somewhere.
- I have found that it is helpful if I try to address concerns and resistances that I
  feel in an innovation process in group meetings in a very person-centered way of
  positive regard and congruence. I tried this in a meeting with civil servants when

we discussed responsibilities and competences and I saw the civil servants being relieved that I had provided them with at least the means to talk about the issue.

- I have found that it is helpful to reveal my personal feelings about a lack of transparency in a negotiation process about future collaboration of two networks. As a consequence, I saw more willingness to open up and to share more information about purposes and actions.
- I have found that working groups in clusters and networks become much more creative and innovative when they learn to practice a self-revealing communication and to give emotional feedback. I also practice this in group sessions with employees and I am still overwhelmed by the great results we achieve.

6 Conclusions and Lessons Learnt in Person-Centered Innovation Management

I would like to summarize my experience in innovation and collaboration management. While it is difficult to distill 16 years of experience in designing and developing flourishing and constructive innovation processes in innovation systems, organizations, networks, and regions, I nevertheless offer the following:

- **Process over Project**
  I learned that "process" is always underestimated. I learned that many persons in their wish to be output oriented plan a meeting by always looking at the project facts. Only rarely do they consider the process of the meeting, for example how do we begin, how can people open up, how can they start to share experiences, how should decisions being taken?
- **Context over Text**
  I learned that in innovation and cluster management, the context of behavior and feelings and the special environment often is much more important than what has been said, planned, and scheduled. The mental and physical environment of an innovation or collaboration process is very important for success.
- **Dialog over Discussion**
  I learned that it is more important to listen to others and to try to understand the realities of the others. If this is understood it is possible to work on a common reality in the group, the partnership, the cluster, or the organization.
- **Innovating means rule breaking**
  I learned that innovation and change mean breaking rules and this can sometimes mean disturbing the realities of other persons, which causes anxiety and leads to conflicts with them. I learned that conflicts are part of my life as an innovator and a change maker. This learning helped me to show more empathy and positive regard towards people in a conflict and to understand that the conflict does not reflect on me as a person.

- **Self-revealing communication style**

  I learned to work on my communication style. According to a quote of one of my trainers, "Language is the house of thinking." I learned that it is often helpful to open up and reveal my feelings, my concerns, and my thoughts to build up trust. And I learned how important it is to use I-messages, to stay true to myself, and to talk always about my feelings, my perception and what I had heard—especially in conflicts and anxious situations brought by innovation tasks.

- **… and one tip at the end: "No Tables"**

  There is one action, which is really a "low hanging fruit": Do not sit around tables. They are barriers and individual shelters, which inhibit a collaborative and open atmosphere and can reduce the flow of constructive energy in a room. In many meetings, I have achieved much better, appreciative, and cooperative results when the group of participants was sitting in a circle of chairs without table barriers between each other. Throw the tables out of your meeting rooms.

Now that I have gone through this process of writing down my experiences and learnings in innovation management I feel even more like Carl Rogers who gave the aforementioned chapter "Speaking Personally" in his book "On Becoming a Person" the subtitle "This is Me." In his fourteen learnings, he writes: "Experience is, for me, the highest authority … What is most personal is most general …. The facts are friendly" (Rogers 1961, pp. 23, 25, 26). The knowledge and the experiences I have had through the PCA have enriched my professional and private life enormously. I am now on my way to deeply "trust the process!"

Acknowledgments I want to thank Daniela Tausch for recommending Helmut Beutel to me. I would like to thank Helmut Beutel, Dorothea Kunze, Hans Jellouschek, and Schorsch Wilms for great educational courses, Dr. Klaus Antons for empathic and constructive supervision, Renate Motschnig for inviting me to write this article and my team, especially Bianca Kolb and Jonas Lander, for supporting me in my role as a person-centered rule breaker.

References

Patterson, M. G., West, M. A., Shackleton, V. J., Dawson, J. F., Lawthom, R., Maitlis, S., et al. (2005). Validating the organizational climate measure: Links to managerial practices, productivity and innovation. *Journal of Organizational Behavior, 26*(4), 379–408.

Rogers, R. C. (1961). *On becoming a person: A therapist's view of psychotherapy.* New York: Houghton Mifflin Company.

Thom, N., & Etienne, M. (2000). Organisatorische und personelle Ansatzpunkte zur Förderung eines Innovationsklimas im Unternehmen. (Organisational and personal starting points for the facilitation of the innovation climate in an enterprise). In G. E. Häfliger & J. Meier (Eds.), *Aktuelle Tendenzen im Innovationsmanagement* (Current trends in innovation management) (pp. 269–281). Heidelberg: Physica-Verlag. http://www.innopool.ch/pdf/I-Th-Et-00-Innkl.pdf . Accessed 07 March 2012.

Part VI
Conflict and Constructive Communication

The Person-Centered Approach and its Capacity to Enhance Constructive International Communication

Colin Lago

1 Introduction

> I have found that when I speak from my heart, then people from many different cultures can understand me (Carl Rogers, personal communication).

This chapter explores the potential for the enhancement of international communication informed by person-centered principles. Nevertheless, the question 'does the person-centered approach (PCA) have a capacity to enhance constructive international communication?' remains critical to our enquiry.

An immediate response to this question can easily be provided by the following references:

- In 1922, Carl Rogers travelled to China and several Southeast Asian countries, interacted with people from all populated continents, and worked for intercultural peace on a large scale as described in a diary that showed how instrumental cross-cultural experiences characterized by authenticity and empathy were crucial to the development of his identity, ideas, and lifework (Cornelius-White 2012).
- In a seminal paper entitled 'Significant Aspects of Client-Centered Therapy,' Rogers (1946) was already noting that he and his colleagues were learning an approach that had 'deep implications for the handling of social and group conflicts' and, he felt, that 'a significant clue to the constructive solutions of interpersonal and intercultural frictions in the group may be in our hands.'
- Almost 25 years later, Rogers proposed potential areas of application for the group (communication) process that included the fields of race relations and international tensions (Rogers 1969).
- Rogers and colleagues commenced exploring the implications of the PCA in small encounter groups from the 1950s onwards. Radical developments of this

C. Lago (✉)
University of Sheffield, 6, Moorcroft Drive, Fulwood, Sheffield S10 4GW, UK
e-mail: email@colinlago.co.uk

J. H. D. Cornelius-White et al. (eds.), *Interdisciplinary Applications of the Person-Centered Approach*, DOI: 10.1007/978-1-4614-7144-8_18,
© Springer Science+Business Media New York 2013

work were then pursued in much larger gatherings held both in the USA and in other countries around the world. See, for example, John K Wood's description of the large group meetings convened in 1977 in Brazil comprising between 300 and 1,000 persons! (Wood 2008).

- This list of previous meetings involving international participants is easily extended by referring to many other 'international' workshops such as in Zinal (1981), Witwatersrand (1982, 1986), Moscow (1986), the 'Rust' workshop (1985), a series of annual PCA 'cross-cultural communication' workshops held from 1983, many 'world' PCA conferences and international forums and so on. Further details on many of these meetings may be found in MacMillan and Lago (1993), Lago and MacMillan (1999), Wood (2008), McIlduff and Coghlan (1989, 1993), and Rogers (1986a, b).
- Rosenberg's (e.g., 2003) model of nonviolent communication grew out of the person-centered approach has been practiced around the world in mediation settings.

These brief references to international gatherings based upon the PCA already serve to indicate that Rogers' radical ideas originating in the discipline of one-to-one psychotherapy soon burst forth in many forms as an approach to meaningful communication with others, wherever and whoever they were in the world. That said, however, it is important also to note that there are many examples from around the world where beliefs in the PCA have brought people together yet there have been breakdowns and splits in relationships that have continued over long periods of time. I would, however, offer a cautious note here that it is, perhaps, not the fault of the theory that rifts have occurred but rather of the persons and personalities involved. This final paragraph captures one essential element of this chapter and that is, however, well intentioned and noble are the intentions toward constructive international communication, there are also many challenges and no guarantees of successful outcome!

As Hesse (1972) wrote: 'It might be asserted that every human being on earth can fundamentally hold a dialogue with every other human being, and it might also be asserted that there are no two persons in the world between whom genuine, whole, intimate understanding is possible—the one statement is as true as the other. It is Yin and Yang, day and night: both are right and at times we have to be reminded of both' (p. 275).

2 The Relative Role of (Social Science) Theory: An Initial and Cautious Note

What is theory after all? It is a model of behaviour that tries to approximate what is operative in actual behaviour. But no theory at the present time can comprehensively explain all instances of a complex behaviour. Realistically, all contemporary theories are compromises of one sort or another (Goldberg 1996, p. 15).

While the overall thrust of this chapter is dedicated to an exploration of how the PCA (one such theory) might enhance international communication, we perhaps have to ask several bigger questions: What is the value of theory to the practitioner? If communication breaks down what are the implications of this for the theory... and the practitioner? Theory offers no guarantee of success in practice. The relationship of theory to each practitioner, their personalities and their communication styles, is a complex and multifaceted phenomenon. It is possible to imagine a negative outcome to a piece of communication where a theory was adopted in good faith as a basis for the interaction (perhaps by both or more practitioners), yet this theoretical symmetry somehow still failed to ensure a positive outcome to the communication.

From the perspective of the PCA, Rogers and Wood (1974) wrote: *First there is experiencing, then there is a theory* (p). In their particular case, Rogers and Wood were the theory makers from their own experience. In direct contrast, for all later generations of students of the approach, the theory has been expounded and learned first within their training and professional development. That is, in the majority of circumstances (e.g., for later students of the PCA), the theory has generally preceded experiencing! Interestingly (and please note here that I am talking very generally and am thus in danger of making enormous assumptions!), what then seems to happen around this time of training and early clinical experiencing for many students is that they, perhaps inevitably, begin to assess the theory in terms of their own prior and current experiencing. Depending upon the sense of 'fit' between the theory and their experiencing, some will enthusiastically embrace it, while others will be cautious and/or actively seek other theoretical approaches that sit more consistently within their own experiencing.

Theory can be most helpful in simplifying the complexities of real life and offering a view, a 'modus operandi' or template for behaving. Theory, particularly when it has been substantiated from research and practice, can thus assist the practitioner's confidence in 'knowing what they are doing' and can act as a guide to practice. Nevertheless, theory yet cannot offer any guarantee of ultimate success. Theory is of value but it does not substitute for practice (communication), commitment, openness, stamina of purpose, willingness to relate, risk taking, and so on. Whatever we believe we are doing (theory), we still have to convert that into a form of practice (communication) that can be successfully received and engaged with by the other person/s in the interaction. Even with the aid of a map, the explorer still has to make the journey!

3 The Person-Centered Approach: An Introduction to the Ground and Context of the Theory

A view of psychotherapy as one specialized example of all constructive interpersonal relationships, with the consequent generalized applicability of all knowledge gained from the field of psychotherapy (Rogers and Sanford 1989).

The PCA to counselling and psychotherapy advanced a series of theoretical hypotheses and their efficacy, which were explored in ground-breaking, radical research programs geared to understanding more deeply the various elements of relationship and communication that facilitated clients' explorations of their own difficult issues and past traumas. Such concepts included:

- The and formative tendencies.
- The 19 propositions of personality development.
- The (6) necessary and sufficient conditions for therapeutic relationships.
- A (7 stage) process conception of psychotherapy.
- A definition of the 'fully functioning person.'

This all too brief list reflects and represents several decades of clinical experience, research, development and writing, both by Rogers and his colleagues.

Despite its twentieth century formulations and popularization, the underpinning philosophical tenets of the approach may be found in ancient philosophic and religious writings. Examples include: Mhairi MacMillan's (1999) work comparing Rogers' writings with those of Ibn-el-Arabi—a thirteenth century Sufi mystic, Rogers' acknowledgment of the influence of the teachings of Lao Tzu and Soren Kierkegaard upon his development of ideas (see Tudor and Worrall 2006, p. 8.) Indeed, these latter authors also cite quotations by Aristotle (384–322 BCE), Marcus Aurelius (121–180 ACE) and Shakespeare (1564–1616) that demonstrate earlier conceptualizations of terms he frequently utilized: 'actualization,' 'congruence,' and 'empathy.'

Rogers and Sanford (1989) created a list of distinctive characteristics that distinguished the PCA from other forms of psychotherapy and included among these are:

- The hypothesis that certain attitudes in therapists constitute the necessary and sufficient conditions for therapeutic effectiveness.
- The concept of therapists' functions as those of being immediately present and accessible to clients and of relying on their moment to moment experiencing in their relationships with clients.
- The intensive and continuing focus on the phenomenological world of the client.
- A developing theory that therapeutic process is marked by change in the client's manner and immediacy of experiencing, with increasing ability to live more fully in the moment.
- Continued stress on the self-actualizing quality of the human organism as the motivational force in therapy.
- Emphasis on the need for continuing research to gain essential learning's regarding psychotherapy.

A closer inspection of the above list reveals key pointers toward Rogers' belief that these specific characteristics, derived from the specialist field of counselling and psychotherapy could be applied to human relationships more generally. However, it is necessary for us to note that both Rogers (1959) and Wood (2008) make the specific distinction between the application of theory (within the therapy setting) and applications of the underlying approach within the many other settings in which humans relate. It is not sufficient for therapeutic practitioners to assume that what they do within the therapy setting is adequate for other settings and applications. As Wood (2008) notes:

> Unlike applying the principles of therapy, applying the person-centred approach means confronting a phenomenon (such as… classroom learning, large groups,…)with a certain 'way of being'… which may also include not only respecting others, but being able to deal with their hostility and skepticism. It may mean facing the unknown and one's own fear and doubt. It may mean fighting for one's own ideas, but giving them up for better ones. It frequently requires an active patience: to allow various perspectives to become apparent before deciding, while, at the same time, not withholding one's vital participation while data was accumulating (p. 72).

The PCA then outlines a 'way of being' (Rogers 1980). This way of being is relational, is respectful, is open to others, is open to being changed by the encounter, is willing to take risks, is willing to listen to others (even when what they say is not agreed with), is being authentic and willing and able to communicate that authenticity, is committed to the process of communication, not any specific outcomes, is generally trusting in the capacity of human beings to know what is right for them, and is secure enough in their own being to face fear and unknowing. Phrased in this manner, we can readily appreciate that the PCA can make tough demands upon the person. However, beautiful and attractive it is as a philosophy (and thousands of people around the world enthusiastically embrace its teachings), the sustained practice of PCA requires stamina, fortitude and belief. As such, it is *a way of looking at the world.*

> The word 'theory' derives from the Greek 'theoria', which has the same root as 'theatre', in a word meaning to 'view' or 'to make a spectacle'. Thus it might be said that a theory is primarily a form of insight, i.e. a way of looking at the world, and not a form of knowledge of how the world is (Bohm 1980 p. 3).

4 What is International Communication? Examples, Challenges, and Emerging Ideas

When I reflect upon the rich 'international experiences' I have had in my life, I consider myself to be extremely fortunate. Once, in Japan, on my own on a Sunday morning, walking down a completely empty street, turning a corner, I noticed a woman walking toward me. There was no-one else around. We were both on the same side of the street and naturally walked past each other, with the slightest of smiles and nods. I had only gone about 10 steps after passing her when I heard a 'yahoo' obviously coming from her. I turned and she started to walk toward me and then said: *Welcome to Japan. I hope you enjoy being here.* I was most touched by this generosity of welcome and her spontaneity. We then proceeded to have a warm and gentle conversation before moving on. I have never forgotten this extraordinary moment of kindness and generosity. In this example, we have to note that the woman was not trained in PCA! Nevertheless, we could argue that she naturally embodied something of the PCA philosophy in her openness and reception of me that was natural or indeed may have come from her own religious or philosophic or internationalist beliefs.

On another occasion, I was attending an international workshop with delegates there from approximately 30 countries. The organizers had kindly provided translators to facilitate the communication process. During the proceedings, one afternoon a woman began to share her experiences of being imprisoned in her country for political reasons. She was speaking in German but was from another country. I neither understand German nor her native language. I found myself internally feeling extremely sympathetic to her circumstances. After translation into a couple of other languages, the English translation of what she had said was offered... and I immediately couldn't work out why this was being made because I realized that I already knew what she had said! I was then struck by the thought of how did I know what she had said when I don't speak either of the languages she was fluent in? And yet, at that moment, I realized from what the translator had said that I had fully grasped the content and the details of her story.

As a student counselor who worked in an university for many years, students from all over the world frequently consulted me. Despite the worldwide origin of these different clients, and by implication, how we were potentially separated by our languages and different cultural heritage, many expressed gratitude that they had felt accepted and understood by me and that our communication had been helpful to them.

Within the context of this chapter then, I personally have had to consider what do we mean here by international communication? There are so many differing scenarios and settings in which we could imagine international communication taking place. I have already referred above to the many meetings of PCA practitioners that have been and continue to be held around the world. In the world of business and politics, international communication is occurring all the time. The electronic world of mobile phones, the internet, 'Facebook,' Twitter, and so on is a working manifestation of the fact that international communication, that is, communication between people of differing linguistic, religious, political, and cultural origins is happening between millions of people every day. We are thus left with the questions: where might PCA fit in, usefully, to such communications?'

One general response that I have to this question is to suggest that someone (or a team) of persons skilled in PCA might usefully be able to contribute to international communications where there already exists some tensions, disagreements and conflict between those involved. These would, perhaps, be a continuation of the aspirational workshops Rogers and his colleagues were involved in South Africa, Ireland, Russia, and Austria (the Rust workshop) in the 1970s and 1980s, and for which Rogers was nominated for the Nobel Peace Prize. Such workshops would have to have been organized by someone motivated to bring the 'sides' together and the PCA team invited by the hosts to be there.

In a recorded conversation with Rogers, he was asked about how his political views may have differed from the group of people he was working with—as they had a history of violence toward others and so on. The question proceeded to explore how could Rogers therefore work with this group if they had such a history? His response was illuminating. He said that over the years of his career, he had come to understand something about communication and that his task within this group was to facilitate the possibility of genuine communication and understanding between the different factions, despite their long histories of difference. Rogers was keen to ensure that the persons within the group were offered the opportunity to hear other persons within the group. To hear each other as humans, not enemies, not projections of stereotypes, but as humans, with families and communities, trying to do the best they could. From this, we can infer three very important components of facilitating international communication. Firstly, that it is important that the person/s with the PCA skills, if and when invited to work in such gatherings, are able to stay dedicated to their task of facilitating the communication, rather than being drawn into the argument of one side or the other. Secondly, it will be important for the facilitator/s to not have their own personal investment in any particular outcome from the meeting. Thirdly, that it is important that they are able to create a 'psychologically conducive' climate in which the various participants can come to meet and hear each other fully as humans, rather than as 'one of them!'

While somewhat optimistic in general tone so far in this chapter, I believe the person contributing to constructive international communication needs also to be widely knowledgeable about the challenges of communicating cross-culturally. The following brief section only hints at this enormous range of issues prevalent in the task of communicating.

5 Some Barriers to International Communication: Preparation and Cultural Literacy

5.1 Lack of Preparation

As an introductory story to this section, I remember well two particular instances of an international PCA facilitating team not creating the optimum psychological conditions for the workshop participants. As an aside, it is important to note that the configuration of an international team is, of course, an important symbol for the group—an example of a team of staff coming from quite different backgrounds and origins working together. However, on these two occasions, the staff team failed to prepare themselves well for the work. In the one instance, working in a country that none of them had been to before, their combined lack of knowledge of recent history and politics in that country eventually resulted in their not being taken too seriously, and consequently, their contribution to the communication process was not valued. In the other circumstance, the staff team did not pay sufficient ongoing attention to their own dynamics and the larger group process. When working in teams (or even as individuals), it is so necessary for the individual or team to spend time in preparation for and in ongoing reflection of the unfolding communication process within the participant community. In not preparing well or working reflectively, the facilitator/s are not caring for the communication participants or process. International communication, at this organized level, is a professional task with high demands.

5.2 The Need for 'Cultural Literacy'

> Honest and sincere persons in the field continue to fail to grasp the true significance of the fact that culture controls behaviour in deep and pointing ways, many of which are outside of awareness and therefore beyond conscious control of the individual (E. T. Hall-quoted in Casse (1980), p. 51).

The history of the world is, of course, replete with incidents, stories, politics, battles, wars, and treaties, and so on that reflects and reveals the complex and frequently troubled nature of communication between culturally different peoples. E. T. Hall, through his many publications (1969, 1973, 1976, 1983), demonstrated the very real need for 'cultural literacy,' for understanding others at the behavioral as well as linguistic levels. Attention must be given to:

- The situation and location of the meeting: the effect of place.
- The culturally different determinants of behaviors and attitudes.
- The complexities of the communication process. (Meanings are in people, not in words!)
- Languages, meanings, metaphors, and understandings.

This all too brief section on the need for cultural literacy has only afforded us the opportunity to merely hint at the vast array of materials, research, and publications generated in many of the social sciences dedicated to cross-cultural communication and understanding. Readers interested in developing their skills within the international arena are strongly encouraged to access this data.

6 The Potential of the Group for the Group!

The preceding section has provided us with a range of perspectives that indicate that communication itself, let alone in the international field, can prove a problematic issue. In general terms, it is argued here that, besides a fluency in the PCA, the more one can learn about and be comfortable with different culturally deter-mined linguistic and behavioral patterns the more one is likely to be successful in international communication.

The PCA is a relationship-based approach. Indeed, Rogers briefly used the term 'Relationship therapy' to describe the approach in 1942. In her recent academic exploration of the parallels between Rogers' six conditions for the establishment of therapeutic relationships and the early relationship between the infant and its primary caregiver (most frequently the mother), Evleen Mann quoted extensive research that substantiates the view that the human infant resonates with a rela-tional capacity which triggers chemical and neurological signals within the brain of the mother. This profound research indicates that it is not just the mother fostering the relationship but that both parties (mother and infant) co-create their relationship together (Mann 2011). From this perspective, we have to hypothesize that human beings are, somehow, genetically 'pre-programmed' to relate. We are pro-social beings.

Rogers (1959) himself states: *Assuming a minimal mutual willingness to be in contact and to receive communications, we may say that the greater the com-municated congruence of experience, awareness, and behaviour on the part of one individual, the more the ensuing relationship will involve a tendency toward reciprocal communication with the same qualities, mutually accurate under-standing of the communications, improved psychological adjustment and func-tioning in both parties, and mutual satisfaction in the relationship* (p. 51). In short, if one person within the relationship is able to embody and model the relationship conditions postulated by the PCA, then it is likely that the other person will reciprocate, will come into relationship... indeed, the research into primary rela-tionships (cited in Mann (2011) suggests that the other will actively co-create the relationship).

Within a group setting Sanford postulated that it is important for the facilitator to be totally 'present' and demonstrate a willingness to hear each person, and have a deep understanding of the PCA on the part of the facilitators is important. She also adds that it is important that 'someone' provide the facilitative conditions (Sanford 1999, pp. 15–16). Please note here that Sanford, in specifying the word 'someone' rather than the term 'facilitator,' recognizes the capacity for all members in the group to be facilitative to other group members at different times. I return to this theme two paragraphs below.

Again, quoting Rogers' (1959) rather more formal academic language,

Building upon the postulate regarding the nature of the individual (therapist) and extending this to apply to groups, it has been hypothesized that to the extent that a perceived leader provides the conditions of therapy (specified above)..., certain phe-nomena will occur in the group. Among these are the following: the perceptual resources of the group will be more widely used, more differentiated data will be provided by the group, thinking and perceptions will become more extensional, self-responsible, thinking and action will increase, a greater degree of distributive leadership will develop, and there will be more effective long-range problem solving. All of these consequences flow logi-cally from the theory thus far presented (p. 52).

This quotation from Rogers already amplifies the capacity, through the group work process, of the 'co-creation of relationships.' This view posits that members joining any group already arrive in the group with a capacity for and skills in relational competence. As such, groups could come together without a leader/facilitator and function perfectly well as the relational potential and capacity are already within any group of human beings. This is a position that has been strongly debated within person-centered theory, particularly with reference to larger groups (Bozarth 1998). 'It's hard to say what is facilitative behavior/or who is facilitative as it's impossible to know what behavior at any one time is facilitative or not for someone' (Coulson 1994). Acknowledging how frequently group members can be more facilitative than the facilitator, Rogers himself was not fixed to the idea of completely dominating the role of facilitator all the time. In his film on conducting encounter groups, he notes the wish to: 'free himself of the burden of being the facilitator, of the feeling of being totally responsible.'

Within the field of international business and negotiations, some training manuals advocate the desirability and involvement of someone they call a 'cultural interpreter'. This person does not have to be a professionally assigned person, but certainly is someone with the reflective capacity to be able to understand and explain behaviors and assumptions of the host country personnel that might not be shared by the visiting team. Such 'insider' explanations can be of immense value to enhancing the empathic capacities of the facilitating team, thus contributing to their capacity to work sensitively and effectively.

7 A Summary of Concluding Thoughts

In this chapter, I have introduced:

- Rogers held a belief in the value of speaking from one's heart, speaking one's truth and that this direct expression of humanity communicates across cultural differences.
- The history of research within the PCA supports the hypothesis of its viability to assist cross-cultural communication.
- Acknowledging commitment to the ideals of PCA does not guarantee successful outcomes!
- The interface between theory and practice is a complex one, and ultimately, the practitioner has to find their own way in practice, though hopefully assisted by the 'map' of the theory.
- Additionally, I have suggested that PCA persons invited to work in other cultural regions need to prepare well for this work to enhance their cross-cultural sensitivity. (Lago 2010; Charura and Lago forthcoming).
- There are a huge range of potential barriers to successful communication (let alone international communication) that exist and which, at any moment, can 'ambush' the proceedings.

- Human beings moving inevitably move toward relationship and thus communication. (See also a forthcoming chapter by Lago et al. (2012) looking at the possibility of 'relational depth across diversity').

In short, PCA theory highlights the value of certain attitudes toward others to enhance communication, including the capacity of being real and fully present, of fully accepting the other, of striving for a respectful understanding-seeking stance toward the other without giving up on one's own ideas and values. The 'approach' involves not only being fully open to others but also being open to the possibility of being changed by the encounter. This is a challenging proposition in itself and demands of the practitioner a deep sense of security in themselves. It implies a willingness to take interpersonal risks without being able to predict outcomes. The 'approach' requires a patient capacity to listen deeply to others and to be committed to the process of communication rather than any specific outcome. It requires a deep trust in the other's motivations and capacities. Overall the 'approach,' when embodied and practiced by sincere committed persons, has the potential to offer added value to any (international) communication moment or event.

When I reflect upon my own experiences within the PCA, of attendance at many meetings and workshops around the world, I am deeply grateful to those whom I have met person-to-person and thosewith whom I have subsequently developed committed and long-term friendships in the USA, Australia, many European countries, Japan and Brazil. PCA is an inspirational theory. People in circumstances of international communication can frequently hold high aspirational goals for their work and commitment. And yet, each new relationship and communication process has its potential challenges as well as rewards. Ultimately, I believe we all have to try 'to turn the best of ourselves toward the best in the other to produce more than either of us could have achieved alone' (Wood 2008).

As Hesse (1972) writes:

> To be sure, I too do not believe that you and I will ever be able to communicate fully and without some residue of misunderstanding, with each other. But though you may be an Occidental and I a Chinese, though we may speak different languages, if we are persons of good will we shall have a great deal to say to each other, and beyond what is precisely communicable we can guess and sense a great deal about each other. At any rate, let us try (p. 275).

References

Bohm, D. (1980). *Wholeness and the implicate order.* London: Boston & Henley.

Bozarth, J. D. (1998) . The person-centered approach : A revolutionary paradigm . Ross-On-Wye, UK: PCCS Books.

Casse, P. (1980). *Training for the cross cultural mind. A handbook for cross cultural trainers and consultants.* Society for Intercultural Education, Training and research, Washington, DC.

Charura, D., & Lago, C. (In press). Culturally Tailored Person Centered Therapy. In: L. M. Hooper. (Ed.) *Culturally Competent Counseling and Psychotherapy: From Research and Theory to Action.* Thousand Oaks, Sage, CA.

Cornelius-White, J. H. D. (Ed.). (2012). *Carl Rogers: The China Diary.* Ross-on-Wye: PCCS Books.

Coulson, A. (1994) Cited in Lago. C, & Macmillan, M "Moments of Facilitation in Large Groups".Paper presented at the 3rd. International Conference on Client-Centred & ExperientialPsychotherapy, Austria.

Goldberg, C. (1996). *Speaking with the evil: A dialogue with evil.* Harmondsworth: Viking Penguin Books.

Hesse, H. (1972). *The glass bead game.* Harmondsworth: Penguin.

Lago, C. (2010). On developing our empathic capacities to work inter-culturally and inter-ethnically: Attempting a map for personal and professional development. *Psychotherapy and Politics International.* 8 (*1*) Published online at Wiley Interscience. (www.interscience.wiley.com) DO1: 10-1002/Pp1213.

Lago, C., & MacMillan, M. (1999). *Experiences in relatedness: Group work and the Person Centred Approach.* Ross: PCCS Books.

Lago, C., Christodoulidi, F., Dhingra, S., & Mudadi-Billings, S. (2013). Aspiring towards relational depth when working with client-therapist diversity. Manuscript in preparation for M. Cooper, R. Knox, D. Murphy. & S. Wiggins. (Eds.) *Contemporary perspectives in relational depth.* Palgrave MacMillan, London.

MacMillan, M. (1999). In you there is a universe: person-centred counselling as a manifestation of the Breath of the Merciful. In I. Fairhurst (Ed.), *Women writing in the person-centred approach.* Ross: PCCS Books.

MacMillan, M. & Lago, C. (1993). Large groups: Critical reflections and some concerns. *The Person Centered Approach and Cross Cultural Communication. An International Review Vol. 2.*

Mann, E. (2011). Does the first relationship support Carl Rogers' theory of interpersonal relationship? Unpublished Dissertation. Temenos/Middlesex University.

McIlduff, E., Coghlan, D. (1989). Process and facilitation in a cross cultural communication workshop. *Person-Centered Review*, 4(1), 77–98.

McIlduff, E., Coghlan, D. (1993). The cross-cultural communication workshops in Europe: Reflections and review. *The Person-Centered Approach and Cross Cultural Communication. An International Review. Vol. 2.*

Rogers, C. R. (1946). Significant aspects of client–centered therapy. *The American Psychologist, 1*(10), 415–422.

Rogers, C. R. (1959). A Theory of Therapy, Personality and Interpersonal Relationships as developed in the Client Centered Framework. In Koch, S. (Ed.). *Psychology: A Study of Science.* Study 1. *Formulations of the Person and the Social Context. Vol. 3.* (pp. 184–256.) New York: Mc-Graw-Hill.

Rogers, C. R. (1969). *Encounter groups.* Harmondsworth: Penguin.

Rogers, C. R. (1980). *A way of being.* Boston: Houghton Mifflin.

Rogers (1986a). The dilemmas of a South African white. *Person-Centered Review, 1*(1), 15–35.

Rogers, C. R. (1986b). The Rust workshop: A personal overview. *The Journal of Humanistic Psychology, 26*(3), 23–45.

Rogers, C. R., & Sanford, R. C. (1989). Client Centred Psychotherapy. In H. I. Kaplan & B. J. Sadock (Eds.), *The comprehensive textbook of psychiatry* (Vol. 2, pp. 1482–1501). Baltimore: Williams & Wilkins.

Rogers, C.R., & Wood, J.K. (1974). Client- Centered Theory: Carl Rogers. In A. Burton (Ed.) *Operational theories of personality.* (pp. 211–258.) New York: Brunner/Mazel.

Rosenberg, M. (2003). *Nonviolent communication: A language of life* (2nd ed.). Encinitas: Puddle Dancer Press.

Tudor, K., & Worrall, M. (2006). *Person Centred Therapy: A clinical philosophy.* Hove: Routledge.

Wood, J. K. (2008). *Carl Rogers' Person-Centered Approach: Towards an understanding of its implications.* Ross-on-Wye: PCCS Books.

Conflict Transformation

Will Stillwell

1 Introduction

I come to write this essay from a career working with and reflecting upon individual lives and small group behaviors. I have noticed that often many of us divide our psychosocial world into alternative centers of experience, a "self" and an "other." It seems to me that only by responding to the call across the divide from the other side will our imagination overcome the divisions we have made. Then integration can occur in that moment.

I believe that in Carl Rogers' movement from "non-directive therapy" to a "person-centered approach" (PCA), he realized something of this divided nature as it concerned human conflict. Rogers understood that conflict within a person, between people, and between groups of people all have a common feature (Rogers 1965). All involve presumed "entities" operating in the same arena such as within the person, a "self-concept" and an "experiential self"; between people, "myself" and "others"; and between groups, a "we" and a "them." In conflict, these entities within one realm bestow incompatibility to their respective desires and develop emotion-charged opposition toward each other.

In general, I think Rogers' conflict resolution process was psychological—that is, was aimed at change within the "internal worlds" of persons involved. He facilitated individuals to learn—respond and re-assess their circumstances in light of trusting new information. New information, he proposed, emerges for an individual as participants of an ongoing situation share experiences of their organismic selves and their conceptions of the meanings. "...[P]eople...desire more personal contact, deeper communication, more closeness, and more searching and intimate dialogue" (Rogers 1986), we desire less mistrust.

In this essay, I will provide an example from each of these three realms of conflict: within a person, between people, and between groups of people. I shall

W. Stillwell (✉)
Center for Studies of the Person, 1150 Silverado St., Suite 217, La Jolla, CA, USA
e-mail: awstillwell@sbcglobal.net

J. H. D. Cornelius-White et al. (eds.), *Interdisciplinary Applications of the Person-Centered Approach*, DOI: 10.1007/978-1-4614-7144-8_19,
© Springer Science+Business Media New York 2013

link each to a particular "core condition"—congruence, unconditional positive regard, and empathy—that Rogers proposed in concert comprise a personal authentic being effective in constructively dealing with conflict. I refer the reader to the editors' introduction where appear definitions of the attitudes in being known as congruence, unconditional positive regard, and empathy.

All of Rogers' effective conditions of being might well occur in any and all of these conflict realms. I am not implying that one attitude particularly occurs in the single realm in which I illustrate some of its expressions. My purpose is to describe how these attitudes might be expressed in anyone's efforts to transform a conflict from impeded movement to fresh possibilities. Any person or party who is attempting to move through a situation of impasse (including those who adjudicate or facilitate) can venture to approach other involved parties in attitudes of congruence, unconditional positive regard, and empathy.

2 Conflict Within a Person: Illustrating the Expression of Congruence

Dadisi's interview with Rogers (presented in the chapter on an Experiential Example of the PCA) will be used to illustrate the role of congruence as it was manifested in a situation of intrapersonal conflict. Dadisi here represents to me a fine example of what—in all its forms—conflict is: he is the archetypal "protesting man" seeking to move his life-world into right order. From his initial statement of his conflict concerning his schooling and career, Dadisi is working on his inner conflict progress. I will point to what I take as some manifestations of Dadisi's personal congruent attitude.

Some of us find it difficult to maintain our own congruence through shifting life situations. Congruence concerns the relation between one's actions and *self-conceptions*. Dadisi demonstrates these in #31, "And I feel with the experience I've had in **public** school, I've been of the belief that the higher in the, this white educational system you be- you went…the more assimilated that one became. So part of my avoidance is to being assimilated." A bit later in #33, "I…I think it's probably **taken** me…**probably** just about to this time, to feel set in myself and set enough in my identity that I could take that on with a probably greater strength…and…know that I won't necessarily, **lose** me."

In their exchange #11 through #14, Dadisi and Rogers work together clarifying Dadisi's own *definition of reality*. Dadisi ties together his experiences: "Yeah, well, part of me feels like I need to do that, and it's quote-unquote 'paying the dues.' Um, I hear this quite often to, to me with some staff people that I work with…and at times I agree with that and still its frustrating to feel like I'd be backtracking…I don't feel like it's going to be catching up, I feel like it's just gonna be **documenting**…in a **sense** [I] have type-of over-compensated for not having the educational background, ah, to back-up, um, the skills…that what I do with the anger is…go out and 'do,' uh, instead of feeling limited."

Dadisi in his #28 and #30 shows he believes himself *neither absolutely sovereign nor absolutely dependent* regarding his social world. "Yeah it makes me mad, but it also motivates me to go and get it...for myself...and not expect...white people to... A totally white system with what felt like totally white interests at heart." Nonetheless, he claims his determination to be the *agent making his own existential choices*: "But I've chosen, often chosen to do that learning, and do that inquisitiveness in other arenas...you know, real life, practical kinds of situations, working with, um, **people**..." (# 16); "Um, when I think, my way, I'm thinking of what I want to do, what I want to accomplish as a self-determining **person**..." (#17); "I say, 'Why can't I **do** that?' but I notice that I'm not, 'can't' 'can't,' 'not being able to...' it's, sometimes it's a **choice**" (#18). And it may be that waiting for, rather than acting upon, is a better expression for him of his personal agency in this situation at this time.

Self-conceiving, defining reality, existential choosing in a non-dependent, non-sovereign social world are some possible elements of a person's congruent attitude. Other potential markers that Dadisi shows include *not giving up on what one wants*. He speaks of his own working, "I criticize, re-prioritize..." (#20) as he remains in or revisits his quandary *without rushing to resolve* by taking a false resolution or refuge. For the entire interview, Dadisi is focusing on his "hard struggle" whether to continue his schooling. He does *not back away from greater congruence*. In exchange #10 between the two men, both demonstrate *trust in their emotions*. Rogers: "It does make you mad." Dadisi: "Uh huh. I'm getting mad thinking about it." In #27, Dadisi approaches a subject suddenly full of emotion, *responsibly allowing his own presence in the immediacy*. "It's a little hard, difficult for me because this is still a **live** issue for me that I'm dealing with now. Um, it has to do with you, the fact that you're white, it has to do with...also how I feel about school..." In #43, we hear that Dadisi's immediate congruence has resulted in at least one *new creative understanding*—that white people need him!

Congruence is approached by a person querying himself, "*Why is this issue important to **me***?" "***Who** am I here, now; and shall that person I am venture into public?*" These questions to "self" can be missed if one is primarily attending and valuing "other's" opinions and perceptions.

3 Conflict Between People: Illustrating the Expression of Unconditional Positive Regard

Dear Amy;

My Lover is a close friend and has been in a sexless marriage for almost 20 years. After 10 years she told her husband she couldn't be celibate any longer, although she views him as her 'true love.' She is not sneaking around. He calls my phone knowing she's at my place. She doesn't lie about what we do..

Being intimate isn't all there is to our relationship; mostly we enjoy spending time together. If we weren't with each other we'd find others to be intimate with.. Her husband likes having time alone, and the three of us spend time together. Her husband and I like each other. Now her family is saying that our relationship has to end, and if it doesn't she'll be kicked out of the family. She has told them that she won't leave either of us, but I am feeling guilty about her losing contact with her family—not to mention losing a decent inheritance.. Is it fair for her family to do this? If the three of us are happy with how things are, then why does it matter to others? Wondering   (Dickinson 2011).

In this letter to an advice columnist, an interpersonal conflict is described among four parties—Wondering (the writer), a Lover, her Husband, and her Family. They are presented as two oppositional positions: three individuals making choices and Family unified in demand for change. Lover and Husband and Wondering are said to be "happy with how things are," but in response to the challenge Wondering begins to newly notice some greater costs of what he had believed was utopian living. He says, he is "feeling guilty," perhaps also he is feeling responsible or vulnerable in their unorthodox situation, maybe he has doubts about his alliance with his partners. But at this point, Wondering first wonders at the moral shortcomings of the opposition, "Is it fair for them to do this?"

Many a person when alarmed starts his attempt to control a conflict by defending self with an attitude of negative moral judgment toward any who opposes him as he is. In this situation, Family is presumed to have begun by morally condemning Lover and her companions. "But in our group we are righteous, just, fair, and loving. Those guys who seem to aim for some other outcome than what we want, must themselves be morally reprehensible" (unfair). A negative judgment toward the other seems to magically polarize our group: we enhance our competitive tendencies, exaggerate our positive self-conception, and choose to be impervious to criticism in our attempt to ignore the costs to our remaining secure.

Unconditional positive regard is an attitude that a person can inhabit as she approaches an other, friend or foe. In fact, appreciating the other *neither as friend nor as foe* is more like the unconditionality of the attitude. "Unconditional" is not "indifferent." Unconditional attitude drops that usual kind of agency which attempts to foresee the outcomes by controlling others' behaviors or the situation itself. Unconditional positive regard *trusts an emerging comprehensive sense of* satisfying *wholesomeness* from and for all the participants. The potential of positive relations with the other (i.e., at least moderated conflict) is enhanced if we *regard them as persons like ourselves* of our own group. They too, are seeking their own truth and congruence, seeking to live manifesting their own reality. They too, wish to regard themselves and be regarded as right-living human beings. They too, legitimately feel security protection needs. Unconditional positive regard is the *covenant we offer to persevere together* with all the people involved. It includes *acknowledging the other's existence and their interest in my actions*.

Two other markers of the attitude, *expecting relationships to evolve and change*, and *not clinging to one's own expectations*, can enable us to clearly notice similarities and differences between us. If we move to *make actual our common interests*, we approach the sources of our creativity together.

In the situation described by Wondering, his most important next move is to accept how Lover feels about staying together with her partners and about being kicked out of her family. If Lover wants something other than family expulsion, it will be helpful for her to be able to be at ease with her family members, whatever they choose to do. *Relationship comfort* such as this applies all around, to Husband, Family, and Wondering, but does not imply that a person gives up on the content of what she wants.

I believe there can be no guarantee (it is "unconditional") that the whole affair will resolve to everyone's complete satisfaction without pain. But when we feel wounded by acts of other people, one of healing's balms is *our own profound respect for our own attitude* and behavior in regard to the other persons. Ceasing our judgment of the other may entail our continued fearlessness in being so, even as others continue in their judgments of us.

4 Conflict Between Groups: Illustrating the Expression of Empathy

Forty years ago, I was co-author of research which demonstrated that prison parolees in the United States have acute physical and material needs, but even more importantly lack the personal support that other people enjoy from domestic partnerships, work groups, or relatives. Parolees are not closely connected with their communities of residence through social groups or organizations. (Erickson et al. 1971) This state of affairs seems to continue today.

Patrice Gains is a woman who served prison time for her criminal behavior. Recently paroled, she was unprepared for meeting the rest of society:

> "Once I committed my crime, I never felt as if I was part of a community. No one saw the power in getting me to realize the harm I had caused to my family. My parents were ashamed. I disappointed friends and neighbors who had helped me over the years. I knew that some of them probably even felt I had brought shame to our close-knit neighborhood...I had wanted to change my life, so I could be a good daughter, sister, and mother. But I didn't know how to change...No one ever considered finding a way for me to give back, to feel forgiven and accepted again, I had to put all of the pieces together myself— find a way to repair the harm I caused, forgive myself, and be a part of the community again—a process that took years." (Gains 2011).

Intergroup conflict, in common with the other types, divides an inner (we) from other, the outsider (not-us); in this case, people who have not been convicted of crime separate from former felons. In conflict, such divisions frequently become rigid. We allow ourselves to declare the feared outsiders as "enemy." They are so wrongfully different from who we are that we are willing to violate and victimize them in our defense. We increasingly admire and support our own forcefulness and seek allies to aid us in these actions. We cling to or even intensify the apple-pie order of our group's internal social relationships.

We do not conceive in empathy those persons convicted of criminal offenses. We who have suffered at their hands do not *understand their stance*. Their presence seemingly brings us feared negative consequences; we deduce alien-to-us motives on their part.

People in search of healing who have brought together perpetrators and their victims tell that victims wish for the convicted criminal to express remorse and to pay restitution for the offenses. They tell also that the offenders too feel alienated from their victims and other non-convicted citizens, these offenders wish *someone would be willing to hear from their inner lives*. Unresolved feelings generate defensive attitudes and ambitions to control outcomes. Each group can become mired in their own sufferings and victimhood. In their mutual stand-off, both ex-felons and righteous people suffer from their narrow attachment to punishment responses, and their deep poverty in ways of empathic relating.

May I invite you to read again at the statements just above by Patrice Gains to ask yourself, "How might I respond empathically to her plight?"

Trying my own hand, I say: *Hear that to which she gives importance. Listen for her sense of consequences and proposals for change. Hear the thoughts and feelings she says, and those you sense she might wish to imply to you about her sense of herself. Then confirm with her to assure us all that we heard all that she hoped to communicate.* Figure 1 provides actual responses I might have made.

Empathy is a way of knowing other people, feeling how their lives might be experienced, and a way of living that invites others to share themselves. It takes energy and dedication for a person to continue empathically among other people who do not reciprocate and continue to choose defensive attitudes.

5 Concluding Thoughts

In these pages, I have presented instances from three human conflict arenas. I have highlighted particular manifestations in action that have been useful in my practice within conflicts. The markers I chose might be manifestations indicating the presence of certain personal attitudes, those orientations toward conflict and peace that Carl Rogers claimed were essential to practice more mature, constructive, peaceful, and fulfilling relationships.

I believe it important to reaffirm that Rogers himself eschews pointing toward such manifestations. His experience taught him that emphasizing practical measures could induce people to trust checklist behavioral routines as themselves sufficient, to the neglect of trusting their personal approach—"inside, psychological attitudes"—necessary for effective being-in-conflict. This emphasis on attitudes is what in today's behavioral measuring world still makes Rogers' approach "radical."

Confirming What Patrice Said	Did I hear These Consequences?	Did you Propose These Remedies?
No one knew how,	So you feel	You want to repair the harm.
knew that you could use help	disappointment and shame,	You want to be a good person.
in understanding the harm	maybe you feel vulnerable.	
youbroughtyourlovedones		
and those who		
had supported you.		
No one initiated an opening	The dry legal remedies	You want to forgive yourself.
with you to even get the idea	of probation and restitution	You want to join the moral
that you wanted to "give back"	are not substitutes for	community.
and be forgiven.	sisterhood and brotherly love.	
No one offered to guide,	You are feeling excluded and	You want people
support or welcome you	negatively judged by others.	of the community to invite
into the community.		you to be part of the
		community, that will help
		you regain your self-esteem.

Fig. 1 One attempt at confirmations, consequences, and remedies with Patrice

Rogers particularly address these attitudes for himself and for other practitioners. He looks toward personal and social growth possibilities, I am not aware that he published assessments of his individual clients or co-participants as to whether or not they had "good attitude." However, they may be manifested, effective attitudes occur when participants "...are experiencing and communicating their own realness...and a deeply sensitive nonjudgmental understanding of every attitude, feeling and opinion expressed." (Rogers 1986) Such participants are trusting—risking and confirming in a process of undeterminable outcome—that living these attitudes in the midst of conflicts is the most likely opening to an interactional process leading to constructive movement.

Do I trust me, my "self" (a self that I identify; our group)? *Do I trust you, my "other"* (a separated part of myself; an other person; an other group)? People struggling in a conflict and third-party mediators can manifest in their initiatives and reactions their own embodied trust of "self," of "other," of inclusive possibilities. Persons who provide openings in which conflictual parties may nurture their own trusting feelings, are those persons who will transform conflict's inherent divisiveness toward tolerable or fulfilling integration.

References

Dickinson, A. (2011). Ask Amy newspaper column *Chicago Tribune* September 29.

Erickson, R. J., Crow, W., Zurcher, L., Connett, A., & Stillwell, W. (1971). *The offender looks at his own needs,* La Jolla:Western Behavioral Sciences Institute.

Gains, P. (2011). Beyond prisons yes magazine (Summer) Positive futures network, Bainbridge Island.

Rogers, C. (1965). Dealing with psychological tensions. *Journal of Applied Behavioral Science, 1*(1), 6–24.

Rogers, C. (1986). The rust workshop a personal overview. *Journal of Humanistic Psychology, 26*(3), 23–45.

PCA Encounter Groups: Transformative Learning for Individuals and Communities

Maureen O'Hara

1 Introduction

The person-centered approach (PCA) is a relational practice that trusts the transformative power of attunement within human relationships to facilitate spontaneous movement toward health, undo long-standing psychological patterns that create problems and cause pain, and expand individual and collective consciousness to sustain well-being, joy, creativity, and efficacy at ever higher orders of complexity and vitality. A core component of PCA—indeed a *sine qua non*—is the view that there exists in nature an intrinsic movement toward growth, complexity, and transcendence. Rogers, after (Goldstein 1934), referred to this drive at different times as an actualizing tendency, formative tendency, and self-actualizing tendency. The actualizing tendency manifests as the self-healing capacity of individuals, in the power of person-to-person connections and in the wisdom of groups. For Rogers, the formative tendency transcends the human domain and includes everything in nature—from atoms to galaxies and beyond. In Rogers' view, the universe is not cold, random, and soulless but is "up to something," and this something could be trusted. The PCA though today known mostly as an approach to individual psychological healing and growth has always carried a larger theme of social transformation. At a time in history when established, mainstream modes of thought are proving inadequate to the challenges before us, a new worldview is needed that is aligned with the universal force that drives being. Person-centered encounters may have potential as sites where such a new worldview can be developed and where faith in the wisdom of the life force can be restored and strengthened.

M. O'Hara (✉)
Department of Psychology, National University, 11255 N. Torrey Pines Road,
La Jolla, CA 92037, USA
e-mail: mohara@nu.edu

J. H. D. Cornelius-White et al. (eds.), *Interdisciplinary Applications of the Person-Centered Approach*, DOI: 10.1007/978-1-4614-7144-8_20, © Springer Science+Business Media New York 2013

2 Relationality, Holism, and Autopoiesis

Peter Schmid has argued that PCA is best understood as a group process even when working one-on-one with individuals and many analyses of PCA practice now place it within holistic, relational, and systems science paradigms (Schmid and O'Hara 2007). O'Hara and Wood (1983; 2004) introduced Koestler's concept of holons and systems science to describe patterns of self-assertive and self-transcendent awareness at individual and collective levels in the development of group wisdom and a conscious group "mind" in PCA groups. Kriz considers the actualizing tendency as an example of autopoiesis. He regards PCA as a systems theory (Kriz 2008) and describes person-centered relationships and groups as self-organizing systems, best understood using complexity science (see also Hulgus and Kriz chapters in this book). Recently, João Hipólito has expanded this discussion (Hipólito 2011). Likewise, (Natiello 2001; Wood 2008), (O'Hara 1984), and (Wood 2008) have all described the nonlinear, emergent phenomena to account for processes that arise in PCA encounters.

3 The Power of Groups

Rogers' faith in the power of groups to facilitate deep learning began as a young man on his trip to China in 1922 (Cornelius-White 2012) and continued throughout his long career. His trust in relationships as sites for transformative change can be seen in his descriptions of counseling with individuals and couples, encounter groups, large community encounters, and encounters with diplomats and peacemakers. His insights from group experiences contributed to the development of core PCA theory and practice (Schmid and O'Hara 2007). During the heyday of the human potential movement, when encounter groups, sensitivity training, marathons, T-groups, TORI process groups, and a raft of personal growth workshops of many orientations were drawing thousands of participants, Rogers concluded that the intensive group experience was "probably the most potent social intervention of the century" (Rogers 1970, p. 9).

Rogers (1970) identified 15 patterns in the PCA encounter group process that resemble those described in the classical group dynamics literature (Bradford et al. 1964; Tuckman 1965). Rogers' initial description was of small groups (6–12 members). Others have detailed the process of group development in community encounter groups with between 150–800 participants (Bowen et al. 1979; Coulson et al. 1977; Devonshire 1991; MacMillan 2004; MacMillan and Lago 1999; McIlduff and Coghlan 1991; Natiello 1987; O'Hara and Wood 1984, 2004; Rogers 1970, 1978).

Encounter groups were first valued in PCA circles as opportunities for personal growth.[1] Published accounts focus on individual stories of emotional risk-taking and deep personal sharing leading to deep and often complex psychological transformation. The movie *Journey Into Self* (Kramer et al. 1968) won its Oscar© largely because of the emotional power of the personal breakthroughs of the seven participants. This individual emphasis is carried over into organization and community interventions using encounter groups where personal sharing, expression of strong emotions, and the development of interpersonal understanding and closeness were highly valued. In early encounters, little attention was given to analysis of group dynamics or of issues and processes beyond the personal and interpersonal. When participants interested in political and social issues would try to insert group-level observations, they were frequently discouraged. This bias in favor of expression of personal feelings prompted some observers to question the emphasis in encounter groups on emotionality at the expense of analysis (Farson 1978), charging "self-indulgence" (Coulson 1994) and "cult of the individual" (MacMillan 2004). Notwithstanding these concerns, for many years, encounter groups were popular sites for growth. Research strongly supported their effectiveness when facilitation styles were those characteristic of PCA, that is, non-directive, caring, empathic, and accepting of personal meaning making (Bates and Goodman 1986).

Encounter groups contributed greatly to advances in conceptualization of person-centered processes. The expansion of the concept of "fully functioning person" from autonomous individual to a self as part of larger systems such as relationships, groups, societies, and ecologies emerged from work in groups. So did the shift from considering the approach "client-centered" to the broader frame of "person-centered" (see below). The flattened hierarchy of the PCA group, where each person's contribution is valued as much as anyone else including the facilitator's, empowers participants, affirms them as uniquely valued, and provides a setting where they may find their own voice. It is often the very public display of unconditional acceptance and belonging in a community group that makes it so meaningful to people and amplifies the effects the core conditions might have in a one-to-one relationship with a therapist.

4 Learning in Large Encounter Groups

Nothing distinguishes PCA from other systems of therapy and counseling more than does the continued investment in the large group community encounter process. Working in large groups began in 1968 as part of the La Jolla Program[2]

---

[1] This contrasts with team building, communication skills, Tavistock training, organizational development applications in vogue at the same time.

[2] The La Jolla Program (LJP) was the first PCA project that used large group encounters. It began as a "leadership training institute" at Western Behavioral Sciences Institute in 1968 and

when the facilitators discovered that when given a choice between staying in a big group or splitting into smaller groups, many people were drawn to the large group, which they saw as a "community." The La Jolla Program in Austria was a spin-off from this program and still occurs. The Facilitator Development Institute (FDI), founded by Charles Devonshire, also an outgrowth of the La Jolla Program, offered large encounter groups in several countries including the United Kingdom and went on to focus on cross-cultural communications. Person-centered organizations in many countries continue to offer encounter groups to the public.

In 1974, Rogers' daughter Natalie convinced her dad to take a risk and move beyond the focus on individual growth to focus on big picture, social, and political issues. Natalie, a feminist peace activist and trained group facilitator, wanted to find out whether the core conditions of client-centered therapy that had been shown to be so powerful for transformation of individuals might also apply to groups and be effective as strategies for social transformation. She, Rogers, and John K. Wood brought a team of facilitators together who came from client-centered therapy, gestalt therapy, expressive arts, organizational psychology, and sociology to convene an encounter that was to be a radical experiment with a non-directive, self-organizing group process.[3] The core PCA facilitation team with additional colleagues from around the world went on to convene a series of over forty large encounters. These "PCA workshops" were distinct from the FDI groups and the La Jolla Program groups in that they were less structured, less focused on individual growth or the application of any predetermined psychological principles, and placed radical trust in the actualizing tendency.[4]

Pushing the boundaries of large group encounters even further, in 1977, a team of PCA facilitators which included Carl Rogers partnered with Brazilian colleagues to experiment with encounters with 800 participants over a span of two days. Bowen et al. (1979) suggested that these remarkable events or "ciclos" which took place during Brazil's transition from dictatorship to democracy might provide experiential settings where long suppressed people might reclaim their capacity to speak out and in an atmosphere of respect, listening, unconditional regard, congruence, empathy and guided by trust in an actualizing tendency, resolve the many cultural dissonances that threaten contemporary societies. Colin Lago echoed this two decades later in his work with culturally diverse groups, when he observed that "Group work in general and large groups in particular offer a forum in which the complex issues of relatedness, the management of power, and active democracy can be explored by participants" (Lago 1994 quoted in Wood 2008).

(Footnote 2 continued)

moved to the Center for Studies of the Person in 1970. The book *The La Jolla Experiment: Eight personal views* (1978) Coulson, B., Land, D., Meador B.(Eds.) offers first-hand case stories.

[3] It was after the first of these events in 1974 that the team realized the term "client-centered" was inappropriate in a process where everyone was both participant and facilitator, so subsequent workshops were called "person-centered approach" workshops. The term PCA stuck.

[4] For a more detailed discussion of what differentiated these encounters from other large group processes run by Rogers' colleagues, see Wood 2008; Bowen et al. 1979).

From field notes and participant feedback from large PCA workshops in several cultures, O'Hara and Wood (1984) acknowledge the importance of encounters for personal growth, education, training, and even psychotherapy, but over time came to believe that even more significant was their potential to "provide opportunities for people to experience and develop the capacities... crucial for our evolution and survival" (p. 103) as a civilization and maybe even as a species. In particular, they demonstrate that not only individuals can become wise, but under the right circumstances, groups and communities may also become wise (Maureen O'Hara and Wood 1984). Rogers' believed that "groups have within themselves vast resources for understanding and accepting their dynamics. They can draw on this wisdom for reduction and resolution of conflicts, and for constructive change in the group's goals, ways of being and behavior" (personal conversation, June 1984). O'Hara and Wood developed a theoretical framework that balances the emphasis on individual psychological process with awareness of higher-order relational processes. For more detailed descriptions, see O'Hara and Wood (1984); O'Hara (1984); O'Hara and Wood (2004); and Wood (2008). Using Koestler's concept of holons and their relationship to increasing orders of complexity,[5] they describe the process of self-organization of the community groups into increasingly complex organization that is both honoring of each person's subjectivity as a unique and sovereign center of consciousness and at the same time is fully attuned to the configurations and flows within the group as a whole. Sometimes a state of collective attunement is reached where participants have extraordinary experiences. This experience resembles the moments when sports teams are in the "zone" and individuals play beyond their usual best, or when an orchestra shifts into a higher level of performance. The "flow" experience (Csikszentmihalyi 1993) lifts individuals and collectives into higher orders of capacity. Importantly, this shift does not always occur nor does it occur automatically. Impasses are potential transition points for groups and it is often after a period of conflict and frustration, when people give up trying to *make* things happen and tune in more deeply and align to what is already actually trying to happen, that a shift in group consciousness occurs. Directive interventions, especially by influential people, though they may offer temporary comfort ultimately undermine the group's faith in its own capacity to work its way through to a resolution. Even when interventions appear to solve the problem, they are often pseudo-solutions and by short-circuiting the learning process hold the group back from reaching its full potential. When driven by anxiety and aimed at controlling the process, directive interventions may actually create more incoherence and turbulence such that the whole becomes less than the sum of its parts. Research with complex systems shows that perturbation may

---

[5] A "holon" is any entity that is differentiated from others by some kind of boundary. Holons have one aspect which maintains and expresses their uniqueness, wholeness or integrity, identities, and boundaries, and an aspect that transcends these to participate in and become part of a larger entity. Koestler calls configurations that are bounded and that define identity, "self-assertive," and those configurations that are porous, easily entered, and permit participation into an entity or system with a higher order of complexity, "self-transcendent."

result either in disintegration to lower orders of complexity—breaking into smaller fragments, sometimes violently—or in self-organization to a higher order, more complex system. Both these movements may occur in PCA encounters (O'Hara 1995). In our experience, what makes the difference is if the group itself has faith in itself and in the actualizing tendency and is able to recognize and accept each person as a legitimate and valued member of the whole. When frustration runs high, this can be difficult, but when there are even a few individuals, people present that instead of trying to control the flow, recognize it, affirm it, and align with it, magic happens. Recent studies in the dynamics of complex systems have confirmed that local interactions within a smart part of a larger system (such as a single person or a conversation) can lead to "emergence of large scale or even global complexity" (Kosse 2001, p. 61). Small acts of hope can have widespread systemic effects suggested that the ability to create conscious groups made up of persons who are at one and the same time beings for themselves and competent participants in greater human collectivities is an essential competence for addressing life in the twenty-first century (O'Hara and Leicester 2012).

5 The Future of Encounter Groups

Most of the problems facing humanity are beyond the scope of individual actors, no matter how brilliant. Tracing back to Rogers' early thinking about social justice, PCA has always included a strong commitment to creating the enabling conditions for personal transformation and higher-order cultural evolution (O'Hara 2009). Many now believe that humanity may have reached a tipping point—its own impasse where the challenges have outstripped our capacity to deal with them from within the worldview that created them. This impasse offers both threat of disintegration and opportunity for transformation. With stunning foresight, in 1970, Rogers worried about the "increasingly impersonal milieu" created by "bigness" of industry, science, and education, and the use of computers in the implementation of deterministic and behavioristic thinking and hoped that encounter groups might become a "counterforce to the dehumanization of our culture" (p. 161).

A sign of hope today lies in the radical interconnectedness made possible by the Internet and social networking that has produced digital natives who talk casually of self-organizing systems, wholes that are "greater than the sum of their parts," Twitter flocks, flash mobs, and smart crowds. The idea of "the wise group" is in common currency. Digital natives who prize the possible synergies in self-transcendent modes such as collaboration, sharing, and co-creation eagerly repeat the mantra "no one is as smart as everyone." But the experience from PCA encounters suggests that group wisdom is most likely to emerge when individuals in them are free to and are willing to participate fully, sometimes to struggle, sometimes to listen, and sometime to love—not as faceless and voiceless parts, but as unique, authentic, and sovereign persons. Wise groups require participants who are fully present to themselves and to each other and who consciously and conscientiously (not automatically or manipulatively) engage with the search for collective welfare. Encounter groups offer a site where such capacities can be developed.

References

Bates, B., & Goodman, A. (1986). The effectiveness of encounter groups: Implications of research from counselling practice. *British Journal of Guidance and Counselling, 14*(3), 24–251.

Bowen, M., O'Hara, M. M., Rogers, C. R., & Wood, J. K. (1979). Learning in large groups:Implications for the future. *Education, 100,* 108–117.

Bradford, L., Gibb, J. R., & Benne, K. D. (1964). *T-group theory and laboratory method.* New York: Wiley.

Cornelius-White, J. H. D. (Ed.) (2012) Carl Rogers: China diary. Ross-on-Wye, UK: PCCS Books

Coulson, W. (1994). Repentant psychologist: How I wrecked the immaculate heart of Mary nuns. The Latin mass: The Journal of Catholic Culture and Tradition(Winter).

Coulson, W., Land, D., & Meador, B. (Eds.). (1977). *The La Jolla Experiment* La Jolla: The La Jolla Program.

Csikszentmihalyi, M. (1993). *The evolving self: A psychology for the third millennium.* New York: Harper Perennial.

Devonshire, C. (1991). The person-centered approach and cross cultural communication. In E. McIllduff & D. Coghlan (Eds.), *The person-centered a and cross cultural communication: An international review* (Vol. 1, pp. 15–42). Dublin: Center for Cross-Cultural Communication.

Farson, R. (1978). The technology of humanism. *Journal of Humanistic Psychology, 18*(April), 5–35.

Goldstein, K. (1934). *The organism: A holistic approach to biology derived from pathological data in man.* New York: Zone Books.

Hipólito, J. (2011). [Auto-organização e Complexidade: Evolução e desenvolvimento do pensamento Rogeriano.].

Kosse, K. (2001). Some regularities in human group formation and the evolution of social complexity. *Complexity, 6*(1), 60–64.

Kramer, S. (Writer) & S. Kramer (Director). (1968). Journey Into Self. In B. Mcgaw (Producer).

Kriz, J. (2008). *Self-actualization: Person-centered approach and systems theory.* Herefordshire: PCCS Books.

MacMillan, M. (2004). Who am I am who are all these other people? In D. W. Bower (Ed.), *Person-centered/client-centered: Discovering the self that one truly is* (pp. 64–80). Lincoln: IUniverse.

MacMillan, M., & Lago, C. (Eds.). (1999). *Experiences in relatedness: Groupwork and the person-centered approach.* Ross-on-Wye: PCCS Books.

McIllduff, E., & Coghlan, D. (1991). Dublin, 1985: Perception of a cross-cultural communications workshop *The Person-centered Approach and cross cultural communication: An international review* (Vol. 11, pp. 21-34). Dublin: Center for Cross-Cultural Communication.

Natiello, P. (1987). The person-centered approach: From theory to practice. *Person-Centered Review, 2*(2), 203–216.

Natiello, P. (2001). *The person-centered approach: A passionate presence.* Ross-on-Wye: PCCS Books.

O'Hara, M., & Wood, J. K. (1983). Patterns of awareness: Consciousness and the group mind. *The Gestalt Journal, 6,* 103–117.

O'Hara, M. (1984). Person-centered gestalt: Toward a holistic synthesis. In R. F. Levant & J. M. Shlien (Eds.), *Client-centered therapy and the person-centered approach*. New York: Praeger.

O'Hara, M. (1995). Streams. In M.L.Suhd (Ed.), *Positive regard: Carl Rogers and other notables he influenced*. Palo Alto: Science and Behavior Books.

O'Hara, M. (2009). Another inconvenient truth and the developmental role for psychology in a threatened world. *The Humanistic Psychologist, 38*(2), 101–119.

O'Hara, M., & Leicester, G. (2012). *Dancing at the Edge:Competence, culture and organization for the 21st century*. Axminster: Triarchy.

O'Hara, M., & Wood, J. K. (1984). Patterns of awareness: Consciousness and the group mind. *The Gestalt Journal, 6*(2), 103–116.

O'Hara, M., & Wood, J.K. (2004). Transforming communities: Person-centered encounters and the creation of integral conscious groups. In B. A. Banathy & J. P. (Eds.): Plenum.

Rogers, C. R. (1970). *Carl Rogers on encounter groups*. New York: Harper and Row.

Rogers, C. R. (1978). *Carl Rogers on personal power:Inner strength and its revolutionary impact*. New York: Dell.

Schmid, P. F., & O'Hara, M. (2007). Group therapy and encounter groups. In M. Cooper, M. O'Hara, P. F. Schmid, & G. Wyatt (Eds.), *Handbook of Person-Centered psychotherapy and counseling*. London: Palgrave-McMillan, UK.

Tuckman, B. (1965). Developmental sequence in small groups. *Psychological Bulletin, 63*(6), 384–399.

Wood, J.K. (2008). *Carl Rogers' Person-Centered Approach: Towards and understanding of its implications* Ross-on-Wye: PCCS Books.

Staying Human: Experiences of a Therapist and Political Activist

Rosemary Hopkins

In campaigning for freedom and democratic change during and since the racist apartheid era in South Africa, Archbishop Desmond Tutu has a charisma that radiates. While talking with him at a conference in St Andrews, Scotland in 1995, we had a lively exchange of views on his father's expressed wisdom: '*Don't raise your voice, improve your argument*'. I shared how powerfully this had influenced me as a political activist. The Archbishop was adamant that to fulfil my potential, I should return to my birthplace, South Africa. I was equally adamant that Scotland was my adopted home and that I could be a vigorous activist here. When he actually raised his voice, it was in delight; when he spoke of a role for me in South Africa, it was with passion; when he listened to me, he showed respect, even when he disagreed with me. We met as strangers, with different views of the world and different roles in it, vividly demonstrating how not to *raise your voice*, but to offer passionate arguments and yet recognise each other. We parted with our different commitments and aspects of patriotism acknowledged and allowed, and with a strong sense of two worlds meeting and connecting.

That is the crucial issue in following the person-centred approach to political activism—to be able to hear another view without becoming detached (Proctor et al. 2006; Rogers 1967). When 'them' or 'us', the oppressors or the oppressed, the exploiters or the exploited, the careless or the careful are perceived as 'other', our interconnectedness can be obscured. When people are dehumanised and perceived as 'them' to another's 'us', those who practise non-violent direct action will emerge challenging the power of dehumanisation, discrimination and disconnection.

Political activism brings me in contact with a great many people from different backgrounds, nationalities and views, and the language used to express these views plays a significant part in how to make connections. It is easy to fall into naming, blaming and shaming, and so easy to judge others as wrong rather than different. And it is easy to be overwhelmed or disheartened by the circumstances or the

R. Hopkins (✉)
9 Drummond Park, Crook of Devon, Kinross KY13 0UX, Scotland, UK
e-mail: rosemaryhopkins@mac.com

J. H. D. Cornelius-White et al. (eds.), *Interdisciplinary Applications of the Person-Centered Approach*, DOI: 10.1007/978-1-4614-7144-8_21, © Springer Science+Business Media New York 2013

cause. Despair can evoke huge rage, which going outward can alienate and provoke more anger and violence, or turning inward can also alienate by sapping energy and storing bitterness. One danger is apathy, the feeling of alienation and helplessness. Bruce Kent is a veteran anti-nuclear campaigner and co-founder of the Movement for the Abolition of War with whom I have spent time with in schools. He is reassuring that *a very normal reaction of people when they think about getting rid of war and warfare is this is quite beyond me. Too big.* He inspires with his orchestra metaphor, in which he says to young people *You don't have to do it all. You need to decide which instrument you can play, big or small, in the peace orchestra and get on with playing it… You can't do it all. Just do your bit and encourage other players to do their bit.* This offered wisdom does not come from training in the person-centred approach, but from an instinctive love of humankind to which Bruce Kent has devoted his life, and which has all the hallmarks of Carl Rogers' kindness, willingness to listen and trust in the inherent wisdom of individuals, alone and in groups.

It is an odd contradiction. The times I feel most resilient as an activist standing silent vigil with Women in Black in Edinburgh every Saturday for an hour, since spring 2002, are when I am out front offering informative leaflets to passers-by and particularly when listening to someone who challenges our vigil. I mean the sort of listening I was trained to do as a PC counsellor—to listen for what lies behind the attack or hopelessness, to acknowledge what I hear, often misplaced anger, fear or low self-worth and then to engage in some sort of discussion. This sometimes finishes with the protagonist's dismay that we do not agree, but often with a better understanding between us about what we each value. Our message is one of peace and justice, against violence and war as a means of solving conflict, so we are occasionally challenged as traitors, disgraceful, a waste of time, pathetic or pointless. I have learnt to accept the attacks and the praise, and there are many expressions of appreciation for our stance in solidarity with **all** victims of conflict.

Standing vigil is very different to lock-ons, sit-ins and canoeing across the Gairloch to board a Trident nuclear-armed submarine, non-violent direct actions of friends who have more courage and daring than I do and who choose, in Bruce Kent's words, to play a different instrument. And yet, spending time with these people at demonstrations, peace camps and the inevitable bus journeys, we share a deep valuing of human beings and the planet, and concern that what anyone does at any time effects others, and we do not know for sure how or for how long. As human beings, we have a responsibility to challenge and be challenged by existing conditions and values expressed and imposed by those in authority and also to be nourished and inspired by others and by the collective response of activists.

I recognise the teachings of Carl Rogers' in colleagues who are politically active and have discovered how these principles emerge in many guises. To my knowledge, Vittorio Arrigoni, journalist and human rights defender, had no specific training in the person-centred approach. I knew him from a distance through his writings and videos and through people who knew him well, following him from 2008 on the first international boat to break the 40-year Israeli naval blockade of Gaza. He stayed on in Gaza with the International Solidarity Movement to accompany ambulances, farmers, fishermen and children under fire. His blogs from inside Gaza describe the devastation of Palestinian lives and livelihoods in the 2008–2009 Israeli attack that killed and injured thousands of civilians (Arrigoni 2010). Viktor was taken hostage on 14 April 2011 and executed the following day by an anti-Hamas faction in Gaza. Huwaida Arraf, co-founder of the International Solidarity Movement, entitled her tribute to him the following day: *Humanity Has No Nationality* (Lock and Irving 2010). Viktor was an inspiration to the blockaded people of Gaza, his colleagues, and friends worldwide who continue to aspire to *Stay Human*, to value interconnectedness—combining kindness, willingness to understand and love with a commitment to risk-taking so as to live congruently.

1 Vittorio Arrigoni's Message

25 August 2008, on arrival by boat in Gaza with Free Gaza

'...History is made by ordinary people. Everyday people, with family at home and a regular job, who are committed to peace as a great ideal—to the rights of all—to staying human.

History is us—who risked our lives to bring utopia within reach, to offer a dream, a hope, to hundreds of thousands of people who cried with us as we reached the port of Gaza.

...Our message of peace is a call to action for other ordinary people like ourselves: not to hand over your lives to whatever puppeteer is in charge this time round, but to take responsibility for the revolution. First, the inner revolution—to give love, to give empathy. It is this that will change the world.

We have shown that peace is not an impossible utopia... Believe this, stand firm against intimidation, fear, and despair and simply remain human'.

References

Arrigoni, V. (2010). *Gaza: Stay human*. England: Kube. [Originally published as *Gaza: Restiamo Umani* (2009). Rome: Il Manifesto, Manifestolibri].

Arrigoni, V. (2008, August). Blog 23, (Translated by Leila, 2011). Retrieved November 12, 2011 from guerrillaradio.iobloggo.com/.

Lock, S., & Irving, S. (2010). *Gaza: Beneath the bombs*. London: Pluto Press.

Proctor, G., Cooper, M., Sanders, P., & Malcolm, B. (Eds.). (2006). *Politicizing the person-centred approach*. Ross-on-Wye: PCCS Books.

Rogers, C. R. (1967). *On becoming a person*. London: Constable.

Part VII
Conclusion and Meta-View

The Person-Centered Approach: An Emergent Paradigm

Renate Motschnig-Pitrik, Michael Lux
and Jeffrey H. D. Cornelius-White

This chapter aims to provide a concise yet encompassing meta-view on the theory, scope, practice, and meaning of the Person-Centered Approach (PCA) and connect it to the "messages" coming from the authors of the "sibling books" on the interdisciplinarity of the PCA: *The Interdisciplinary Handbook of the Person-Centered Approach: Research and Theory* (Cornelius-White, Motschnig-Pitrik, & Lux 2013) *and the Interdisciplinary Applications of the Person-Centered Approach* (this volume). Since the PCA as illustrated in both books is far more than a theory, a meta-theory—in the sense of a theory about a theory—might still be too restrictive to describe the phenomenon in sufficient richness as to capture some of the experienced meaning associated with it. This is why our conceptual enterprise needed to be extended to encompass all kinds of meta-statements. It draws from the experience of preparing, editing, and accompanying the chapters of the interdisciplinary volumes, iteratively checking back with Rogers' writing, our own thoughts, and the visual mapping of concepts and their relationships. In other words, our process was one to reflect on the PCA such that the reflection of its theories yields a meta-theory and captures essential aspects of this overarching phenomenon. These being very rich, indeed, we cautiously propose to refer to the interdisciplinary PCA as an *emerging, overarching paradigm*. Readers will find evidence in this chapter to form their own view.

R. Motschnig-Pitrik (✉)
Computer Science Didactics and Learning Research Center, University of Vienna,
Währinger Strasse 29/6.41 1090 Vienna, Austria
e-mail: renate.motschnig@univie.ac.at

M. Lux
Neurologisches Rehabilitationszentrum Quellenhof, Kuranlagenallee 2,
75323 Bad Wildbad, Germany
e-mail: luxbw@yahoo.de

J. H. D. Cornelius-White
Counseling, Leadership and Special Education, University of Missouri,
S. National Avenue 901, Springfield, MO 65897, USA
e-mail: JCornelius-White@MissouriState.edu

J. H. D. Cornelius-White et al. (eds.), *Interdisciplinary Applications*
of the Person-Centered Approach, DOI: 10.1007/978-1-4614-7144-8_22,
© Springer Science+Business Media New York 2013

However, note that the emergent paradigm, or indeed any theory or research, will *not* substitute for *experiencing* the PCA as it happens in person-centered relationships and encounter groups. The lived, subjective experience of the PCA is primary. It precedes any conceptualization and requires channels that underlie, complement, and enrich the conceptual. This can be compared with giving another hug, looking in their eyes, hearing their voice, or sitting side by side: The best description can never fully substitute for the subjective richness of the genuine experience.

Let us start the meta-view description with the first insight that crystallized during the book-editing process with thanks to Colin Lago for explicating a significant part of the idea.

1 The PCA is Far more than a Theory

As illustrated in Fig. 1, the PCA has an enormous scope. Not only does it transcend traditional disciplines such as psychology, philosophy, education, neuroscience, being transdisciplinary as well as interdisciplinary, it also attracts various applications, expressive arts, and the search for meaning in the philosophical and spiritual dimension of (the) human being.

Importantly, the PCA "starts" even before we think of a theory. It has an important pre-theoretical source: experience. *Experience* is as much at the core of

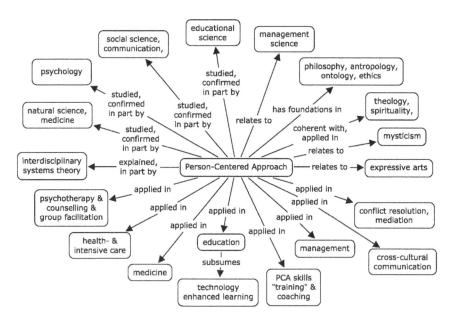

Fig. 1 The scope of the PCA. The arrows help the reader link the concepts

the PCA as are its empirically derived, philosophically grounded, and scientifically confirmed theories (see for example Rogers (1959) and the chapters by Ikemi, Lux, Motschnig-Pitrik and Nykl, Schmid, Silani, Zucconi and Lamm. Wolter-Gustafson, and others in *Interdisciplinary Handbook*). Therefore, the next statement is devoted to highlighting the vital or even primary function of experience in the PCA.

2 Experience Comes First: Otherwise no Theory and no Becoming a Person

It is necessary to engage with a person who lives the person-centered attitudes for the PCA to be fully appreciated. In particular, the PCA cannot be learned purely receptively and you cannot train (in the sense of conditioning) a human being to become person-centered (see also chapters by Lago, McCombs, Motschnig-Pitrik, and Kunze in this volume).

Rogers and Wood (1974) wrote: "First there is experiencing, then there is a theory" (p. 274). According to Rogers (1959), "Both the research and theory are being aimed toward the inward ordering of significant experience…It is the persistent, disciplined effort to make sense and order out of the phenomena of subjective experience" (p. 188). For Rogers, the construct of experience has a total quality: It includes pre-conceptual, bodily experience up to highly differentiated sensory experiences, feelings, recollections from memory, as well as deliberate and abstract thinking.

It is not by chance that person-centered practitioners frequently engage in person-centered encounter groups—a setting primarily aimed at experiencing self and relationship in the purest form and thereby allowing for deep and significant learning (Barrett-Lennard 1998; Rogers 1970; Lago and McMillan 1998; O'Hara in this volume). Will Stillwell referred to the experience during an encounter group (2003) as follows: "It helps to shape intuitions."

Very distinctly Rogers (1961) realized:

> "*Experience is, for me, the highest authority*. No other person's ideas, and none of my own ideas, are as authoritative as my experience. It is to experience that I must return again and again, to discover a closer approximation to truth as it is in the process of becoming in me. … My experience is not authoritative because it is infallible. It is the basis of authority because it can always be checked in new primary ways. In this way its frequent error or fallibility is always open to correction." (p. 23)

Such a high value of experience impacts Person-Centered Approaches to empirical research as elaborated, for example, in the chapter by Haselberger and Hutterer in *Interdisciplinary Handbook*. But what is it that motivates or drives us to experience?

3 The Actualizing Tendency as the Only Motive and "Inner Compass" Toward Growth

The actualizing tendency is the only "substratum of all motivation" (Rogers 1980, p. 123) that is postulated in the theoretical system. There are no other sources of energy in the system. The actualizing tendency is a directional tendency inherent in each organism as a whole, "involving not only the maintenance but also the enhancement of the organism" (Rogers 1980, p. 123).

Taking the actualizing tendency as a fundamental construct has far-reaching implications. These include an explicitly formulated assumption or image as to the nature of the human being, viewing life as a process of change and adaptation, and an inherent direction in each person that, furthermore, can be seen in coherence with the direction of the universe (to be described later in this chapter).

3.1 Explicitly Expressed Image of the Human Being

Along with humanistic psychology, the PCA builds upon an *explicitly* postulated and *expressed image of the human being* as basically constructive, forward moving, self-organizing, and social, when functioning freely (Rogers 1961, p. 194). This image or basic belief per se is meta-empirical (e.g., the chapter by Peter Schmid in *Interdisciplinary Handbook*); it cannot be verified or falsified directly in its entirety since holding or not holding the belief would influence the outcome. However, given we regard human beings as basically constructive, conditions are known under which human beings tend to unfold optimally.

3.2 Life is a Process of Change Needing Flexibility of Structures

The PCA acknowledges *life as a changing process* in which nothing is fixed (Rogers 1961). *Flexibility* is a vital goal and quality of enhancement to ensure adaptability to changes and thus survival (Damasio 2012; Rogers 1961). In the context of person-centered psychotherapy, Rogers (1961) observed that in the process of developing toward the "Fully Functioning Person" clients tend to move away from rigidity. He described the changes as follows: "The process involves a loosening of the cognitive maps of experience. From construing experience in rigid ways, which are perceived as external facts, the client moves toward developing changing, loosely held construing of meaning in experience, constructs which are modifiable by each new experience" (p. 64). In this regard, the chapters by Lux, Motschnig and Nykl, Ryback, Sheldon, Silani, Zucconi and Lamm, Sheldon, and Wolter-Gustafson in *Interdisciplinary Handbook* offer insight on how self-exploration can be fostered by person-centered relationships. Additionally, as shown by chapters in *Interdisciplinary Handbook*, the process view of the self which is held by the PCA is shared by Eastern philosophies (see chapter by Bundschuh-Müller) and is also implicit in Christian spirituality (see chapter by Fruehwirth) and social ethics (see chapter by Schmid). Last but not least, the chapter by O'Brien, Afzal, and Tronick uses the lens of relational psychophysiology to illuminate the effects and changes that our relational being has on us.

Hence, the primary goal of Person-Centered Approaches to psychotherapy, counseling, and education (as indicated by the majority of chapters and emphasized by Stumm, McCombs, Harbaugh and Cornelius-White, Kunze, and Motschnig-Pitrik in this volume) is the *facilitation of change*. Interestingly, the *promotive* inclusion of new media such as computers and the Internet in person-centered education can be seen as a further indication of the openness of the PCA toward new developments (Cornelius-White and Harbaugh 2010). If applied thoughtfully, these tools can be used to enhance constructive interaction, if only through a limited channel, and also the effectiveness of human beings, very much in line with the direction of the actualizing tendency.

Consequently, if change is ubiquitous, also theory about life has to be developed further, such as to mirror the developments and accommodate for changes (see the chapter by Haselberger and Hutterer, and McCombs in the research and theory Handbook (Cornelius-White et al. 2013)). For example, the effects of using new media on the human psyche and on interaction need to be better understood. The chapters by Harbaugh and Cornelius-White, McCombs, Motschnig-Pitrik and Ryback in this volume address this novel issue.

3.3 The Actualizing Tendency has an Inherent Direction Orienting Organismic Valuing

Life as a changing process has an inherent direction. Changes are guided by the actualizing tendency directed toward the survival/maintenance and enhancement of the person as a whole, or, in other words, as a self-organizing system in interaction with other such systems. Non-directivity is a logical consequence of trusting the actualization process. However, since the actualizing tendency—as the term indicates—is a tendency and not an imperative, trusting its direction must not be confused with a laissez-faire attitude. Furthermore, although the actualizing tendency is selective and has an inherent direction, the process of actualization does not proceed in a linear way. Neither is it a smooth process. It is better characterized as proceeding through ups and downs and as involving struggle to reach the goal (Rogers 1951, 1959). Rogers (1959) illustrates this by describing the way a little child learns to walk. He or she often stumbles and falls, but gets up and continues trying again and again until they masters the skill.

As an expression of the directional, actualizing tendency, human beings come equipped with an *organismic valuing process* in which each element, each moment of what one is experiencing is weighed, and selected or rejected, depending on whether, at this moment, it tends to actualize the organism or not. According to Rogers (1983): "This valuing process in the human being is effective in achieving self-enhancement to the degree that the individual is open to the experiencing that is going on within" (p. 264).

In his chapter in *Interdisciplinary Handbook*, Sheldon cites evidence of the organismic valuing process as leading us, in the long run, in the direction of beneficial goal choices (Sheldon et al. 2003). Additionally, neuroscience begins to explore the biologic foundations being involved in the organismic valuing process, with phenomenon such as "somatic markers" (see Lux 2007, 2010, and chapter by Lux) the "integrative function of the insula" (see chapter by Ryback) both in the research and theory Handbook (Cornelius-White et al. 2013).

In an infant, this complicated self-organized weighing of experience is clearly an organismic, not a conscious or symbolic process. The only difference to a mature person is that they can use the wisdom of their organism knowingly and integrate it with all the richness of cognitive learning and functioning (Rogers 1983, p. 264). Bohart and Tallmann (2010), citing Wood (2008), refer to this phenomenon designatively as "self-organizing wisdom of the person" (p. 122).

Furthermore, the actualizing tendency adheres to the *self-organizing principles* of complex, open, dynamic systems of which humans, groups, and higher-level relational systems are instances of. We will address this wider, structural scope after describing further meta-theoretical observations that more specifically characterize the human species. In this context, let us ask: "What is it that supports the actualizing tendency to unfold optimally and what is it that hinders its unfolding?"

4 The Person-Centered Approach Focuses on the Quality of Interpersonal Interaction

Free unfolding of the actualizing tendency for the human species, in other words a person's openness to experience, is facilitated by empirically derived and specified but unspecific *socio-environmental conditions* (Rogers 1959; Patterson and Joseph 2007). When perceiving these conditions, human beings tend to move in *common, internally generated directions* regarding qualities and values that are associated with *healthy psychological functioning and well-being*. "These common value directions are of such kinds as to enhance the development of the individual himself, of others in his community, and to make for the survival and evolution of his species" (Rogers 1964, p. 165). In particular, these directions include: "Fluidity, changingness, immediacy of feeling and experience, acceptance of feelings and experience, tentativeness of constructs, discovery of a changing self in one's changing experience, realness and closeness of relationships, a unity and integration of functioning" (Rogers 1961, pp. 64). Various chapters in both books demonstrate how the person-centered principles facilitate healthy psychological and social functioning, for example, from the perspectives of psychotherapy (Stumm) in this volume, or cognitive science (Motschnig and Nykl), neuroscience (Silani, Zucconi and Lamm; Lux; Ryback), positive psychology (Joseph and Murphy; Sheldon), developmental relating (Höger; O'Brien, Afzal, and Tronick; Mann), mindfulness and Eastern philosophies (Bundschuh-Müller), Christian spirituality (Fruehwirth), game theory (Fisher), and other disciplines in *Interdisciplinary Handbook*.

Adverse conditions such as *putting regard under conditions* or not being sufficiently genuine and empathically accepting of the other (in particular, in infancy and young age) thwart the organismic valuing process such that humans tend to distort or deny to awareness aspects of their experience. This alienates us from our genuine experience and results in negative consequences for psychological well-being/health as well as in deteriorating relationships. In Rogers' words (1961): "[W]hen man is less fully man—when he denies to awareness various aspects of his experience—then indeed we have all too often reason to fear him and his behavior, as the present world situation testifies" (p. 105).

In his chapter in *Interdisciplinary Handbook*, Lux mentions that such a view can also be found in considerations of neuroscientists. Furthermore, the detrimental effect of parental conditional regard was repeatedly empirically demonstrated (see for example Assor, Roth and Deci 2004; Assor and Tal 2012).

More generally, what most critics of the PCA who devalue the approach as "too individualistic" overlook is that proposition IX of Rogers's Theory of Personality and Behavior (Rogers 1951, p. 481–533) testifies Rogers' early emphasis on interaction that is broadly confirmed by the neurosciences (see chapters by Lux, Motschnig-Pitrik and Nykl, O'Brien, Afzal, and Tronick or Damasio 2012) as well as attachment theory (see chapters by Höger; Mann) all in *Interdisciplinary Handbook*. Rogers (1951) writes: IX) As a result of the interaction with the environment, and particularly as a result of evolutional interaction with others, the structure of self is formed ... (p. 498). Later, Rogers (1980) most clearly expressed his focus on interaction when he wrote: "I discern more sharply the concern of my life as having been built around the desire of *clarity of communication*, with all its ramifying results" (p. 66).

But how can such clarity of communication be conceptualized and understood? In Fig. 2, we abstracted and interconnected key constructs of Rogers' theories - for their definitions, see the introductory chapter in the research and theory Handbook or (Rogers 1959) - in order to capture the most essential (reciprocal) associations between these constructs. Despite the incompleteness of the figure (e.g., constructs like defense or subception are not shown) and its complexity, which we perceive to be inherent in the "subject matter," Fig. 2 depicts essential *psychological* "circuitries." For example, readers can follow the "path," (or spiral since travelled iteratively) in which relationships (see the right-hand side of the figure) and the

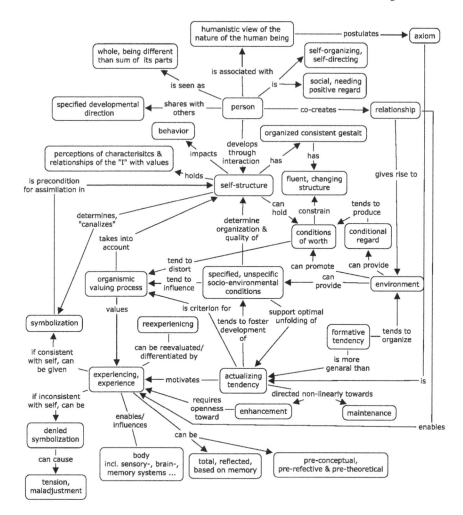

Fig. 2 Selected constructs of the PCA and their associations. Note that the arrowheads help the reader link the concepts in one direction for ease of understanding, but the associations do tend to disclose meaning if followed in either direction

environment influence a person's self-structure via his or her experience (shown on the bottom right side). Likewise, the self-structure, via conditions of worth, influences the "processing" (e.g., assimilation, re-evaluation, differentiation, or distortion) of experience. Thus, it is our hope that Fig. 2 allows to introduce—in coherence with Rogers' constructs—some complex order and regularities in the interdependence between experience and the self-structure.

5 The PCA is a Whole-Person Approach, a Generative Framework for Integrity

The PCA acknowledges that the whole-human organism, that is, the totality of experience is wiser and more trustworthy than the intellect alone. According to Rogers (1983): "Significant learning combines the logical and the intuitive, the intellect and the feelings, the concept and the experience, the idea and the meaning. When we learn in that way, we are whole ..." (p. 20).

This view is confirmed, for example, by the neuroscientist Damasio (2000) who posits that each relationship that comes to mind is initially perceived as a *feeling* (Damasio 2000; Motschnig-Pitrik and Lux 2008). Furthermore, it has been confirmed by several researchers that complex problem solving needs a good collaboration between (among others) affective and cognitive processes and the respective brain structures. (e.g., Claxton 1998; Goleman 1995; Ryback 1998; see also the chapter by Ryback in *Interdisciplinary Handbook*). In this regard, we refer to Timothy Wilson (Wilson 2002; Hofmann and Wilson 2010) whose view on adaptive unconscious and consciousness seems to be closely related to the theories of the PCA.

As an example illustrating the necessity of integrating psychological and physiological processes at various levels, consider the phenomenon of empathic understanding (Rogers 1961). The term alone implies an affective aspect ("empathic") as well as a cognitive one engaging higher-level thought processes ("understanding"). Investigations on the neural circuitry of empathy as described, for example, in the chapter in *Interdisciplinary Handbook* by Silani, Zucconi, and Lamm confirm that empathy—even without the yet more sophisticated "understanding" component—is a complex social phenomenon engaging the organism and its environment (typically other persons) from the biologic (Marci et al. 2007) to the whole-person level and beyond (see also chapter by Lux (in *Interdisciplinary Handbook*); Watson 2007).

Staying with the neurosciences, Wolter-Gustafson (in *Interdisciplinary Handbook*) cites evidence that neural plasticity—our very capacity to flexibly adapt neural pathways and synapses to current challenges and thus to adapt our behavior—is a whole-person endeavor: It depends to a significant degree on our organism's "minute physiological phenomena at the cellular level" (Wolter-Gustafson in *Interdisciplinary Handbook*, citing Pert 1997, p. 24).

But it is not the neural interconnections and the cellular processes per se that contribute to the whole-person view of the PCA. Both volumes, in particular, attend to philosophical and systemic foundations regarding wholeness (see for example chapters in *Interdisciplinary Handbook* by Schmid, Cavalcante, Kriz, and Hulgus). Furthermore, intentionally calming our minds (see e.g., chapters in *Interdisciplinary Handbook* by Bundschuh-Müller, Flender, and Ryback, or by Rao and Umesh in this volume) to become more open and receptive for any impulses from within and receiving bodily shifts along with pre-conceptual *felt meaning* potentially leading to articulated *felt sense* is a well-acknowledged process in focusing (see (Gendlin 1978) and the chapter by Ikemi in *Interdisciplinary Handbook*).

However, while whole-person perspectives are quite straightforward to argue, they tend to be difficult to achieve in practice. Rogers (1980) wrote:

> It is the overstress on the conscious and the rational and the underestimation of the wisdom of our total reacting organism that prevent us from living as unified, whole human beings. Yet, I can testify from personal experience that it is not easy for people whose lives have been dichotomized for decades to achieve this unity. I have conducted courses in which the whole group, including myself, have agreed that our feelings are as important a part of the curriculum as our ideas. Yet, if a member starts exploring some highly emotionalized experiences into which he is beginning to gain understanding, other members hesitate to bring up anything like feeling reactions. And if one person starts a class meeting excitedly propounding the ideas involved in a budding theory he is just beginning to develop, that session tends to be intellectual in focus. Only occasionally has a group been able to be whole persons in the experience. Yet, when they have achieved this, the results have been unforgettable. (p. 250)

Summarizing, in line with Seeman (1984) (as described in the chapter by Wolter-Gustafson in *Interdisciplinary Handbook*), we see "organismic integration" is a whole-organism activity of various "subsystems" working in a "transactional process that blends...biochemical, physiological, perceptual, cognitive, and interpersonal" in ways that are "congruent, harmonious, and adaptive" (Levant and Shlien 1984, p. 146).

More fully, Rogers (1961) describes advanced stages of therapy as follows:

> "The client has now incorporated the quality of motion, of flow, of changingness, into every aspect of his psychological life, and this becomes its outstanding characteristic. He lives in his feelings knowingly and with basic trust in them and acceptance of them. The ways in which he construes experience are continually changing in his personal constructs and modified by each new living event. His experiencing is process in nature, feeling the new in each situation and interpreting it anew in terms of the past only to the extent that the now is identical with the past. [...] His internal communication between various aspects of himself is free and unblocked. He communicates with himself freely in relationships with others, and these relationships are not stereotyped, but person to person. He is aware of himself, but not as an object. Rather it is a reflexive awareness, a subjective living in himself in motion. (pp. 154–155)

Further evidence for the importance of an integration of subsystems for mental health, that is, in Rogers' words an unblocked internal communication between various aspects of himself, can be found from the perspective of a person's coherence of self-organization (see chapter by O'Brien, Afzal, and Tronick in *Interdisciplinary Handbook*) and neuroscience (see chapter by Lux also in *Interdisciplinary Handbook*; Siegel 2010).

6 The Person-Centered Approach is a Way of Being

The PCA encompasses conscious and subconscious phenomena as well as their interconnection (interdependence, acting in concert) and reaching out. Openness to present experiences, that is, being attentive to messages of thoughts, feelings, body, and senses is central to this way of being. This has a number of consequences.

- The PCA as a holistic, socially attuned approach acknowledges the *expressive arts* and *spiritual dimension* of the human being. Currently, this cannot be captured purely scientifically. The scientific perspective on humanity—how significant and foresighted so ever—is necessarily only a reduction in the complex phenomena inhabiting the PCA. Current scientific approaches need to be extended or complemented by other paths expressing regularities and "truths" if we want to capture more of the whole-person and interpersonal relationship phenomena inherent in the PCA.
- The PCA addresses human beings in all stages of their lives, from infancy to intensive care in old age (See Fig. 3). This is illustrated in chapters that explore infants' development and patterns of attachment (see chapters by Höger and Mann in *Interdisciplinary Handbook*) and those referring to special care (see chapter by Pörtner in this volume). Additionally, the PCA is regarded by Daniela Tausch (2009), one of the main representatives of hospice movement in Germany, as "the most appropriate approach in care for the dying" (p. 69, translation by Lux).
- Current, *mechanistically influenced language* does not adequately serve to describe the full range of phenomena characterizing the PCA. Expressions such as "providing training," "applying the PCA," and "processing emotions" evidently do not satisfactorily describe the whole intended meaning but are hard to be substituted in texts that require clear, succinct language to be understood broadly. (see, for example, the chapter by Jürgen Kriz in *Interdisciplinary*

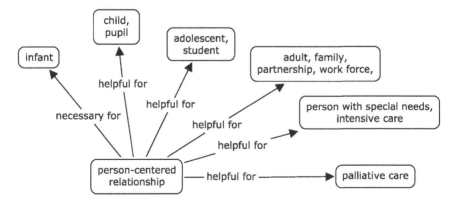

Fig. 3 The life span of person-centered relationships

Handbook. Thanks also to Ladislav Nykl and Leslie Simonfalvi for repeatedly drawing attention to such precision with language). Thus, the PCA community needs to be particularly sensitive, careful, and creative in expressing their thought and experience.

- The PCA to psychotherapy is just one specialized, well-researched subtheme of the PCA. While conceptually closely related, other areas of life, such as education, group work, management, cross-cultural communication, require *context-sensitive adaptations of the PCA*, sharing the basic principles but respecting the qualities and focuses of the other area, respectively (Wood 2006). Hence, a kind of "complex empathy for the environment" and particular forms or emphases of empathic understanding become ever more essential as the PCA moves into further fields (Barrett-Lennard 2005; Nykl 2012). As shown in chapters of the this volume, this applies in particular to encounter groups (see chapters by Lago, O'Hara), to person-centered medicine (see chapter by Botbol and Lecic-Tosevski), and to coaching that at times calls for selectively attending to various work-related aspects of the coachees inner world without ever losing the whole sense of it (see chapter by Sollarova and Sollar, and chapter by van Zyl and Stander in *Interdisciplinary Handbook*).
- Furthermore, the PCA may offer new perspectives for constructive political activism (see chapter by Hopkins in this volume).

7 Interdisciplinary Systems Theory Captures Structural Aspects of the PCA

The PCA acknowledges the *self-organizing principles* and *nonlinear evolution of complex, open, dynamic systems* of which humans, groups, and higher-level relational systems are instances of. At a structural level, humans share generic patterns with other organisms and inorganic matter, as further elaborated in the chapters by Kriz and Hulgus in *Interdisciplinary Handbook*.

In the last decade of his life, Rogers expanded the actualizing tendency with the term formative tendency, still postulating only one motivational construct, but seeing it as more systemically oriented. The formative tendency conceptualization suggests that the uniform directional tendency can be viewed at levels both smaller (e.g., biologic processes) and larger (e.g., social systems) than the organism. In fact, in the decades to follow Rogers' formulation, the PCA has been received to work at most versatile levels, as the chapters in both books testify. This wide spectrum is visualized in Fig. 4.

Rogers wrote (1980): "There appears to be a formative tendency at work in the universe, which can be observed at any level" (p. 124). "Thus, without ignoring the tendency toward deterioration, we need to recognize fully... the ever operating trend toward increased order and interrelated complexity evident at both the inorganic and the organic level" (p. 126). Consequently, the so often assumed

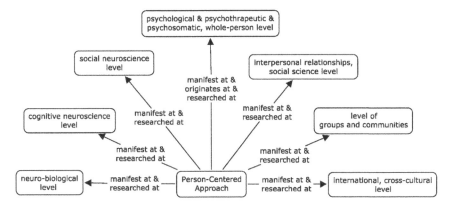

Fig. 4 The multiple levels at which the PCA is studied and present

linear relationship between cause and effect that underlies wide areas of science is questioned. Several real-world phenomena need to consider that the change in a small part of a system can lead to a change in the whole system and that effects tend to be reciprocal. For example, many contributors wrote about mirror neurons. These provide a parsimonious example of interest in systems that can be both smaller and larger than the individual, but also are understandable at a whole-person level (see also in *Interdisciplinary Handbook* the chapter by Barrett-Lennard on self-diversity).

An example of a ubiquitous phenomenon is that of interpersonal relationship. Typically, it tends to be reciprocal, as indicated, for example, by Rogers' preliminary law of interpersonal relationship. Strongly simplified, it says that if one partner in the relationship is congruent, this will foster the congruence of the other partner and vice versa such that the ensuing relationship will improve and both partners will experience personal growth. Many authors of both books referred to reciprocal effects between persons involved in interpersonal relationships (e.g., see the chapters by O'Brien, Afzal, and Tronick; Hulgus; Kriz; Lux; Mann; Motschnig-Pitrik and Nykl in *Interdisciplinary Handbook*).

However, the traditional construct of the actualizing tendency appears to be too constrained to describe this phenomenon. This is because the *actualizing tendency* is defined to be operational at the level of an *individual organism*. In order to describe the *reciprocal* actualization of two (or more) partners in a person-centered relationship *along with* the forming of their relationship, the new construct of *co-actualization* has been introduced (see in *Interdisciplinary Handbook* the chapter by Motschnig-Pitrik and Nykl; Motschnig-Pitrik and Barrett-Lennard 2010). This construct is aimed to spur interest and research in the "reciprocal impact" of person-centered attitudes in collaborative settings such as partnerships, teams, and organizations.

A further prominent example of system dynamic is the group process, for instance taking place in person-centered encounter groups. The basic encounter group—a setting for self-experience and problem solving, typically unstructured and vastly self-organizing—if well facilitated, has been regarded as one of the most potent social inventions of the twentieth century. The group as a whole and its participants as members move through a group process that is characterized by small talk, superficial conversation, and a resistance against expressing own feelings in its beginning. As the group process continues, participants move toward trust, open, and respectful interaction, deep understanding, and helpful relationships inside and outside the group setting, without having been told or instructed to do so. More on encounter groups and their transformative potential is shared in this volume in the chapter by Maureen O'Hara.

Likewise in this volume, readers can find another example of the dynamics of self-organizing systems (Kriz 2007, 2008) in the chapter by Bert Rice on oppression. The author illustrates in which ways imposing order or control by external forces can work counter to a (human) system's self-organizing direction and thus harm or at least slowdown its development. This tends to hold true, particularly for children who depend on their parents for love and care. Thus, the free development of their selves is particularly under risk.

8 The PCA Implies a Culture-Transcending Way of Relating

The quality of interpersonal relationship is a decisive factor not only for approaching optimal being, but it is also essential for reciprocally and collaboratively moving forward within and across cultures (Cain 2010). Interestingly, the commonality of the value directions, perhaps most prominently the felt sense of congruence as a desirable feeling of well-being, does not seem to be due to the influences of any one culture (Rogers 1983, Wood 2006). This cross-cultural coherence of value directions is observed in several chapters of both books, for example in the writings of Lago (this volume, see also Lago 2011) and Ikemi (*Interdisciplinary Handbook*, see also Ikemi 2010) and can be logically derived from neurobiological processes that appear not to differ across cultures (see in *Interdisciplinary Handbook* (Cornelius-White et al. 2013) the chapters by Lux and Silani, Zucconi and Lamm)

More particularly, Sheldon et al. (2004) found empirical evidence on the fact that *self-concordance*—owning one's actions or feeling one's goals being consistent with one's self—predicted subjective well-being across 4 cultures. It thus can be hypothesized that it is true for most (if not all) cultures. The construct *of self-concordance* is closely related to *congruence*. Evidence for a cross-cultural relationship between well-being and another aspect of congruence, namely the discrepancy between self-ideal and actual self-concept, was found in a study by Lynch, La Guardia, and Ryan (2009). This study also revealed that in non-professional relationships, a partner's autonomy support, a crucial aspect of person-centered relationships, is associated with higher well-being and a smaller degree of incongruence between ideal self and actual self in the other partner. However, we hope that soon, further research will be conducted to *empirically* confirm the hypothesis that Rogers' socio-environmental conditions (Rogers 1959) are valid cross-culturally.

Hence, it seems reasonable and not overly bold to hypothesize that—for the human species—the person-centered *way of being* appears to rest on a definable but unspecific person-centered *way of relating*. It is characterized by accepting the other as a person, endeavoring to understand them within their context in a profound and complex way—based on an undistorted flow of experiencing within oneself and the transparent communication of the felt sense, if appropriate. Thus, it is the way we relate to oneself and the other that is decisive whether an experience or relationship is growth promoting, "co-actualizing" or the opposite. Carl Rogers, his team, and the community that evolved from their "heritage" have researched and expressed the conditions as accurately as possible and left it up to us to keep them alive and developing in our ever changing, increasingly interconnected and globalized society. With his work, Carl Rogers opened up a path toward a "we" enriched by and enriching others regardless of color, race, or gender—an *interpersonal basis for a social ethic*.

From what has been said so far, it follows that the meta-theoretical and meta-empirical statements describing the PCA apply *regardless of a specific cultural background* even though the way the socio-environmental conditions are communicated may differ from culture to culture. Thus, it seems we propose to consider the PCA also as a psychosocial *"meta-culture,"* a most promising candidate for a uniting, overarching level of "culture" for the human inhabitants of our planet (Lago 2011). A level that emerges when living the person-centered core conditions and that exists beyond "traditional" cultures. The appreciation of the PCA across all continents and numerous nations and religions nicely confirms this statement. The fact that authors from 6 continents contributed to both books certainly is friendly.[1]

9 An Emergent Paradigm

As summarized in Fig. 5, the PCA can be seen as an emergent paradigm, providing a meta-view for interdisciplinary work consistent with interdisciplinary systems theory. It uses research to link theory with experience, posits a unitary motivation construct, and focuses on quality of interpersonal interaction and a whole-person approach. The PCA advocates for a way of being and relating that is culturally respectful yet culturally transcendent.

---

[1] We as co-editors are aware that our nationalities, more naturally than by intention, influenced the "choice" of authors we had asked to contribute and we beg our pardon to those we did not contact due to limited resources and knowledge.

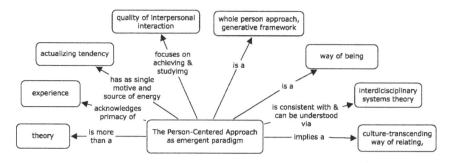

Fig. 5 Overview of the PCA as an emergent paradigm

A look back at Figs. 1 and 4 shows how the ideas and findings of the PCA are studied and applied through diverse disciplines, providing bridges that can help advance a variety of fields. Figure 3 depicts its applicability across the life span, and Fig. 2 shows the associations among many of its core concepts. While these figures cannot capture much of what the sibling books on the interdisciplinarity of the PCA share, they aim to help the reader appreciate the breadth and potential of the PCA for continuing collaborations among researchers and practitioners across settings, disciplines, cultures, and continents.

References

Assor, A., & Tal, K. (2012). When parents' affection depends on child's achievement: Parental conditional positive regard, self-aggrandizement, shame and coping in adolescents. *Journal of Adolescence, 35*, 249–260.

Assor, A., Roth, G., & Deci, E. L. (2004). The emotional costs of parents' conditional regard: A self-determination theory analysis. *Journal of Personality, 72*, 47–88.

Barret-Lennard, G. T. (1998). *Carl Rogers' helping system journey and substance*. London: Sage.

Barret-Lennard, G. T. (2005). *Relationship at the centre, healing in a troubled world*. Philadelphia: Whurr Publishers.

Bohart, A. C., & Tallmann, K. (2010). Clients as active self-healers: Implications for the Person-Centered Approach. In M. Cooper, J. C, Watson & D. Nuding (Eds.), *Person-centered and experiential therapies work*. Ross-on-Wye: PCCS-books.

Cain, D. J. (2010). *Person-centered psychotherapies*. Washington, DC: American Psychological Association (APA).

Claxton, G. (1998). *Hare brain and tortoise mind—why intelligence increases when we think less*. London: Fourth Estate.

Cornelius-White, J. H., & Harbaugh, A. P. (2010). *Learner-centered instruction: Building relationships for student success*. Thousand Oaks: Sage Publications.

Cornelius-White, J. H. D., Motschnig-Pitrik, R., & Lux, M. (2013). *Interdisciplinary handbook of the Person-Centered Approach: Research and theory*. New York: Springer.

Damasio, A. (2000). *The feeling of what happens—body, emotion and the making of consciousness*. London: Vintage.

Damasio, A. R. (2012). *The self comes to mind*. London: Vintage.

Gendlin, E. (1978). *Focusing*. New York: Bantam Books.

Goleman, D. (1995). *Emotional intelligence*. Bantam Books.

Hofmann, W., & Wilson, T. (2010). Consciousness, introspection, and the adaptive unconscious. In B. Gawronski & B. K. Payne (Eds.), *Handbook of implicit social cognition: Measurement, theory, and applications* (pp. 197–215). New York: Guilford Publications.

Ikemi, A. (2010). Empowering the implicitly functioning relationship. *Person-Centered and Experiential Psychotherapies, 10*(1), 28–42. Routledge.

Kriz, J. (2007). Actualizing tendency: The link between PCE and interdisciplinary systems theory. *Person-Centered and Experiential Psychotherapies, 6*(1), 30–44.

Kriz, J. (2008). *Self-actualization: Person-Centered Approach and systems theory*. Ross-on-Wye: PCCS-books.

Lago, C. (2011). *The handbook of transcultural counselling and psychotherapy*. UK: McGraw Hill.

Levant, R., & Shlien, J. (Eds.). (1984). *Client-centered therapy and the Person-Centered Approach: New directions in theory, research and practice*. New York: Praeger.

Lux, M. (2007). Der Personzentrierte Ansatz und die Neurowissenschaften [The Person Centered Approach and neuroscience, in German]. Ernst Reinhard Verlag: München.

Lux, M. (2010). The magic of encounter: The Person-Centered Approach and the neurosciences. *Person-Centered and Experiential Psychotherapies, 9*(4), 274–289.

Lynch, M. F., La Guardia, J. G., & Ryan, R. M. (2009). On being yourself in different cultures: Ideal and actual self-concept, autonomy support, and well-being, in China, Russia, and the United States. *Journal of Positive Psychology, 4*(4), 290–304.

Marci, C. D., Ham, J., Moran, E., & Orr, S. P. (2007). Physiologic correlates of perceived therapist empathy and social-emotional process during psychotherapy. *Journal of Nervous and Mental Disease, 195*, 103–111.

Motschnig-Pitrik, R., & Barrett-Lennard, G. T. (2010). Co-actualization: A new construct for understanding well-functioning relationships. *Journal of Humanistic Psychology, 50*(3), 374–398.

Nykl, L. (2012). *Carl Ransom Rogers a jeho teorie. Přístup zaměřený na člověka*. [Carl Ransom Rogers and his theories. Person-Centered Approach. (In czech)]. Grada, Praha.

Patterson, T. G., & Joseph, S. (2007). Person-centered personality theory: Support from self-determination theory and positive psychology. *Journal of Humanistic Psychology, 47*(1), 117–139.

Pert, C. (1997). *Molecules of emotion: Why you feel the way you feel*. New York: Scribner.

Rogers, C. R. (1951). *Client-Centered Therapy*. London: Constable.

Rogers, C. R. (1959). A theory of therapy, personality, and interpersonal relationships, as developed in the client-centered framework. In S. Koch (Ed.), *Psychology: A study of a science*. Vol. 3, (pp. 184–256). New York: McGraw-Hill.

Rogers, C. R. (1961). *On becoming a person—a psychotherapists' view of psychotherapy*. London: Constable.

Rogers, C. R. (1980). *A way of being*. Boston: Houghton Mifflin Co.

Rogers, C. R. (1983). *Freedom to Learn for the 80's*. Columbus: Merrill Publishing Company.

Rogers, C. R., & Wood, J. K. (1974). Client-centered theory: Carl Rogers. In A. Burton (Ed.), *Operational theories of personality* (pp. 211–258). New York: Brunner/Mazel.

Ryback, D. (1998). *Putting emotional intelligence to work*. Butterworth-Heinemann.

Sheldon, K. M., Arndt, J., & Houser-Marko, L. (2003). In search of the organismic valuing process: The human tendency to move towards beneficial goal choices. *Journal of Personality, 71*(5), 835–869.

Sheldon, K. M., Elliot, A. J., Ryan, R. M., Chirkov, V., Kim, Y., Wu, C., et al. (2004). Self-concordance and subjective well-being in four cultures. *Journal of Cross-Cultural Psychology, 35*, 209–223.

Tausch, D. (2009). Das Nicht-Aushaltbare aushalten. Wirklich als Person anwesend sein (Interview) [Stand what is unsustainable. Being really present as a person]. *Gesprächspsychotherapie und personzentrierte Beratung, 40*(2), 66–70.

Watson, J. C. (2007). Facilitating empathy. *European Psychotherapy, 7*, 61–76.

Wilson, T. (2002). *Strangers to ourselves. Discovering the adaptive unconscious.* Cambridge: Belknap press.

Wood, J. K. (2008). Carl Rogers' Person-Centered Approach: Toward an understanding of its implications. Ross-on-Wye: PCCS-books.

Editors Biography

The Editors

Jeffrey H. D. Cornelius-White Psy.D., LPC, is a Professor of Counseling at Missouri State University and Doctoral Faculty at the University of Missouri-Columbia. He is a former editor of *The Person-Centered Journal* and former chair of the World Association for Person-Centered and Experiential Psychotherapy and Counseling. He has published more than 75 works, including *Learner-Centered Instruction* (Sage 2010 with Adam Harbaugh), *Facilitating Young People's Development* (PCCS 2008 with Michael Behr), and *Carl Rogers: The China Diary* (PCCS 2012). Jef studied at the Chicago Counseling Center and the Pre-Therapy Institute and is a graduate of Argosy University-Chicago. He enjoys cycling, volleyball, his friends and family.

Michael Lux born in Stuttgart, Germany, has master's degrees in psychology and gerontology. He is a certified person-centered psychotherapist and works as a psychotherapist and neuropsychologist in the Neurological Rehabilitation Center Quellenhof in Bad Wildbad, Germany. Over the past few years, he has been intensively engaged with linkages between the person-centered approach (PCA) and neuroscience. As a result, he developed the model of a neuroscientifically based person-centered psychotherapy, which he described in a book and in scientific articles. Furthermore, he gives lectures and workshops on the neuroscientific bases of the PCA at conferences and training institutes.

Renate Motschnig-Pitrik born in Ostrava, Czech Republic, is a Professor of Computer Science and Head of the Computer Science Didactics and Learning Research Center at the University of Vienna, Austria. Renate held positions at the RWTH Aachen in Germany, the University of Toronto, Canada, and teaches and cooperates with the Masaryk University in Brno, Czech Republic. She participated in encounter groups and several events based on the person-centered approach. She is deeply interested in the multiple ways in which mutual understanding and

J. H. D. Cornelius-White et al. (eds.), *Interdisciplinary Applications of the Person-Centered Approach*, DOI: 10.1007/978-1-4614-7144-8,
© Springer Science+Business Media New York 2013

whole-person learning happen. She is an author/co-author of more than 130 scientific articles, one book, and is determined to foster a style in education that is based on person-centered attitudes, our co-actualizing potential, and thoughtful support by web-based technology. She appreciates synergies between presence and distance, and a multitude of (scientific) disciplines and cultures.

Additional Contributors

Pr Michel Botbol MD, is Professor of Child and Adolescent Psychiatry at the University of Western Brittany, France, Chief of the Department of Child and Adolescent Psychiatry at the University Hospital of Brest and Psychoanalyst of the Paris Psychoanalytic Society. He is a member of the board of the International College of Person-Centered Medicine, Co-Chair of the WPA Section on Psychoanalysis in Psychiatry and Secretary General of the French Association of Psychiatry, since 2007. He was previously a Consultant of the French Ministry of Justice for the Juvenile Justice System and Medical Director of a leading psychiatric clinic for students near Paris.

Klaus Haasis With degrees in media engineering and journalism, Klaus Haasis now brings to his current initiatives more than 35 years of experience in designing communication architecture, innovation processes, and relationship systems. His career has spanned creative industries, the ICT sector, chemical and pharmaceutical industry and politics, and he has also worked as a photographer and advertiser. In 1995, he was founding CEO of MFG Baden-Württemberg, (www.innovation.mfg.de/en), which today is one of the leading innovation agencies in Europe fostering Creative Industries, Media and ICT. Klaus Haasis has successfully built cluster initiatives and networks like Baden-Württemberg: Connected, www.bwcon.de, and the Open Source Solutions Network, www.osba.org. He is Director and Secretary of The Competitiveness Institute–TCI, the global network for practitioners dealing with competitiveness, clusters and innovation, www.tci-network.org, and a member of the European Cluster Collaboration Forum. He is a qualified person-centered counselor and coach and is a lecturer on the MSc program for the management of creativity and innovation at the University of Popular Music and Music Business in Mannheim.

Adam P. Harbaugh is an Assistant Professor of Mathematics at Missouri State University. He primarily teaches middle and secondary methods courses. Adam holds a master's and Ph.D. degree in curriculum and instruction from Texas A&M University and bachelor's and master's degrees in mathematics. Adam is also a certified middle grades and secondary mathematics teacher with experience in middle and high school mathematics classrooms. Adam's publications and research interest are centered on supporting teachers' effective use of communications, problem solving, and technology in their mathematics classrooms. He enjoys running, photography, racquetball, and spending time with his family.

Rosemary Hopkins born and educated in South Africa, has lived and loved on three continents—Africa, North America and Europe—as wife, mother, and grandmother and teacher, trainer, person-centered counselor, and supervisor. After 44 years in Scotland, her retirement is more akin to ongoing reinvention, and she is broadening her activities as a peace and justice activist, writer, poet, and student of the natural world.

Dorothea Hüsson (born 1959) has a master's degree in social pedagogy, is trained as person-centered therapist for children and adolescents (GwG), and as trauma therapist (ZPTN). She works as a trainer at the Stuttgart Institute for the person-centered approach and at the University of Education in Schwäbisch Gmünd (Germany). As a therapist, she works in a free practice in Stuttgart with children, young people, and parents.

Grace Harlow Klein is a psychotherapist, writer, and artist in the Center for Human Encouragement, created with her husband, Armin Klein. The Center offers person-centered psychotherapy services and workshops. Grace earned bachelor's and master's degrees in nursing and a PhD in human development from the University of Maryland. She is a Professor Emeritus, former Dean of the Syracuse University School of Nursing, and a Fellow of the American Academy of Nursing.

Dorothea Kunze is based in Germany and has a master's degree in social pedagogy from the University of Applied Sciences, Heidenheim, a master's degree in adult education science from University of Tuebingen and is a doctoral candidate there. She is a person-centered psychotherapist, supervisor, internal family systems therapist, coach, and supervisor. Additionally, she is a freelance trainer for person-centered communication, person-centered coaching, person-centered psychosocial counseling, person-centered organizational psychological development counseling, person-centered adult learning and leadership.

Colin Lago was a Director of the Counselling Service at the University of Sheffield, U.K., from 1987 to 2003. He now works as an independent counselor, trainer, supervisor, and consultant. He is a Fellow of the British Association for Counselling and Psychotherapy, being an accredited counselor with that organization. He is currently a visiting lecturer to the Universities of East Anglia and Strathclyde. Deeply committed to "transcultural concerns," he has had articles, videos and books published on the subject. He has recently been awarded a D.Litt and Hon. Prof. for his contributions to the literature on multicultural therapy. (For further details, see: www.colinlago.co.uk)

Pr Dusica Lecic-Tosevski MD, PhD, is neuropsychiatrist, psychoanalytic psychotherapist, and Professor of Psychiatry at the School of Medicine,

University of Belgrade. She is corresponding member of the Serbian Academy of Sciences and Arts, Director of the Institute of Mental Health and Head of the WHO Collaborating Centre. She is WPA honorary member, APA distinguished fellow, and International Associate of the Royal College of Psychiatry. Dr Dusica Lecic-Tosevski has focused her research on personality disorders, traumatic stress, and comorbidity of mental disorders, and she was investigator and coordinator in many international and national research projects. She is an editor-in-chief of the journal *Psychiatry Today*, and member of the editorial board of many national and international journals. As Chair of the National Committee for Mental Health, she is involved in the reform of mental health care in the country. Her hobbies are literature (she has translated 6 books—K. G. Jung, W. H. Auden, M. Serrano, etc.) and yoga.

Barbara McCombs PhD, is a Senior Research Scientist and Director of the Center for Human Motivation, Learning, and Development (HMLD) with the Applied Research and Technology Institute (ARTI), University of Denver, Denver, CO, USA (email: bmccombs@du.edu). She is the author of several works on the learner-centered model including *A School Leader's Guide to Creating Learner-Centered Education: From Complexity to Simplicity* (2008). She has served in leadership capacities within the American Psychological Association and the American Educational Research Association, such as being the primary author of the Learner-Centered Psychological Principles (LCPs): Guidelines for School Redesign and Reform. Much research has utilized several forms of the Assessment of Learner-Centered Practices (ALCP) she developed. McCombs' research encourages new leadership models for redesigning schooling and learning.

Dagmar Nuding (born 1980) has a master's degree in educational science and works as a lecturer and researcher at the University of Education in Schwäbisch Gmünd (Germany). As a person-centered (play) therapist, she practices in Stuttgart where she mainly works with children, young people, and families. She is a member of the board of the German Association for the person-centered approach and received the Virginia Axline Junior Award 2012.

Maureen O'Hara PhD., Professor of Psychology, National University, President Emerita, Saybrook University, and President International Futures Forum-US worked closely with Carl Rogers and the PCA team facilitating large group events and training counselors in many countries. Maureen's current work explores the impact of global cultural shifts on psychological development and emotional well-being. Books include, *Em busca da vida* with C.R. Rogers, J.K. Wood, and A. Fonseca (Summus1983), *10 Things to Do in a Conceptual Emergency* with G. Leicester (Triarchy 2009), and *Handbook of Person-Centered Psychotherapy and Counseling* with M. Cooper, P. Schmid, and G.Wyatt (Palgrave Macmillan 2007).

Marlis Pörtner psychologist, psychotherapist, and author, lives in Zurich, Switzerland. After other professions and family years, she studied psychology and was trained as a person-centered psychotherapist. Marlis worked for 30 years in private practice with many persons with mental disabilities among other clients. In addition, she has been a consultant and trainer for staff members of social services in Switzerland, Germany, Austria, and Belgium. She developed person-centered conceptions for everyday care in different fields and published several books in German. Some were translated and published in English, French, Dutch, Danish, and Czech. Her main focus now is on writing and occasionally presenting lectures, seminars, and workshops.

Umesh Rao born 1939, heads the Department of Counselling at the Sri Sathya Sai Institute of Higher Medical Sciences, Bangalore, India. A strong believer of spirituality-based integrative medical care, he partnered in developing the SAI way counselling program in a modern tertiary care hospital. He has made extensive presentations in India and abroad at academic and medical forums such as the PCE 2008 World Conference and the 2010 Mayo Spiritual Care Research Conference. He is the editor of the book *Spirituality in Healthcare - Perspectives* and also teaches a course on spirituality, health and nursing ethics at the Sri Sathya Sai Nursing College.

Bert Rice is married to Kathryn Moon, and they have a son, Ivan Rice, who is 24 years old. Bert is a compulsive list maker with a great passion for the consumption of popular culture, including movies, rock 'n' roll, and sports. Major influences include Ayn Rand and John Lennon. Bert believes that Alfred Hitchcock is the greatest artist of the twentieth century, and that Polly Jean Harvey is god. Bert holds degrees in economics, law, and counseling.

David Ryback received his Ph.D. from the University of Hawaii and then traveled through Europe and Asia for a couple of years to further his education in human nature. He returned to Georgia to direct a conference on humanistic education to which he invited Carl Rogers as keynote speaker, and then a working friendship ensued, resulting in a co-authored paper, "One alternative to nuclear planetary suicide." After years as associate editor of the *Journal of Humanistic Psychology*, David settled into consulting with business and government organizations on applying the principles that Rogers engendered to make bottom-line success more easily attainable. He is the author of *Putting Emotional Intelligence to Work* (Butterworth-Heinemann) and *Connect Ability: 8 Keys to Building Strong Partnerships with Your Colleagues* (McGraw-Hill) and is book review editor for *The American Journal of Family Therapy*. With fiction writing as his hobby, David is under contract with Tiger Iron Press to publish his first novel, *Beethoven in Love,* due out in 2013.

Antonio M. Santos is a Brazilian professor, lecturer, writer, coach, organizational and school consultant, and a licensed psychologist in the USA. He is the author of the book *Miracle Moments*, co-author with Dr. Carl Rogers and Dr. Maria Bowen of the book *When the Heart Speaks* and collaborator on the *Clinical Handbook of*

Schizophrenia. He is currently involved in researching the power of silence to help people uncover inner power, resilience and inner wisdom in a personal, organizational and educational levels of experiencing.

Tomáš Sollár is an Assistant Professor at the Constantine the Philosopher University in Nitra, Slovakia and Deputy Director of the Institute of Applied Psychology at the Faculty of Social Sciences and Health Care. For the past decade, he has participated in several encounter groups, trainings and workshops based on the person-centered approach. Currently, he is leading several courses on the person-centered approach, especially in nontherapeutic settings. He is deeply interested in applying person-centered approach principles in the context of education, work relationships and everyday life. He is also interested in researching these applications, measuring outcomes of person-centered approach trainings and studying the relationship of a person-centered way of being and health.

Eva Sollárová is a Professor of Psychology and Dean of the Faculty of Social Sciences and Health Care at Constantine the Philosopher University in Nitra, Slovakia. She graduated with trainings in client-centered psychotherapy and PCA applications for organizations. For the past two decades, she has been intensively engaged with establishing the PCA within university study programs for helping professionals as well as lifelong education and trainings of helping professionals and managers on national level within the Ministry of Work and Family and the Ministry of Education. She has published books, research articles, and book chapters on applications of the PCA beyond therapy, the PCA coaching model, the effects of trainings facilitating PCA competence for various professional roles, and facilitating the psychological integration in persons.

William Stillwell PhD, trained as an anthropologist and psychologist, has associated himself with humanistic psychology for more than forty years at The Center for Studies of the Person in La Jolla, California. There in the conflict transformations group he works with people in organizations: as coach to individuals, facilitator to groups, and mediator in conflict situations. His book written with colleague Jere Moorman on conflict transformations is *Conflict is Inevitable-War is Optional*. He is a longtime staff member of the Center's The La Jolla Program and Director of the Carl R. Rogers Memorial Library at the Center. He teaches as an adjunct faculty member at San Diego University for Integrative Studies. 'I am a person concerned with optimal qualities of life and work in today's organizations. I aim to liberate creative excellence. I apply my skills and heart with individuals and small work groups. Together we find new ways for us to deal with conflict, morale, leadership, quality of work and accountability.'

Gerhard Stumm PhD, 1950, is a freelance psychotherapist (person-centered psychotherapy) in Vienna, Austria, clinical and health psychologist, trainer of the Forum of the 'Arbeitsgemeinschaft Personenzentrierte Gesprächsführung, Psychotherapie und Supervision (APG).' He is author or editor of numerous publications on psychotherapy, including *'Wörterbuch der Psychotherapie'* (Dictionary of Psychotherapy) (2000), *'Die vielen Gesichter der Personzentrierten Psychotherapie'* (The many faces of person-centered psychotherapy) (2002), *'Grundbegriffe der Personzentrierten und Focusing-orientierten Psychotherapie'* (Basic concepts of Person-centered and Focusing-oriented psychotherapy) (2003), *'Personenlexikon der Psychotherapie'* (2005), and *'Psychotherapie: Schulen und Methoden'* (Psychotherapy: schools and methods) (2011).

Gita Umesh born 1950, has been a senior counselor since 2001 in the Department of Counselling at the Sri Sathya Sai Institute of Higher Medical Sciences, Bangalore, India. She has contributed significantly in the experiential development of the SAI way counselling program and made presentations at university medical schools and hospitals in the USA and Europe. She has extensive clinical experience having counseled over ten thousand patients, including terminally ill patients in a hospice, during the past decade. She is a faculty member at the Sri Sathya Sai Nursing College and a co-founder of the Nurturing Grace program group promoting sustainability, spirituality, and service.

Christopher C. Wagner PhD, is Associate Professor and Vice-Chair of the Department of Rehabilitation Counseling at Virginia Commonwealth University, with appointments in the Departments of Psychology and Psychiatry. A licensed clinical psychologist, he has worked in outpatient, inpatient, residential and hospital settings with a wide range of clinical concerns. Dr. Wagner is past president of the Society for Interpersonal Theory and Research (SITAR) and is a member of the Motivational Interviewing Network of Trainers (MINT). His scholarship focuses on developing motivational interviewing theory and the use of MI in groups, and studying interpersonal processes in MI and other therapies.

Index

A
Abuse, 141, 142
Acceptance, 89, 147, 149
Active listening, 147, 148
Actualizing, 204
Actualizing tendency, 25, 26, 29
Actualizing theory, 239
Adult education, 116, 119
Advocacy, 32
Ambivalence, 32
Anxiety, 183, 187
Applied positive psychology, 182
Assimilation of self-image, 184
Attachment, 146
Attitude, 189, 190
Authenticity, 201, 205
Authority, 237
Autonomy support, 89
Autopoeisis, 222
Awareness of the audience, 166
A way of being, 205

B
Barrier, 201, 207, 210
Behavior, 201, 208, 210
Behaviorism, 158–160, 162
Black educational systems, 16
Blended instruction, 134
Body, 63, 64, 66–70
Body reflections, 31
Body work, 33
Breakdown, 202
Business, 155–157, 162–167, 169–175, 193,
    195

C
Cardinal human values, 65
Care-giver, 58–61, 73
Carl R. Rogers, 258
Carl Rogers, 11–19, 23, 129, 155–160, 162,
    164, 167, 173–175, 179–181, 201
Centre of evaluation, 184
Change, 44–46, 148, 195, 197, 213, 218, 238,
    247
Change talk, 43
Children, 7, 141–143
Choice, 60, 92, 98
Clarity, 241
Classical client-centered therapy, 24
Client-centered therapy, 43, 45
Cluster management, 197
Co-actualization, 247
Co-create, 209
Collaboration, 97, 101, 133, 135, 136
Collaboration culture, 195
Communication, 126, 128, 146, 148, 193, 197,
    198, 201–211, 241, 244, 249
Community, 221–223, 225
Community engagement, 96
Conflict, 213–215, 217–220
Conflict resolution, 94, 178, 188, 213
Conflicting relationships, 217
Congruence, 64, 77, 117, 118, 214–216, 247,
    248
Congruent, 60, 61
Connectedness, 179
Constellation work, 33, 34
Constructive, 238, 239
Constructive communication, 8
Contact, 58

J. H. D. Cornelius-White et al. (eds.), *Interdisciplinary Applications*
of the Person-Centered Approach, DOI: 10.1007/978-1-4614-7144-8,
© Springer Science+Business Media New York 2013

Lightning Source UK Ltd.
Milton Keynes UK
UKOW07n0416100215

245986UK00015B/221/P